DATE DUE

JAN 0 2 2001	

MICHEL FOUCAULT

Critical Studies in Education and Culture Series

Postmodern Philosophical Critique and the Pursuit of Knowledge in Higher Education
Roger P. Mourad, Jr.

Naming the Multiple: Poststructuralism and Education
Michael Peters, editor

Literacy in the Library: Negotiating the Spaces Between Order and Desire
Mark Dressman

Thinking Again: Education After Postmodernism
Nigel Blake, Paul Smeyers, Richard Smith, and Paul Standish

Racial Categorization of Multiracial Children in Schools
Jane Ayers Chiong

bell hooks' Engaged Pedagogy: Education for Critical Consciousness
Namulundah Florence

Wittgenstein: Philosophy, Postmodernism, Pedagogy
Michael Peters and James Marshall

Policy, Pedagogy, and Social Inequality: Community College Student Realities in Post-Industrial America
Penelope E. Herideen

Psychoanalysis and Pedagogy
Stephen Appel, editor

The Rhetoric of Diversity and the Traditions of American Literary Study: Critical Multiculturalism in English
Lesliee Antonette

Becoming and Unbecoming White: Owning and Disowning a Racial Identity
Christine Clark and James O'Donnell

Critical Pedagogy: An Introduction, 2nd Edition
Barry Kanpol

MICHEL FOUCAULT

Materialism and Education

Mark Olssen

Critical Studies in Education and Culture Series
Edited by Henry A. Giroux

BERGIN & GARVEY
Westport, Connecticut • London

Library of Congress Cataloging-in-Publication Data

Olssen, Mark.
    Michel Foucault : materialism and education / Mark Olssen.
       p. cm.—(Critical studies in education and culture series,
  ISSN 1064–8615)
    Includes bibliographical references and index.
    ISBN 0–89789–587–8 (alk. paper)
    1. Foucault, Michel—Contributions in education. 2. Education—
Philosophy. 3. Historical materialism. I. Title. II. Series.
  LB880.F682O47 1999
  370'.1—dc21   98–49933

British Library Cataloguing in Publication Data is available.

Library of Congress Catalog Card Number: 98–49933
ISBN: 0–89789–587–8
ISSN: 1064–8615

First published in 1999

Bergin & Garvey, 88 Post Road West, Westport, CT 06881
An imprint of Greenwood Publishing Group, Inc.
www.greenwood.com

Printed in the United States of America

The paper used in this book complies with the
Permanent Paper Standard issued by the National
Information Standards Organization (Z39.48–1984).

10 9 8 7 6 5 4 3 2

Copyright Acknowledgments

The author and publisher are grateful for permission to reproduce portions
of the following copyrighted material:

Balibar, E. (1992). Foucault and Marx: The question of nominalism. In
T. J. Armstrong (Ed.), *Michel Foucault: Philosopher*. New York and London:
Harvester/Wheatsheaf.

Foucault, M. (1972). *The Archaeology of Knowledge* (trans. A. Sheridan).
London: Tavistock.

Foucault, M. (1991b). *Remarks on Marx: Conversations with Duccio
Trombadori* (trans. R. J. Goldstein & J. Cascaito). New York: Semiotext(e).

Contents

Series Foreword

Educational reform has fallen upon hard times. The traditional assumption that schooling is fundamentally tied to the imperatives of citizenship designed to educate students to exercise civic leadership and public service has been eroded. The schools are now the key institution for producing professional, technically trained, credentialized workers for whom the demands of citizenship are subordinated to the vicissitudes of the marketplace and the commercial public sphere. Given the current corporate and right wing assault on public and higher education, coupled with the emergence of a moral and political climate that has shifted to a new Social Darwinism, the issues which framed the democratic meaning, purpose, and use to which education might aspire have been displaced by more vocational and narrowly ideological considerations.

The war waged against the possibilities of an education wedded to the precepts of a real democracy is not merely ideological. Against the backdrop of reduced funding for public schooling, the call for privatization, vouchers, cultural uniformity, and choice, there are the often ignored larger social realities of material power and oppression. On the national level, there has been a vast resurgence of racism. This is evident in the passing of anti-immigration laws such as Proposition 187 in California, the dismantling of the welfare state, the demonization of black youth that is taking place in the popular media, and the remarkable attention provided by the media to forms of race talk that argue for the intellectual inferiority of blacks or dismiss calls for racial justice as simply a holdover from the "morally bankrupt" legacy of the 1960s.

Poverty is on the rise among children in the United States, with 20 percent of all children under the age of eighteen living below the poverty line.

Unemployment is growing at an alarming rate for poor youth of color, especially in the urban centers. While black youth are policed and disciplined in and out of the nation's schools, conservative and liberal educators define education through the ethically limp discourses of privatization, national standards, and global competitiveness.

Many writers in the critical education tradition have attempted to challenge the right wing fundamentalism behind educational and social reform in both the United States and abroad while simultaneously providing ethical signposts for a public discourse about education and democracy that is both prophetic and transformative. Eschewing traditional categories, a diverse number of critical theorists and educators have successfully exposed the political and ethical implications of the cynicism and despair that has become endemic to the discourse of schooling and civic life. In its place, such educators strive to provide a language of hope that inextricably links the struggle over schooling to understanding and transforming our present social and cultural dangers.

At the risk of overgeneralizing, both cultural studies theorists and critical educators have emphasized the importance of understanding theory as the grounded basis for "intervening into contexts and power . . . in order to enable people to act more strategically in ways that may change their context for the better."[1] Moreover, theorists in both fields have argued for the primacy of the political by calling for and struggling to produce critical public spaces, regardless of how fleeting they may be, in which "popular cultural resistance is explored as a form of political resistance."[2] Such writers have analyzed the challenges that teachers will have to face in redefining a new mission for education, one that is linked to honoring the experiences, concerns, and diverse histories and languages that give expression to the multiple narratives that engage and challenge the legacy of democracy.

Equally significant is the insight of recent critical educational work that connects the politics of difference with concrete strategies for addressing the crucial relationships between schooling and the economy, and citizenship and the politics of meaning in communities of multicultural, multiracial, and multilingual schools.

Critical Studies in Education and Culture attempts to address and demonstrate how scholars working in the fields of cultural studies and the critical pedagogy might join together in a radical project and practice informed by theoretically rigorous discourses that affirm the critical but refuse the cynical, and establish hope as central to a critical pedagogical and political practice but eschew a romantic utopianism. Central to such a project is the issue of how pedagogy might provide cultural studies theorists and educators with an opportunity to engage pedagogical practices that are not only transdisciplinary, transgressive, and oppositional, but also connected to a wider project designed to further racial, economic, and political democracy.[3] By taking seriously the relations between culture and power, we further the possibilities of resistance, struggle, and change.

Critical Studies in Education and Culture is committed to publishing work that opens a narrative space that affirms the contextual and the specific while simultaneously recognizing the ways in which such spaces are shot through with issues of power. The series attempts to continue an important legacy of theoretical work in cultural studies in which related debates on pedagogy are understood and addressed within the larger context of social responsibility, civic courage, and the reconstruction of democratic public life. We must keep in mind Raymond Williams's insight that the "deepest impulse (informing cultural politics) is the desire to make learning part of the process of social change itself."[4] Education as a cultural pedagogical practice takes place across multiple sites, which include not only schools and universities but also the mass media, popular culture, and other public spheres, and signals how within diverse contexts, education makes us both subjects of and subject to relations of power.

This series challenges the current return to the primacy of market values and simultaneous retreat from politics so evident in the recent work of educational theorists, legislators, and policy analysts. Professional relegitimation in a troubled time seems to be the order of the day as an increasing number of academics both refuse to recognize public and higher education as critical public spheres and offer little or no resistance to the ongoing vocationalization of schooling, the continuing evisceration of the intellectual labor force, and the current assaults on the working poor, the elderly, and women and children.[5]

Emphasizing the centrality of politics, culture, and power, *Critical Studies in Education and Culture* will deal with pedagogical issues that contribute in imaginative and transformative ways to our understanding of how critical knowledge, democratic values, and social practices can provide a basis for teachers, students, and other cultural workers to redefine their role as engaged and public intellectuals. Each volume will attempt to rethink the relationship between language and experience, pedagogy and human agency, and ethics and social responsibility as part of a larger project for engaging and deepening the prospects of democratic schooling in a multiracial and multicultural society. *Critical Studies in Education and Culture* takes on the responsibility of witnessing and addressing the most pressing problems of public schooling and civic life, and engages culture as a crucial site and strategic force for productive social change.

Henry A. Giroux

NOTES

1. Lawrence Grossberg, "Toward a Genealogy of the State of Cultural Studies," in Cary Nelson and Dilip Parameshwar Gaonkar, eds., *Disciplinarity and Dissent in Cultural Studies* (New York: Routledge, 1996), 143.

2. David Bailey and Stuart Hall, "The Vertigo of Displacement," *Ten 8* (2:3) (1992), 19.

3. My notion of transdisciplinary comes from Mas'ud Zavarzadeh and Donald Morton, "Theory, Pedagogy, Politics: The Crisis of the 'Subject' in the Humanities," in Mas'ud Zavarzadeh and Donald Morton, eds., *Theory Pedagogy Politics: Texts for Change* (Urbana: University of Illinois Press, 1992), 10. At issue here is neither ignoring the boundaries of discipline-based knowledge nor simply fusing different disciplines, but creating theoretical paradigms, questions, and knowledge that cannot be taken up within the policed boundaries of the existing disciplines.

4. Raymond Williams, "Adult Education and Social Change," in *What I Came to Say* (London: Hutchinson-Radus, 1989), 158.

5. The term "professional legitimation" comes from a personal correspondence with Professor Jeff Williams of East Carolina University.

Preface

I started writing on Michel Foucault in 1984 while on study leave in London. I had read Foucault's earlier works during the latter 1980s and had been reading *The History of Sexuality*, Volumes 2 and 3 and re-reading *The Archaeology of Knowledge* during the first few weeks of my study leave. I had also become convinced that to read Foucault as part of a general "post-modernist" tradition of thought in the same broad arena as Derrida and Lyotard was a mistake. As I re-read *The Archaeology of Knowledge* and his later works I increasingly took the view that his *oeuvre* as a whole revealed an overall consistency that could be located within a broadly materialist perspective that could be represented as a reconfiguration of the base–superstructure relation, a reconfiguration that altered and rejected certain distinctive features and fundamental axioms of Marxism but nevertheless constituted a viable historical materialist form of analysis. I also became convinced that such a perspective had been understated in accounts of Foucault. His modifications in relation to Marxism and his oppositions in relation to Hegelianism enabled a new resolution of the linkage between metaphysical holism and terror, a linkage which had preoccupied both Western liberal and continental traditions of thought alike. In addition, it enabled a radically different understanding of the processes of education from the dominant technicist and individualist conceptions which prevail in our times. Yet, in that Foucault shared certain affinities with Marxism it is not possible to see him as a Marxist, for he rejected much of the substantive approach of Marxism as well as the broad conception of history in which that perspective was wrapped. In that his work can be better understood in terms of a particular *relation* to Marxism, however, his overall approach draws on Nietzsche, Heidegger, and Greco-Roman and classical Greek thought, and can also be understood in terms of its relation and opposition to Kantianism. As a thinker who dared to challenge many of the dominant intellectual conceptions since the Greeks, his writings have radical implications for our contemporary understandings of what it means to be human, for our understandings of ethical action, and for our understanding of the types of futures that it is possible to create. Having written a number of articles suggesting that Foucault advocated his own distinctive form of historical materialism, in 1997 I was encouraged to develop them into a book-length work, which now appears in this work.

As with all such enterprises, various people have assisted in reading this manuscript or earlier drafts of chapters related to this manuscript. To these ends I would like to thank James Marshall and Michael Peters for their assistance and encouragement with this project, and John Morss for reading over the manuscript. I would also like to thank my partner, Judith McFarlane, for her patience and encouragement, and Christine Gardener for typing and preparing the manuscript.

Chapter 1

Introduction

Jürgen Habermas commented after Michel Foucault's death in 1984 that "within the circle of the philosophers of my generation who diagnose our times, Foucault has most lastingly influenced the *Zeitgeist*" (Habermas, 1986: 107). Given that Habermas was for many years one of Foucault's staunchest critics, this was tribute indeed. Foucault was not only to become France's most prominent post-war philosopher but, as David Macey (1993: xi) has observed, "he . . . successfully crossed the great divide that separates the purely academic world from the broader cultural sphere." In order to answer the questions "what is it he has done?" and "what significance does what he has done have for an understanding of education?", it is necessary first to position Foucault in relation to the dominant intellectual currents of his time.

At one level of abstraction, Foucault's main achievement and goal was to counterpose the philosophy of the concept to the philosophy of consciousness. In this he reacted against the dominance of Sartrean existentialism instancing a dividing line that ran between a philosophy of experience, of meaning, of the subject, and of consciousness on the one hand, and an anti-humanist philosophy of concepts and structures on the other. On the one side stood Sartre and Merleau-Ponty. On the other stood Cavaillès, Bachelard, Koyré, Canguilhem, and Althusser (Macey, 1993: 33).

In a different sense, and within this context, Foucault can be viewed as a sociologist of knowledge, and at the same time as an historian and as a philosopher. Such representations seem plausible given Foucault's self-chosen title of the Chair he occupied at the Collège de France as the "Professor of the History of Systems of Thought." His central works comprise studies of the emergence of phenomena, events, and processes that have come to be seen as taken-for-granted within the history of European culture. Among his earlier works one was concerned with the history of madness during the Classical age, and another with the birth of a discourse of clinical medicine during the late eighteenth century. In the 1960s he wrote on the human sciences and the nature of knowledge. In the 1970s he presented a history of the prison and of new modes of discipline as they occurred in the nineteenth century. Later in the 1970s he wrote on the history of sexuality to oppose the idea that sexuality reveals some "deep truth" about the self and to expose the fallacy of the view that the human sciences are concerned with uncovering rather than constructing the objects of their domain. In an important sense Foucault's work seeks to uncover not the development of rationality, but the ways new forms of control and power are legitimated by complex discourses that stake a claim to rationality and that are embedded in diverse institutional sites.

Foucault's lasting contribution is as an historian and a philosopher of science, though not of the sort who can be neatly labeled in terms of disciplinary home, but rather a scholar who defies neat intellectual classification and who rejects the institutional basis of disciplinary affiliation. Although his works can be considered histories by virtue of their objects and temporal reference, the objectives and conceptual and theoretical resources are drawn from philosophy. According to Clare O'Farrell (1989: 3), a stronger case can be made to consider Foucault's writings as philosophies rather than as histories. There is, she says, a "constancy of philosophical quest" which underpins the historical shifts in emphasis and reinterpretations he makes of his work. While I would agree with O'Farrell on this point, I would argue further that the mix of historical and theoretical concerns means they are not straightforwardly philosophical treatises either. If his work has a coherence, the best designation, in my view, is as a sociologist of knowledge in the traditions of Marx, Durkheim, and Mannheim. The sociology of knowledge seeks to relate patterns of thought to social situations and thereby reveal how knowledge is a product of social structures and social interaction. Foucault's approach fits such a designation as revealed in the illumination as to how the human sciences as forms of power-knowledge have been implicated with social structures, and in the repeated effort on Foucault's part to expose the individualist, and especially bio-medical roots of modern knowledge as expressions of power-knowledge.

To present an account of Foucault's life can only be undertaken against the background that Foucault's own attitude to texts on or about the self mirrored Nietzsche's (1983: 97) distaste for "all the learned dust of biography." There is an important sense, however, in which each of Foucault's books must be seen as part of his biography and related to changes within his life. In their important book *Michel Foucault: Beyond Structuralism and Hermeneutics* (1982), Dreyfus and Rabinow distinguish four stages in Foucault's intellectual development—a Heideggerian stage; an archaeological, quasi-structuralist stage; a genealogical, Nietzschean stage characterized by a general retreat from Marxism and language philosophy; and finally, an ethical stage marked by a new concern with Greek and Stoic thought and the development of a new ethics of the self.

After entering the École Normale Supérieure as a *normalien* in 1946, Foucault's intellectual and personal life was shaped in the shadow of Marxism and his close friendship with Louis Althusser which developed in the 1940s. Although Foucault joined the Parti Communiste Français (PCF) in 1950, under the undoubted influence of Althusser, Foucault's commitment to Marxism extended little beyond the general conviction that material economic conditions were an important influence on social and political life. Disillusioned by the nature of inter-party communist politics, his commitment was to be short-lived, however. Foucault left the PCF in 1953 and embarked on a period of political quietism that lasted until the mid-1960s. From then on there was a renewed interest in politics—this time of a non-communist sort—brought into focus by the events of May–June 1968, and his growing friendship with Gilles Deleuze, the "prime mover" of the Nietzschean renaissance in France. From 1968 through the next decade, Foucault started to work collaboratively with Deleuze on a number of projects. These included joint authorship of the "Introduction" to Pierre Klossowski's 1967 translation of Nietzsche's *Fröhliche Wissenschaft*, being interviewed together during 1972, and Foucault's writing of the "Preface" to the 1977 English translation of *Anti-Oedipus*. Politically from this time Foucault became active in prison reform and in active representation of other subjugated and marginalized groups within French society.

Foucault's writings can also be traced in relation to the varied characterizations he offers of his own work over the course of time. As Paul Patton notes, in his earlier works, written in the 1960s, Foucault represented his project as concerned to define "the limits and exclusions which make up our cultural unconscious" (1987: 227). Later, in the 1970s, he defined his central concern as being related to the issue of power, although he conceded that in his earlier works—*Madness and Civilization* and *The Birth of the Clinic*—he had scarcely used the term (Foucault, 1980b: 115). By the late 1970s, Foucault offered yet another representation of his work, defining his central interest as concerned with the historical origins of "subjectification"—"the process by which, in our culture, human beings are made into subjects" (Patton, 1987: 227). At various times throughout the course of his life, Foucault represented his *oeuvre* as a long-term project of discovering the elements of the "western will to truth." Just before his death in 1984, in what is perhaps an attempt to bring these different characterizations together, he defended an intellectual ethic of "permanent revolution in thought" (1987: 227). Notwithstanding the different accounts Foucault

offered at different times, however, within the broad tradition of the sociology of knowledge, Foucault's work, I will argue, can be seen to have a
more deeply structured coherence.

In terms of the major influences on his work, his intellectual and philosophical precursors, so to speak, it has been commonplace to repeat Foucault's own acknowledgments of his substantial debts to Nietzsche and
Heidegger. As he states, "for me, Heidegger has always been the essential
philosopher. . . . My entire philosophical development was determined by
my reading of Heidegger" (Foucault, 1985b: 8).

Concerning Nietzsche, he says, "I am simply Nietzschean, and I try to
see, on a number of points, and to the extent that it is possible, with the
aid of Nietzsche's texts . . . what can be done in this or that domain"
(1985b: 9).

But, as Hubert Dreyfus tells us, "it was through Heidegger that Foucault
came to appreciate Nietzsche" (1992: 80–81). In Foucault's words, "it is
possible that if I had not read Heidegger, I would not have read Nietzsche.
I had tried to read Nietzsche in the fifties but Nietzsche alone did not appeal
to me—whereas Nietzsche and Heidegger, that was a philosophical shock!"
(Foucault, 1985b: 9).

One of the central themes which Foucault shared with Heidegger and
Nietzsche, as well as with French writers like Althusser, was their challenge
to the Cartesian and Kantian conceptions of the subject, propounding instead the view that our own selves may be the greatest illusion of our time.
This "theoretical anti-humanism" stands in contrast to the phenomenological conception that Foucault rejected. He rejects a view of the subject standing prior to history or society, maintaining that the events and categories of
our world must be analyzed in relation to historical bodies of discourse
"tacitly governed by anonymous rules" (Rajchman, 1985: 44).

To see Foucault as Heideggerian, or as Nietzschean, however, is to exaggerate. Notwithstanding his own views on this matter, and not wishing
to underrate his debt to Nietzsche, he is not *simply* Nietzschean, or *simply*
Heideggerian. Other key influences on his work include French structuralism, as well as the more mainstream French philosophy of science, including
notables such as Koyré, Cavaillès, Bachelard, Canguilhem, and Althusser.
These thinkers had each in their own way sought to challenge the conception of history as a universal, objective, and progressive unfolding of events
governed by a conception of a unified model of science taken on from the
Enlightenment, and sought to replace it with an attempt to discover an
irredeemable plurality of forces and objects of knowledge, characterized, as
Rajchman says, "by anonymous tacit procedures, [each] succeeding one another through breaks and ensuing ruptures—a discontinuous history"
(1985: 53).

Yet another influence on Foucault came from the *Annales* school conception of "new history" identified with the journal *Annales*, which opposed

" 'battle-treaty' narrative" conceptions of history (Rajchman, 1985: 53), replacing it with broad social history. In the introduction to *The Archaeology of Knowledge* (1972: 3–11), Foucault acknowledges the importance of the *Annales* histories, drawing specifically on Braudel's concepts of "serial history" as well as the notion of *longue durée* whereby events were seen not as discrete atoms, but rather as intelligible only within a "series" or "coherent succession" characterized by repetition over a long period and utilized conceptually for the measurement of data on economic agricultural phenomena (such as price fluctuations) (see Dean, 1994: 37–42).

Finally, Foucault was influenced by Marxism. Although he took the view that "Marxist thought is irredeemably confined by an episteme that is coming to an end" (Sheridan, 1980: 73), he could also agree, albeit in a somewhat different sense, to an interviewer's suggestion that "Marx was at work in [his] own methodology" (Foucault, 1988a: 46). As these two instances might suggest, Foucault's relationship to Marxism was not straightforward. Although for the most part he was critical of Marxism, a great deal of what he wrote can be seen as a response to Marxism. As Balibar has noted, "the whole of Foucault's work can be seen in terms of a genuine struggle with Marx and . . . this can be viewed as one of the driving forces of his productiveness" (1992: 39). The main criticisms of Marxism were directed against the methodological models and philosophical conceptions it embraced, especially its attachment to various forms of Hegelianism, as well as its undue emphasis on economic determinants and forms of power. As Foucault states, "to put it very simply, psychiatric internment, the mental normalization of individuals, and penal institutions have no doubt a fairly limited importance if one is only looking for their economic significance" (1980b: 116).

In that Foucault departs from Marxism, his own approach nevertheless constitutes a form of consistent materialism that has theoretical implications for the analysis of social and educational systems. In seeking to demonstrate such an approach as a correct reading of Foucault, linguistic readings of his work such as that of Christopher Norris (1993) which represent him as part of the linguistic turn in French philosophy, where "there is nothing beyond [the] prison-house of language" and where "language (or representation) henceforth defines the very limits of thought" (1993: 30), will be dispelled in the process of being corrected. Rather, Foucault will be represented, as Habermas has suggested, "not merely as a historicist," but at the same time as a "nominalist, materialist and empiricist" (1987: 257).

Because the distinctiveness of Foucault's approach can best be seen in contrast to other major philosophical systems and thinkers, this study directs considerable attention to examining Foucault's relationship to Marxism, as well as to Kant, Gramsci, Habermas, and the Greeks. By so locating Foucault, it is possible, I will argue, to expose the distinctive character of his philosophical contribution. In relation to education, there is in Foucault's approach a double emphasis that constitutes an ordering principle for this work. On the one hand, attention is directed to discursive practices that perform an educative role in the constitution of subjects and of human forms of existence. On the other hand, forms of education are constituted and utilized for the purposes of collective ethical self-creation, a theme Foucault emphasized in his latter works.

This work is divided into three sections. Part I provides an introduction to Foucault as a distinctively materialist thinker, focusing on the distinctiveness of his methods of research (Chapter 2) as well as his theoretical conception of power and of the historical constitution of the subject (Chapter 3).

Part II considers Foucault as an historical materialist. This section seeks to bridge the divide between linguistic receptions of Foucault and historical materialism by pointing to Foucault's developing interest after 1968 in the relationship between discursive and extra-discursive dimensions of reality. In this context it will be argued that Foucault's analysis of the double relation between power and knowledge differs radically from the self-referential textuality of Derrida and his followers (Chapter 4). Chapter 5 goes on to examine the central differences between Foucault's version of historical materialism and Marxist versions, noting the central rejection of the Hegelian conception of a closed "totality" and the developing suggestion of what may be represented as a form of post-structuralist Marxism. Although many authors have criticized Foucault's project on the grounds of epistemological and moral relativism, it is argued in Chapter 6 that relativism is not an insuperable problem for Foucault and that there are various ways to resolve the problem of self-referentiality in his work. Although Foucault's notions of materialism are anti-Marxist in their rejection of modes of production, dialectical method, and ideology critique, such an assessment should not obscure deficiencies in Foucault's account relating to power and structure or to the nominalistic form of analysis adopted. As a consequence, the sources, substances, and dispersal of power are not concretely related to institutional practices. Chapter 7 explores the issue as to whether the addition to Foucault's approach of insights from Gramsci can serve as a corrective to some of these deficiencies.

Part III explores various themes relating Foucault's work to education. Chapter 8 outlines Foucault's critical epistemology and his relationship to Kant, seeking to elucidate Foucault's conception of knowledge in relation to political action and utopian proposals. In Chapter 9 his latter emphasis on ethical self-creation is represented as a distinctively educational form of activity, embodying a form of thin communitarianism that takes us back to the Greek polis. Chapter 10 assesses some of the more interesting recent utilizations of Foucault in educational research. Chapter 11 concludes by focusing on Foucault's distinctive resolution of structure and agency and determinism and free will.

Part I

The Modified Realism
of Michel Foucault

Chapter 2

Foucault's Methods

Methodologically, Foucault's works utilize two approaches: that of *archaeology*, concerned with describing the historical presuppositions of a given system of thought, and that of *genealogy*, concerned with tracing the historical processes of *descent* and *emergence* by which a given thought system or process comes into being and is subsequently transformed.

Foucault's method of archaeology constitutes a way of analyzing the superstructural dimension of language statements constitutive of discourse. A discourse is defined in terms of statements (*énoncés*), of "things said." Statements are events of certain kinds which are at once tied to an historical context and capable of repetition. Statements are not equivalent to propositions or sentences, or "speech acts," neither are they phonemes, morphemes, or syntagms. Rather, as Foucault (1972: 115) states,

In examining the statement what we have discovered is a *function* that has a bearing on groups of signs, which is identified neither with grammatical "acceptability" nor with logical correctness, and which requires if it is to operate: *a referential* (which is not exactly a fact, a state of things, or even an object, but a principle of differentiation); *a subject* (not the speaking consciousness, not the author of the formulation, but a position that may be filled in certain conditions by various individuals); *an associated field* (which is not the real context of the formulation, the situation in which it was articulated, but a domain of coexistence for other statements); *a materiality* (which is not only the substance or support of the articulation, but a status, rules of transcription, possibilities of use and re-use). (emphasis added)[1]

Foucault is interested in serious statements comprising that sub-set of formal knowledge statements, which contain truth claims and which belong to a single system of formation. A "discursive formation" comprises the "regularity" that obtains between "objects, types of statement, concepts, or thematic choices" (Foucault, 1972: 38). It is "the general enunciative system that governs a group of verbal performances" (116).

Archaeological analysis is centrally concerned with uncovering the rules of formation of discourses, or discursive systems. In a technical sense, it proceeds at the level of statements (*énoncés*) searching for rules that explain the appearance of phenomena under study. It examines the forms of regularity, that is, the discursive conditions, which order the structure of a form of discourse and which determine how such orders come into being. It is not an analysis of that which is claimed to be true in knowledge but an analysis of "truth games." Discourse is thus analyzed in terms of the operation of rules that bring it into being. Archaeology attempts to account for the way discourses are *ordered*. As Foucault states, "my object is not language but the archive, that is to say the accumulated existence of discourse. Archaeology, such as I intend it, is kin neither to geology (as analysis of the sub-soil), nor to genealogy (as descriptions of beginnings and sequences); it's the analysis of discourse in its modality of *archive*" (1989a: 25). As such, archaeology focuses attention on the link between perception and action and on why at different periods specialists in knowledge perceive objects differently. The core of archaeology is thus an attempt to establish the discursive practices and rules of formation of discourses through asking, "how is it that one particular statement appeared rather than another" (Foucault, 1972: 27). As Manfred Frank says, "As such, he is more interested in the conditions which make it possible for the structures to arise than in the structures themselves . . . for Foucault the foundation of the constitution of an order is never a subject, but yet another order: in the last instance this would be the order of the discourse with its *regard déjà codé* (already coded look)" (1992: 107).

In *The Order of Things*, for example, Foucault seeks to uncover the regularities that accounted for the emergence of the sciences in the nineteenth century by comparing forms of thought across different historical periods (Renaissance, Classical, and Modern). Archaeology here constitutes a method for examining the historicity of science by describing rules that undergird ways of looking at the world. These rules are regularities that determine the systems of possibility as to what is considered as true and false, and they determine what counts as grounds for assent or dissent, as well as what arguments and data are relevant and legitimate. These "structures of thought" are termed *epistemes*. An "episteme" refers to "the total set of relations that unite, at a given period, the discursive practices. . . . The episteme is not a form of knowledge . . . or type of rationality which, crossing the boundaries of the most varied sciences, manifests the sovereign unity of a subject, a spirit, or a period; it is the totality of relations that can be discovered for a given period, between the sciences when one analyses them at the level of discursive regularities" (Foucault, 1972: 191).

Robert Machado (1992: 14) characterizes an episteme as defined by two features. The first is its depth; an episteme relates to the nature of "deep" knowledge (*savoir*) and to the specific order or configuration that such knowledge assumes in a given period. This is to say that an episteme is governed by a principle prior to and independent of the ordering of discourse such as science, which is constituted of "surface" knowledge (*connaissance*). The second is its general global nature. In any culture, at a particular point in time, there is only one episteme which defines the conditions of possibility of all theoretical knowledge (see Foucault, 1970: 179). Archaeology is an historical analysis of this theoretical knowledge attempting to trace links between the different domains of "life, work, and language," revealing relationships that are not readily apparent. In doing so, it seeks to expose the "historical a priori" of the episteme as it manifests itself in the body of discourses under study. In this sense, Foucault insists that epistemes are not transcendental in the Kantian sense, neither are they origins or foundations. Rather, they are a practice to be encountered; that is, they are time-bound and factual.

Archaeology signals Foucault's affinity to the mainstream tradition of French philosophy as embodied in Bachelard, Koyré, Cavaillès, Canguilhem, and Althusser, who sought to study science in terms of its place in history. Its proper object of analysis in Foucault's work is the historical constitution of the human sciences. It aims to trace, in the manner familiar to French philosophy, sharp but not complete discontinuities between systems of thought. Hence, archaeology seeks to chart ruptures/changes between discursive systems. An archaeological mutation makes a new age possible, that is, the structures of discourse suddenly change at certain crucial junctures in a sudden radical discursive restructuring.

For example, in *The Birth of the Clinic*, Foucault utilizes archaeological methods to extend his study of the human sciences to the study of medicine as a science. In seeking to trace the conditions of possibility of modern medical discourse, Foucault identifies a "mutation" in Western medical thought at the end of the eighteenth century. It is a mutation in medical perception and knowledge from a classificatory medicine, or "medicine of species," based on pathological anatomy, to a "medicine of symptoms" and eventually, a "medicine of tissues," or "anatomo-clinical medicine" (Smart, 1985: 29). Essentially it involves a reconceptualization of the medical gaze from a classification of cases based on "types" to a classification of cases solely in relation to individuals. As Smart (27) maintains, for Foucault medicine is "the first scientific discourse concerning the individual." It is with medical discourse that the individual is constituted as an "object of positive knowledge."

Insofar as archaeology's object of study is discourse, its methods are conceptual and it aims to search for explanations at a deeper level than those provided by science. Archaeology utilizes theoretical knowledge (*savoir*) in order to analyze science. As Machado states, "in short, archaeology analyses the similarities and differences between different forms of theoretical knowledge (*savoirs*), establishing between them a 'unique network of necessary relationships' " (1992: 15). It examines science in its historical context, taking as its starting point the historical constitution of scientific concepts, detailing the types of progress that characterize them, the means by which truth is produced, and the criteria of rationality that they establish (Machado, (1992: 15).

Archaeology has several affinities to structuralism. The main similarities reside in representing discourse as a rule-governed system, as autonomous, and in focusing on both discourse and the speaker as constructed objects, the latter effected through the de-centering the subject. What saves Foucault, ultimately, from lapsing into structuralism is the utilization of Nietzsche's method of genealogy (described below,) which enables him to situate discourse and the locus of its transformation in the context of history.

Crucially, too, archaeology asserts the priority of theoretical knowledge (*theoria*) over science for the purposes of analysis and evaluation. It is because Foucault believes in the superiority of theoretical knowledge that he subordinates science to it. The centrality of theoretical knowledge (*theoria*), as a form of critical interrogation, was displaced with the Scientific Revolution of the sixteenth and seventeenth centuries, and it continued to be dismissed by Kant at the end of the eighteenth century. Until the end of the eighteenth century, the principle that being can always be represented directly was the central characteristic of the episteme, which Foucault calls the "reign of representation." Although Kant challenged the postulate of a directly represented order (which he attributed to a mistake made by Plato), replacing it with an analytic that reflected on limits, he nevertheless safeguarded the continued dominance of the "objectivist" tradition based on mathematization, thus ensuring the retreat of *theoria* as a form of knowledge to a position outside the "space of representation" (Foucault, 1970: 212–213).

In establishing archaeology, Foucault is thus reinstating *theoria* prior to science. Unlike science, archaeology does not contain assumptions about evolution or progress, and it displaces science for providing the authority for knowledge of the past in relation to issues such as progress or truth. Yet, in doing so, it does not invalidate the legitimacy or truth of science either.

GENEALOGY

Genealogical analysis aims to explain the existence and transformation of elements of theoretical knowledge (*savoir*) by situating them within power structures and by tracing their descent and emergence in the context of history. As such, it traces an essential, historically constituted tie between power and knowledge, and it provides a causal explanation for change in discursive formations and epistemes. Because it is more historical, it helps Foucault avoid succumbing to the temptations of structuralism. Yet, like archaeology, it avoids reference to a philosophical conception of the subject, radicalizing Nietzsche and Heidegger's opposition to the post-Cartesian and Kantian conceptions. Like archaeology, too, it is limited and justified as a method in terms of the fruitfulness of its specific applications.

Genealogy thus asserts the historical constitution of our most prized certainties about ourselves and the world in its attempts to de-naturalize explanations for the existence of phenomena. It analyzes discourse in its relation to social structures and has an explicit focus on power and on bodies. It is interested in institutional analysis and technologies of power aiming to isolate the mechanisms by which power operates. Through its focus on power, also, genealogy aims to document how culture attempts to normalize individuals through increasingly rationalized means, by constituting normality, turning them into meaningful subjects and docile objects. Power relations are therefore pivotal. Genealogy thus shifts the model for historical understanding from Marxist science and ideology, or from hermeneutical texts and their interpretation, to a Nietzschean-inspired analysis of strategies and tactics in history.

For Foucault (1977b: 142), then, as for Neitzsche, genealogy opposes itself to the search for origins (*Ursprung*) or essences. To search for origins is to attempt to capture the exact essence of things, which Foucault sees as reinstating Platonic essentialism. Such a search assumes the existence of "immobile forms that precede the external world of accident and succession." Such a search, says Foucault, assumes the existence of a

primordial truth fully adequate to its nature, and it necessitates the removal of every mask to ultimately disclose an original identity. However, if the genealogist refuses to extend his faith in metaphysics, if he listens to history, he finds that there is "something altogether different" behind things: not a timeless and essential secret, but the secret that they have no essence or that their essence was fabricated in a piecemeal fashion from alien forms. (142)

In addition, genealogical analysis does not take history at its word but rather shows that concepts such as liberty, for example, far from being fundamental to human nature, or at the root of human attachment to being and truth, are rather the invention of the ruling classes (142).

Rather than trace origins (*Ursprung*), genealogy traces the processes of *descent* and *emergence*. Foucault defines descent (*herkunft*) as pertaining to practices as a series of events: "To follow the complex course of descent is to maintain passing events in their proper dispersion; it is to identify the accidents, the minute deviations—or conversely, the complete reversals—the errors, the false appraisals, and the faulty calculations that gave birth to those things that continue to exist and have value for us" (Foucault, 1977b: 146).

Unlike the continuities traced by those historians who search for origins, genealogy traces the jolts and surprises of history in terms of the effects of power on the body. Following Nietzsche's nominalism, Foucault's genealogies of the subject constitute an investigation into how we have been fashioned as ethical subjects. Hence, genealogy attaches itself to the body, that "inscribed surface of events . . . and a volume in perpetual disintegration" (1977b: 148). It reveals how history "inscribes itself in the nervous system, in temperament, in the digestive apparatus . . . in faulty respiration, in improper diets, in the debilitated and prostrate body of those whose ancestors commited errors" (147).

In contrast to descent, emergence (*Entstehung*) traces "the movement of arising" (148). "Emergence is thus the entry of forces; it is their eruption, the leap from wings to center stage, each in its youthful strength" (149–150).

Genealogy has a central role in tracing the patterns of descent and emergence of discursive systems. Citing Nietzsche from *The Dawn* and from *Human, All Too Human*, Foucault argues that the forces operating in history that constitute the historical process are not controlled by destiny or by regulative mechanisms, but respond to "haphazard conflicts," and they "always appear through the singular randomness of events" (1977b: 154–155).

In terms of its approach to history, genealogy signals Foucault's affinities to the "new history" of the *Annales* school and the rejection of linear, humanist histories that embodied hermeneutical methods in ascertaining the meaning of documents, and subscribed to conceptions of linearity and succession. Such approaches treat history as a narrative of events in chronological order, assume a feigned neutrality generated more from adherence to a particular style than to worked-out methodological rules, and represent the present as emerging unproblematically from the historical record, recounting the facts as pure description in an assumed phenomenological union between the historian and the past.

In *Nietzsche, Genealogy, History*, Foucault (1977b) invokes the second of Nietzsche's *Untimely Meditations* (Nietzsche, 1983: 57–123) in order to record his debt to Nietzsche concerning the forms of history he rejects. Nietzsche identifies three uses of history which are problematic: the monumental, devoted to a veneration of great events, great men, and great deeds (Foucault, 1977b: 69–72); the antiquarian, dedicated to preservation of the past as a continuity of identity in tradition (72–75); and the critical, dedicated to judgment on and condemnation of parts of the past in the name of the present (74–75). It is to these three conceptions that Foucault argues the historical sense of Nietzsche's genealogy is opposed. Following closely in Nietzsche's footsteps, Foucault summarizes his own approach to reason and history as a "critical inquiry into the history of rationality," "a rational critique of rationality," and "a contingent history of history" (1983a: 201). Drawing on concepts elaborated by Nietzsche, Mitchell Dean summarizes Foucault's histories as "effective" and "critical":

If archaeology displaces the delirium of interpretation with an analysis of the positivity of discourse, then genealogy displaces both the search for ultimate foundations and its opposite, nihilism, with a form of patient criticism and problematisation located in the present. Foucault's critical history forsakes the critique of the past in terms of the truth of the present but not the critical use of history of reason to diagnose the practical issues, necessities, and limits of the present. Let us call history "effective" to the extent that it upsets the colonisation of historical knowledge by the schemas of a transcendental and synthetic philosophy of history, and "critical" in proportion to its capacity to engage in the tireless interrogation of what is held to be given, necessary, natural, or neutral. (1994: 20)

Foucault's genealogical histories thus challenge the presuppositions of past histories, the tendency toward totalizing abstraction, toward closure, toward universalist assumptions regarding the human identity or the nature of existence. His approach also rejects the transcendental turn in philosophy and asserts the radical contingency of discourses in their historical context.

Further insights into Foucault's methods are revealed in his lecture notes at the Collège de France, as published in the four volumes of *Dits et écrits* (1994a). In these volumes, Foucault reveals the importance of analytic method and the philosophy of language in relation to the analysis of discourse. In one essay, "La philosophie analytique de la politique" (1994c), initially delivered in 1978 in Japan, Foucault spells out the superiority of analytical methods as used in Anglo-American philosophy compared to dialectical methodology. What characterizes analytic methods is a concern not with the "deep structures" of language, or the "being" of language but with the "everyday use" made of language in different types of discourse. By extension, Foucault argues that philosophy can similarly analyze what occurs in "everyday relations of power" and in all those other relations that "traverse the social body." Just as language can be seen to underlie thought, so there is a similar grammar underlying social relations and relations of power. Hence, Foucault argues for what he calls an "analytico-political philosophy." Similarly, rather than seeing language as revealing some eternal buried truth that "deceives or reveals," the metaphorical method for understanding that Foucault utilizes is that of a game: "Language, it is played." It is thus a "strategic" metaphor, as well as a linguistic metaphor, that Foucault utilizes to develop a critical approach to society freed from the theory of Marxism: "Relations of power, also, they are played; it is these games of power (*jeux de pouvoir*) that one must study in terms of tactics and strategy, in terms of order and of chance, in terms of stakes and objectives" (Foucault, 1994c, Vol. 3: 541–542).

Foucault's dependence on structural linguistics is also central to understanding the nature of his analysis. Traditionally, the rationality of analytic reason, he says, has been concerned with causality. In structural linguistics, however, the concern is not with causality, but in revealing multiple relations which, in his 1969 article "Linguistique et sciences sociales," Foucault calls "logical relations" (see Foucault, 1994b, Vol. 1: 824). While it is possible to formalize one's treatment of the analysis of relations, it is, says Foucault, the discovery of the "presence of a logic that is not the logic of causal determinism that is currently at the heart of philosophical and theoretical debates" (824).

Foucault's reliance on the model of structural linguistics provides him with a method that avoids both methodological individualism and entrapment by a concern with causalism. Structural linguistics is concerned with "the systematic sets of relations among elements" (Davidson, 1997: 8), and it functions for Foucault as a model that enables him to study social reality as a logical structure, or a set of logical relations revealing relations that are not transparent to consciousness. The methods of structural linguistics also enable Foucault to analyze change. For just as linguistics undertakes synchronic analysis seeking to trace the necessary conditions for an element within the structure of language to undergo change, a similar synchronic analysis applied to social life asks the question, in order for a change to occur, what other changes must also take place in the overall texture of the social configuration? (See Foucault, 1994b, Vol. 1: 827.) Hence, Foucault seeks to identify logical relations where none had previously been thought to exist or where previously one had searched for causal relations. This form of analysis becomes for Foucault a method of analyzing previously invisible determinations (see Davidson, 1997: 1–20).

The methodological strategies common to both archaeology and genealogy were also developed in response to Marxism, which is characterized by a specific, narrow conception of causality (*un causalisme primaire*) and a dialectical logic that has little in common with the logical relations that interest Foucault. Thus he maintains: "what one is trying to recover in Marx is something that is neither the determinist ascription of causality, nor the logic of a Hegelian type, but a logical analysis of reality" (Foucault, 1994b, Vol. 1: 824–825; cited in Davidson, 1997: 10).

Arnold Davidson (1997), in a review of *Dits et écrits* to which my own analysis is indebted, points out that it is through such methodological strategies that Foucault proceeds to advance a non-reductive, holist analysis of social life. According to Davidson, "this kind of analysis is characterised, first, by anti-atomism, by the idea that we should not analyse single or individual elements in isolation but that one must look at the systematic relations among elements; second, it is characterised by the idea that the relations between elements are coherent and transformable, that is, that the elements form a structure" (11). Thus, in his dissertation on the knowledge of heredity as a system of thought, submitted as part of his application for his position at the Collège de France, Foucault seeks to describe the changes, transformations, and conditions of possibility that made genetics possible, that constituted it as a science based on a series of discourses concerning breeding, just as in *The Order of Things* he had done for natural history and biology. What factors led to the emergence of these fields as sciences? What elements changed to make such developments possible? What made them possible as systems of thought? Thus Foucault seeks to describe the relations among elements as structures that change as the component elements change. That is, he endeavors to establish the systematic sets of relations and transformations that enable different forms of knowledge to emerge.

NOTE

1. Unless indicated, all emphases in quotations in this book belong to the original author being cited.

Chapter 3

Power and the Self

For Foucault, at least in *Discipline and Punish* and *The History of Sexuality*, Volume 1, the relationship between discursive systems of knowledge and power and domination becomes critical. Unlike Marxists, he sees no one set of factors as directing human destiny. Rather, he represents power in terms of a *multiplicity of force relations* throughout the entire social formation. Foucault's central critique of traditional approaches to power is against the "juridico-discursive" model of power which underpins not just Marxist theories but liberal theories of power as well. The three features of this model of power are (Sawicki, 1991: 20–21):

- that power is possessed (e.g., by the state, classes, individuals);
- that power flows from a centralized source, from top to bottom; and
- that power is primarily repressive in its exercise.

In contrast, Foucault's alternative conception maintains

- that power is exercised rather than possessed;
- that power is productive, as well as repressive; and
- that power arises from the bottom up.

Foucault's argument vis-à-vis Marxism is that in modern capitalist states power is not significantly determined by economic forces. Furthermore, other institutional sectors, such as psychiatric institutions, schools, and prisons, are increasingly essential to the operations of social power and in the constitutions of subjectivities: roles that have been minimized by Marxists. Thus, in relation to Marxism, Foucault asks a series of questions:

What means are available to us today if we seek to conduct a non-economic analysis of power? Very few, I believe. We have in the first place the assertion that power is neither given, nor exchanged, nor recovered, but rather exercised, and that it only exists in action. Again, we have at our disposal another assertion to the effect that power is not primarily the maintenance and reproduction of economic relations, but is above all a relation of force. The questions to be posed would then be these: if power is exercised, what sort of exercise does it involve? In what does it consist? What is its mechanism? (Foucault, 1980f: 89)

In *The History of Sexuality*, Volume 1, Foucault repeats his view concerning the general nature and exercise of power: "Power . . . is exercised from innumerable points in the interplay of non-egalitarian and mobile relations. . . . Power comes from below; that is, there is no binary and all-encompassing opposition between rulers and ruled at the root of power relations" (1978a: 94). Foucault's rejection of the view that "power is what represses" is also directed against Marxists. As he states it in *Discipline and Punish*: "We must cease once and for all to describe the effects of power in negative terms; it 'excludes', it 'represses', it 'censors', it 'abstracts', it 'masks', it 'conceals'. In fact, power produces, it produces reality; it produces domains of objects and rituals of truth. The individual and the knowledge that may be gained of him belong to this production" (1977a: 194). Foucault also rejects the metaphors of war, struggle, or conflict to explain power. His rejection of the "juridical" conception of power entails the rejection of those conceptions derived from philosophers of the eighteenth century which saw power as an "original right that is given up in the establishment of sovereignty, and the contract" (1980f: 91). Foucault rejects both the juridical conception, which he characterizes as a "contract-oppression" schema, and the "war-repression schema," which sees power in terms of struggle and submission, in preference to an approach that examines the mechanisms (i.e., the "how") of power (1977a: 92). As he puts it, in a lecture given in 1976 "my general project over the past few years has been, in essence, to reverse the modes of analysis followed by the entire discourse of right from the time of the Middle Ages" (1980f: 95). In his view, this juridical theory of power as sovereignty has had four roles to play: as a mechanism that was effective under feudalism; as an instrument and justification for establishing large-scale administrative monarchies; as a theory of sovereignty utilized to reinforce royal power; and as justification for a model of parliamentary democracy (see Foucault, 1980f: 103).

Central to this juridical theory of sovereignty is a concern to explain how power descends from the top to the lower orders of society. When Foucault talks of power, on the other hand, he talks about manifold forms of domination that can be exercised within society: "not the domination of the king in his central position . . . but that of his subjects in their mutual relations . . . [of] the multiple forms of subjugation that have a place and function within the social organism" (1980f: 96).

In his *Two Lectures on Power* (1980f: 96–102), he summarizes several methodological imperatives concerning the study of power. First, analysis should not concern itself with the regulated and legitimate forms of power in central locations, but rather with power at the extremities, at the points where it becomes capillary, that is, regional and local forms and institutions.

Second, analysis should not concern power at the level of conscious intention or decision—that is, not consider power from the internal point of view but rather at the level of real practices, at the level of those continuous and uninterrupted processes which subject our bodies, govern our gestures, and dictate our behaviors (see 1980f: 97).

Third, power is not to be taken as one individual's domination over others, or one group or class over others. That is, it is not a case of those who possess it and those who don't. Power must be analyzed as something that circulates or that functions "in the form of a chain . . . through a net-like organisation" (1980f: 98).

Fourth, power must not be analyzed as a descending analysis, in a deductive manner, starting from the center and aimed at discovering to what extent it permeates its base. Rather, one must conduct an *ascending* analysis of power starting from its infinitesimal mechanisms each of which has its own history, its own trajectory, its own technologies and tactics (1980f: 99).

The descending analysis is again that of the Marxist who will say that the bourgeoisie has been the dominant class since the sixteenth or seventeenth century. Rather than deducing the general phenomenon of power from the domination of the bourgeois class, one needs to investigate historically, beginning from the lowest level, how mechanisms of power have been able to function: "we need to identify the agents responsible . . . and not be content to lump them under the formula of a generalised bourgeoisie" (1980f: 101). In short, says Foucault, we should direct our researches on power not toward the juridical edifice of sovereignty, or the State apparatus, or the ideologies that accompany them but toward the material operations of power, and specific aspects of domination and subjection as they operate in localized systems and apparatuses.

While power may result in dominance, subjection, or violence, it is not primarily a form of domination. As Foucault puts it (1978a: 93), "one needs to be nominalistic, no doubt: power is not an institution, and not a structure; neither is it a certain strength we are endowed with; it is the name that we are endowed with; it is the name that one attributes to a complex strategical situation in a particular society."

As a strategy, the problem is to know how power works in specific locations. Hence, in place of a concept of power as an entity or as a juridical conception which represents power as the emanation of sovereignty, Foucault establishes an analytic of power which makes explicit its purely relational character and which locates the basis of these relations in a "hostile engagement of forces . . . Nietzsche's hypothesis" (Foucault, 1997: xv). Power in this conception, while co-extensive with the social body, is not necessarily directed by a subject. While there is a push, no one is pushing:

Power relations are both intentional and non-subjective . . . there is no power that is exercised without a series of aims and objectives. But this does not mean that it results from the choice or decision of an individual subject. . . . It is often the case that no one is there to have invented them, and who can be said to have formulated them: an implicit characteristic of the great anonymous, almost unspoken strategies which coordinate the loquacious tactics whose "inventors" or decisionmakers are often without hypocrisy. (Foucault, 1978a: 94–95)

The abandonment of the juridical model of power is thus replaced by a concrete analysis of power. The juridical model, which sees the individual subject as endowed with natural rights, primitive powers of antagonism, and proclivities for war, has the consequence that social relations are also seen as examples of warfare, ultimately dependent on an essentialist foundation.

Between 1976 and 1980, Foucault sought to strengthen his views on power, distinguishing more precisely between the *strategic* conception of power and the *states of domination* that people ordinarily call power:

It seems to me we must distinguish between power relations understood as strategic games between liberties—in which some try to control the conduct of others, who in turn try to avoid allowing their conduct to be controlled or try to control the conduct of others—and states of domination that people ordinarily call "power". And between the two, between games of power and states of domination, you have technologies of government—understood, of course, in a very broad sense. (Cited in Foucault, 1997: xvii)

POWER-KNOWLEDGE

In *The Order of Things*, discourses were seen to express the *historical a priori* of an episteme. Later, while they continued to express this, Foucault began to chart the manifold ways that they were related to social structure. It is the fact that knowledge systems are inextricably related to issues of power, that there are always sociological implications to the production of knowledge, and that knowledge systems themselves constitute technologies of power, that Foucault is referring to in the concept of *power-knowledge*, a concept he uses in his genealogical writings to theorize the interconnections between power and knowledge. One of his purposes in this regard is to focus on discourses that claim to be advancing under the banner of legitimate science but that have remained intimately connected to the micro-physics of power. Because the different sciences interact with social structures in different ways, Foucault believes it is necessary to examine each specific discursive formation separately so that one can evaluate its claims to adequately describe reality, as well as assess the particular ways in which interactions with social structure and with power take place (Dreyfus & Rabinow, 1982: ch. 2).

Although any quest for knowledge may produce expertise and technical competence, it is never simply neutral or disinterested. Rather, it is always affected by, and warped by, other factors within the social domain. In this sense, Foucault argues, the Enlightenment discourses of the human sciences—medicine, psychiatry, biology, genetics, psychology—took their shape not simply from the accumulated knowledge that their researchers had produced, but from an interrelation with a series of other elements within the historical field. To show how human populations became objects of positive knowledge and to explore the bio-medical roots of modern knowledge as an expression of power-knowledge became Foucault's principal theoretical interest.

The links between *power* and *knowledge* increasingly occupied Foucault's attention when he sought to explain the rationale for his empirical studies on the sciences as discursive structures of disciplined knowledge. It was the human sciences, what Ian Hacking (1979) calls "immature" sciences, rather than the natural sciences, that occupied most of Foucault's attention. In his early work, *The Order of Things*, Foucault hardly mentions the concept of power and only occasionally refers to social structure. Yet, it is here that Foucault gives his most thorough and systematic critique of the contemporary human sciences. In this work he argues for a radical reconstruction of the way we understand the disciplines, and he suggests a new theory of knowledge, which he expounds more systematically in *The Archaeology of Knowledge*, and elaborates in terms of the interactions with the non-discursive practices of social structure in works like *Discipline and Punish* and *The History of Sexuality*, Volume 1, as well as in interviews which he gave with increasing regularity in the later years of his life.

In methodological terms, the central key to understanding the disciplines as discursive formations is as structures (1) that manifest definite rules and regularities; (2) where these rules and regularities are compatible with the episteme of the age in the sense of establishing limits and exclusions, and are affected by the practical constraints of institutional power and control within the social structure; (3) that determine and limit the "conditions of possibility," that is, what it is possible and legitimate to say or write, what counts as reason, argument, or evidence; (4) that are autonomous in the sense that they do not integrally represent being; (5) that are anonymous in the sense that they are not linked to or embodied in individual subjects but are themselves, ontologically, part of a discursive regularity; (6) that go through transformations and experience radical discontinuities at particular periods which are sharp but not complete; and (7) that constitute forms of power that shape subjects and assist in regulating social life through the process of *normalization*.

The link between power and the disciplines is built on the relation of power and truth. In Foucault's words, "there can be no possible exercise of power without a certain economy of discourses of truth which operates through and on the basis of this association" (1980f: 93). Hence, truth for Foucault is ultimately political in nature and is predicated on knowledge of power strategies operative in a given society at a particular time. In this sense, power promotes truth just as it does falsity. In this regard truth has not set humans free but has instituted subjection since, as Foucault says, "the man described for us, whom we are invited to free, is already himself the effect of a subjection much more profound than himself" (1977a: 30).

In focusing on the "dubious" or "immature" sciences, Foucault brings into question the possible success of the unity of science program. In his early book *Maladie Mentale et Personalité*, first published in 1954,[1] he argues the basic thesis that whereas organic medicine is a genuine science of the body, there cannot be a similar science of human beings. Although, as is now well-known, he opposed republication of this work, owing to the form of anthropological humanism and materialism advanced, there was no major alteration of his views concerning the sciences. As he states in chapter 1 of the revised edition of that work,

My aim . . . is to show that mental pathology requires methods of analysis different from those of organic pathology and that it is only by an artifice of language that the same meaning can be attributed to "illnesses of the body" and "illnesses of the mind". A unitary pathology using the same methods and concepts in the psychological and physiological domains is now purely mythical, even if the unity of body and mind is in the order of reality. (Foucault, 1987b: 10)

Here Foucault argues that while a theoretical, scientific approach had been achieved in organic medicine, a parallel approach in psychiatry had not succeeded. Hence:

Psychology has never been able to offer psychiatry what physiology gave to medicine: a tool of analysis that, in delimiting the disorder, makes it possible to envisage the functional relationship of this damage to the personality as a whole. . . . In psychiatry, on the other hand, the notion of personality makes any distinction between normal and pathological singularly difficult. . . . [In medicine] the notion of organic totality accentuates the individuality of the sick subject; it makes it possible to isolate him in his morbid originality and to determine the particular character of his pathological reactions. In mental pathology, the reality of the patient does not permit such an abstraction and each morbid individuality must be understood through the practices of the environment with regard to him. . . . The dialectic of the relations of the individual to his environment does not operate in the same way in pathological physiology and in pathological psychology. (Foucault, 1987b: 10–13)

Thus Foucault does not view every science as equally problematic. His cynicism is reserved for the human sciences, and especially those whose object of analysis is the "figure of man." Yet, as Dreyfus points out, citing Foucault (1985c: 3), this does not make Foucault an opponent of scientific realism:

Despite his interest in the historical background and social consequences of all truth-claims, Foucault remained throughout his life a scientific realist in the tradition of his teacher, Georges Canguilhem. In an appreciation of the work of Canguilhem, Foucault wrote in 1985: "in the history of science one cannot take truth as given, but neither can one do without a relation to the truth and to the opposition of the true and the false. It is this reference to the order of the true and the false which gives to that history its specificity and its importance." (Dreyfus, 1987b: x–xi)

Although, as Dreyfus points out, Foucault owes a major debt to Canguilhem, as do writers like Bourdieu, Castels, Passeron, Althusser, and Lacan (see Foucault, 1980l), it should be appreciated that in many respects this debt extends through Canguilhem (and also independently of him) back to Bachelard. As Gutting (1989: ch. 1) points out, his recognition of the historicity of scientific conceptions, as well as the notion of discontinuity, that is, of epistemological ruptures and mutations, by which the history of science is understood in terms of breaks, owes a major debt to Bachelard. Like Bachelard, too, Foucault rejects a sharp theory/observation distinction of the sort advanced by naive realisms. He shares Bachelard's emphasis on the need to treat questions of scientific rationality in regional terms, eschewing global theories; to expose the contingent nature of that which imposes itself in the present as necessary; and to seek to expose the "deep structures" of knowledge, which has affinities, as Gutting notes, to Bachelard's conception of a "psychoanalysis of knowledge" (1989: 53).

Although Bachelard's influence must not be underemphasized or discounted, the direct debt to Canguilhem, especially to treatment of the history of science as a history of its concepts, is of central importance. In addition, Foucault frequently sides with Canguilhem against Bachelard on specific issues; notably, he emphasizes with Canguilhem the ways in which continuities can persist over epistemological breaks. Although Canguilhem rejects the idea of science as emergence in the process of a linear unfolding, he has a more nuanced understanding of the process than did Bachelard, tracing the discontinuities internal to the history of science: its ruptures and mutations, wrong turnings, obstacles, unanticipated advances, that characterize the process differently for each and every scientific domain. Hence, rather than seeing error as progressively eliminated by the "natural forces of truth which emerge little by little from the shadows" (Foucault, 1980l: 56), Canguilhem sees the historical link that different moments of a science have with each other as "constituted by . . . successive recastings, reformations, bringing to light of new foundations, changes in scale, transitions to new types of objects" (1980l: 56).

With regard to the relations between the physical and the social sciences, Dreyfus notes that even in *Discipline and Punish*, a later work, Foucault represents the physical and human sciences in much the same way as he did in his early work in the 1950s. Thus, while natural sciences like physics and organic chemistry are seen as mature and as having detached themselves from the power processes in which they originated, the human sciences have been largely unsuited to their subject matters and have remained implicated with the microphysics of power. Although in his works in the 1980s Foucault doesn't write about the physical sciences, "it seems reasonable to suppose," as Dreyfus puts it, "that Foucault retained the view stated in this first book [*Maladie Mentale et Personalité*] that the natural sciences have been able to arrive at relative autonomy because they have found a level of analysis that authorizes valid abstractions corresponding to the causal powers in the physical world" (Dreyfus, 1987b: xi).

Central to Foucault's explanation is his view that human phenomena such as personality can only be understood in relation to historical and cultural domains and thus human beings cannot be studied in the same way that physical phenomena can be. In order to understand "the historical dimension of the human psyche" (Foucault, 1987b: 31), it is not possible to study it as a series of "isolable functional components" (Dreyfus, 1987: xii). Whereas the "natural sciences can be right about the functional components of physical and organic nature . . . there is no human nature for the human sciences to be right about" (Dreyfus, 1987: xii). Hence the "dubious sciences" that focus on the "figure of man" must perpetually struggle with the fact that man's self as well as his consciousness are opaque and foreign to him in spite of the fact that he is the source of all meaning.

Foucault's method thus owes nothing to the methods of the natural sciences. Rather, his attempt to explain the human subject, or any other cultural phenomenon, is by endeavoring to see as much as possible the whole panorama—synchronically and diachronically—by understanding sets of elements as totalities whose elements cannot be dissociated but rather must be articulated through the ensemble of discursive and non-discursive practices which brings something into the interplay of truth and falsehood constituting it into an object of thought. Psychiatry and psychology are, then, for Foucault "pseudo-sciences," whereas disciplines such as natural history are "sciences at the prehistoric stage" (1972: 178). These disciplines, which constitute "groups of statements that borrow their organization from scientific models," constitute the privileged object of archaeological analysis, he tells us in *The Archaeology of Knowledge*. Hence archaeology describes

and analyzes disciplines that are "not really sciences . . . which tend to coherence and demonstrativity, which are accepted, institutionalized, transmitted and sometimes taught as sciences" (178).

In tracing the emergence of discourses of knowledge, including the sciences, Foucault distinguishes several distinct *levels of emergence* of a discursive formation. The first level he mentions is the *threshold of positivity*, which
refers to the point at which a discursive practice achieves individuality and
autonomy, the moment when a single system of the formation of statements
is put into operation (1972: 186). A *threshold of epistemologization* pertains
to the point when, in the operation of a discursive formation, a group of
statements is articulated and claims to validate (even if unsuccessfully) norms
of verification and coherence, and when it exercises a dominant function
over knowledge (186–187). A *threshold of scientificity* is crossed when a
discursive system obeys formal criteria and when its statements comply with
the laws and rules for the construction of propositions and so on (1972:
187). And a *threshold of formalization* is passed when a scientific discourse
is able, in turn, to define and proscribe axioms necessary to it, the elements
that it uses, the propositional structures that are legitimate to it, and the
transformations that it accepts (187).

The chronology of the emergence of these levels is neither regular nor
homogeneous; hence it is not possible to divide the history of human knowledge neatly into different stages. Moreover, not all discursive formations
pass through all these different thresholds, so there are no "natural stages
. . . of maturation." Yet, it is the "distribution in time of these different
thresholds, their succession, their possible coincidence (or lack of it), the
way in which they may govern one another, or become implicated with one
another, the conditions in which, in turn, they are established" (1972: 187)
that constitutes Foucault's theoretical description of his own endeavor. By
recognizing that discursive practices have their own levels, thresholds, ruptures, and the like, he avoids chronological description or the imputation of
a single linear process of emergence in which all the complexities are "reduced to the monotonous act of an endlessly repeated foundation" (1972:
188).

Hence, central to Foucault's analytic endeavor is the task of tracing the
emergence of various discursive formations across different thresholds,
showing how concepts develop, are purified and accredited scientific status,
how a region of experience is accorded scientific status or constituted as a
scientific domain, as well as tracing how science emerges from a pre-scientific
domain or level. Foucault sees mathematics as the only science for which
one can neither distinguish these different thresholds or shifts, as "the only
discursive practice to have crossed at one and the same time the thresholds
of positivity, epistemologization, scientificity, and formalization," although
he concedes that the ability to analyze it thus is partly because its establishment is so "little accessible to analysis" (1972: 188).

In a more general sense Foucault asks the question, "in accordance with what order and what processes is the emergence of a region of scientificity in a given discursive formation accomplished?" (1972: 184), and he traces the processes by which science becomes localized in a field of knowledge at a particular juncture. Here the field of knowledge refers to a more general discursive context made up of elements that are "indispensable to the constitution of a science, although they are not necessarily destined to give rise to one" (182).

What made it possible for psychiatry to appear epistemologized at the beginning of the nineteenth century with Pinel, Heinroth, and Esquirol "was a whole set of relations between hospitalization, internment, the conditions and procedures of social exclusion, the rules of jurisprudence, the norms of industrial labour and bourgeois morality, in short a whole group of relations that characterized for this discursive practice the formation of its statements" (1972: 179). Yet, says Foucault, the discursive formation whose existence was mapped by the psychiatric discipline was not coextensive with it, but rather went beyond its boundaries. Moreover, if one goes back in time and tries to discover what, in the seventeenth and eighteenth centuries, preceded the establishment of psychiatry, one realizes that there was no such prior discipline, but, despite this, a discursive practice, with its own regularity and consistency did operate. Such a discursive practice was present in medicine and could also be found in "administrative regulations, in literary or philosophical texts, in casuistics, in the theories or projects of obligatory labour or assistance to the poor" (1972: 179).

Although one can analyze psychiatry in its epistemological structure, or in terms of the framework of the political institutions in which it operates, or in terms of its ethical implications as regards either the patient or doctor or both, Foucault's objective has not been concerned with such goals; but rather to seek to show

> how the formation of psychiatry as a science, the limitation of its field, and the definition of its object implicated a political structure and a moral practice: in the twofold sense that they were presupposed by the progressive organisation of psychiatry as a science and that they were also changed by this development. Psychiatry as we know it couldn't have existed without a whole interplay of political structures and without a set of ethical attitudes; but inversely, the establishment of madness as a domain of knowledge changed the political practices and the ethical attitudes that concerned it. It was a matter of determining the role of politics and ethics in the establishment of madness as a particular domain of scientific knowledge, and also of analysing the effects of the latter on political and ethical practices. (1984g: 386–387)

BIO-POWER AND GOVERNMENTALITY

At the end of *The History of Sexuality*, Volume 1, Foucault proposes that power in modern society increasingly takes the form of *bio-power*. By "bio-power" he means the "macro-social" functions of "power-knowledge" in the regulation and investigation of populations. It is in this sense that Foucault has identified certain knowledge and attendant practices as crucial to constructing and normalizing modern society. In addition, certain institutions—prisons, mental hospitals, schools, sciences, and the like—have functioned as apparatuses that have been instrumental in constructing the modern conception of the subject and the very idea of what it means to be normal. They are vehicles by which the population is organized and by which productivity and order in modern welfare capitalist states are made possible. Bio-power emerged, says Foucault, in the seventeenth century as a coherent and powerful technology, and it refers to the increasing ordering and regulation of all realms of society by the State under the guise of improving the welfare of individuals—not as individuals as such, but rather as *subjects* of a population. For Foucault, the aim of bio-power is *normalization*. It aims to regulate individuals through increasingly rationalized means, utilizing technologies such as statistics and political arithmetic. The systems of knowledge and the institutional sectors to which they have given rise in turn began to constitute systems of administrative control that replaced harsher forms of control from previous times. In this sense, says Foucault, modern states do not rely on force, but on forms of knowledge that regulate populations by describing, defining, and delivering the forms of normality and educability (Foucault, 1980b).

Increasingly, the State became the ultimate agent in the exercise of bio-power, and as it did it constituted new forms of political rationality or *governmentality*. Foucault first used the concept of governmentality in 1978 in a paper published in English in 1979 (see Foucault, 1979a), and he developed the concept further in lectures given at the Collège de France between 1976 and 1984. The theoretical rationale for the concept was to counter the criticisms of Marxists and liberals that his treatment of power as explicated in works such as *Discipline and Punish* and *The History of Sexuality*, Volume 1 dealt only with the "micro-physics" in terms of which subjects appeared deterministically prefigured by techniques that fashion individuals to lead docile and practical lives in a way that obliterates all possibility of resistance and autonomy. Governmentality thus refers to the global coordination of power at the level of the State as opposed to the micro-physics of power. It refers to discourses concerned with the "arts of government" by which the State politically coordinates power to effect particular constructions of the subject. As Foucault puts it:

The art of government . . . is essentially concerned with . . . how to introduce economy, that is the correct manner of managing individuals, goods and wealth within the family . . . how to introduce this meticulous attention of the father towards his family, into the management of the state. (Foucault, 1979a: 10)

In his lectures on the arts of government, Foucault insists on the importance of a series of discourses that appeared in Europe from the late sixteenth
century onwards and that provided forms of rationalization for new administrative techniques. State reason initially distinguished government by State
from government by the head of a family, a nobleman, or a sovereign prince.
Then a science of policing emerged (*Polizeiwissenschaft*) related to the aim
of completely controlling social life and seeking to adjust the happiness of
individuals to the happiness of the State. Through a complex series of political, economic, and epistemological changes, and especially the Church's
decline in unity and influence, classical liberalism represented a new emergent form of governmentality that constituted for Foucault a political-
epistemological revolution. What he suggests is that a genealogy of the
modern State suggested two modalities of power, which can be distinguished in terms of the directions in relation to which power is exercised.
First are totalizing forms of power, which are aimed at increasing the power
of the State at the level of populations, and that characterize the *Polizeiwissenschaft* of the *ancien regime*. This reason of State is based on a unity
of knowing and governing as embodied in the conception of the State as a
Leviathan where all that was happening in society could be maintained by
the State.

Second are individualizing forms of power, applied to subjects of State
power to which it recognizes a special responsibility, and which characterize
emergent liberal regimes. This conception questioned the unity of knowing
and governing and maintained that the rationality of the State could not be
calculative and regulative of the totality, but instead sought to situate political reason within an unstable politico-epistemological matrix. Hence liberalism represented a new reason of state, and a new individualizing form
of power that aimed to create subjects of certain kinds. It was both an
alternative conception of how things were to be and a critique of what had
gone before (Marshall, 1996a; Burchell, 1996; Rose, 1996).

In developing notions of *bio-power* concerned with populations as aggregates and of *governmentality* concerned with political rule and management,
Foucault also came to argue for a conception of ontological freedom of
individuals through a conception of the *strategic reversibility of power relations* in terms of which individual subjects, though constituted by *power-
knowledge*, can utilize the techniques of power in achieving their own ends.
Such a notion ultimately makes Foucault an optimist about the possibilities
of emancipation and the ability of people to direct the course of human
events, for it is through such a conception of power, together with his in-
sistence on the contingent nature of life, that Foucault underscores the
transformable character of the cultural formation (see Foucault, 1991a).

THE HISTORICAL CONSTITUTION OF THE SELF

Foucault utilizes the concepts concerned with the problematic of power to provide a novel and now influential perspective on the construction of the self. Essentially, what he advocates is a social constructionist account of the self. What this involves, as Deborah Cook states, is that:

the subject is . . . not pregiven, just as sex and the body or man are not "already there" waiting to be discovered. When Foucault speaks of the formation of the subject, he means quite literally that the subject does not exist as a determinate form with specific qualities before the practices that make up the *rapport à soi* in different historical periods bring it into being. (Cook, 1987: 218–219)

For Foucault, the subject is constituted not in language, as Lacan would have it, but through many different types of practices. Some of these individualizing practices are discursive (author function); others are institutional. In this view he stood sharply opposed to the phenomenology of Sartre, opposing any conception of the subject that is prior to and constitutive of history. Hence, life's events must be analyzed not as a consequence of the volition of subjects but in terms of historical bodies of anonymous, rule-governed discourse. In this, Foucault is much closer to Heidegger's anti-humanist understanding of the subject and freedom than to Sartre's conception of the individual as the embodiment of freedom of the will.

For Foucault, the process through which subjects and their identities are formed is deeply ingrained in the culture and, as Racevskis maintains, is "one that is immanent in the dominant epistemological mode of the modern period in particular" (1991: 23) In considering the problems of theorizing identity formation as a function of history and language, Racevskis identifies what he calls the major paradox of Foucault's work, for:

Identity is what is naturally given and is therefore considered as a possession, yet it is also that which possesses the individual. If, on the one hand, identity is constituted by a personal experience and an individual history, it is also and inevitably a product of the otherness of cultural, social, and linguistic determinants. As the individual reconstructs and reflects upon an imaginary identity, he/she cultivates an illusion of conscious control that only serves to occlude the aleatory and contingent nature of this imaginary essence. Thus, in a sense, identity is our metaphysical refuge, it is the gap between our history and History, between our self-conscious and purposeful use of language and the *Logos* that makes our speech possible. We reside in this gap by covering it up with an explanatory system that reconciles our self-image with our being, a system that has also the virtue of placing other humans within the context of a fundamental nature, a teleological design, or a scientific paradigm. (1991: 21)

In order to examine the notion of identity, Foucault, through archaeology and genealogy, challenges what is traditionally considered as given and what-

ever is deemed normal. This challenging of the traditional conception of
identity in modernism, introduced and emphasized from Hobbes onwards,
is part of a massive indoctrination to which individuals have been subjected.
This, as Racevskis (1991: 27) notes, Foucault applies to himself, as evident
in his statements such as "I have been bottle-fed with knowledge." Identity
constitution is derived when through culture and education the dominant
epistemological matrix is internalized. Hence, an identity is linked closely to
notions of essence and being, says Racevskis, and it can be considered to be
"a product of the epistemological configuration that gave rise to the figure
of 'man' at the beginning of the nineteenth century" (22). Identity formation, like other aspects of subjectivity, is therefore inextricably enmeshed
in political strategies and is involved with the power-knowledge effects applied by discourse.

For Foucault, the self is constituted discursively and institutionally by
power-knowledge organized in disciplinary blocks. There are two main
mechanisms: *technologies of domination* and *technologies of self.* Technologies
of domination act on the body from the outside via classification and ob-
jectification. These involve the human sciences, which developed after the
start of the nineteenth century and which ensure the provision of "expert"
and "authoritative" knowledge, and an assortment of "dividing practices"
which objectify the subject, providing classifications for subject positions
(*mad, normal, intelligent, unintelligent, high flyer, slow developer,* etc.). In
education these operate through a whole range of techniques, including
examinations and other forms of assessment, streaming practices, and the
like. "Technologies of the self," Foucault's later interest, are operated by
individuals themselves who have the agency to utilize strategies of power to
manage and affect their constitution as subjects through a recognition of
the possible "subject positions" available, and through resistance, to change
history (Foucault, 1982a: 208).

In *The History of Sexuality*, Volume 1, Foucault outlines his suspicion of
doctrines of liberation that rely on a conception of a "deep self," which can
be uncovered through some privileged form of science. Rather, sexual discourses create subjects from without as an effect of certain regimes of
"power-knowledge." It is through techniques originally deriving from
Christian pastoral power (such as the "confession"), and seeing its modern
form on the psychoanalyst's couch, says Foucault, that knowledge of an
"inner self" is claimed. As such, *The History of Sexuality*, Volume 1 constitutes a genealogy of the forms by which Europeans have recognized themselves as subjects of desire. Although Foucault maintains the constructionist
nature of discursive systems, based on a thesis, as Marshall (1996a, 1996b)
has noted, on the performative function of language, this should not be
seen as amounting to a naive form of linguistic idealism whereby it is claimed
that nothing exists outside of discourse, or that *everything* about ourselves
is constructed by discourse. Foucault's philosophical nominalism ensures

that his constructionist claims vary depending on the object of his analytical focus. While in relation to explaining the constitution of the self Foucault maintains a strong constructionist thesis, in relation to the physical sciences he is much more cautious, and in relation to the physical world he is not a constructionist at all. These facts give his constructionism a "dynamic" quality (Olssen, 1995).

In relation to the history of philosophical conceptions, Foucault's view of the self is premised on a rejection of the Cartesian and Kantian conceptions of subject-centered reason. In this, he follows Nietzsche who rejects the Cartesian *Cogito* as a foundation constitutive of autonomous reasoned thought. Nietzsche questioned the "strangeness" of Descartes' indubitable beliefs—that "thinking exists" (Nietzsche, 1968: 483–484). As Lash explains:

This . . . Nietzsche remarks is a "strong belief," at best "questionable," hardly "indubitable." This shaky assumption is followed by the non-sequitur that the "I" exists. Even if thinking was indubitable, the argument for the "I" would depend on another assumption—that there must be a "substance" which thinks, which itself, observes Nietzsche, is dependent on a belief in "substance" . . . Nietzsche may have, with justification, added that there is no necessity that such a substance be the "I". (Lash, 1984: 12)

Foucault also rejects the Kantian conception of a constitutive subject, accepting Heidegger's (1967) critique of that notion. For Kant rational individuals impose their categorical constructions on the world; that is, they constitute the world imposing categories on sense data through a priori faculties. For Foucault the categories were historically contingent rather than universal, and following Heidegger, he claimed that Kant attributed too much agency to the individual subject, thus neglecting to afford sufficient significance to the context of "background beliefs"—the discourse for Foucault—constitutive of experience.

Kant, says Foucault, placed men at the center of scientific knowledge through locating the levels of knowledge, as well as the basis of rationality, in pure a priori faculties of human reason which were independent of empirical evidence. This "centering of man," Foucault states in *The Order of Things* (1970: 340–341), is Kant's "Copernican revolution" which induced an "anthropological sleep" into the modern systems of knowledge directing attention to the issue: what is man? (see Simons, 1995: 13).

While in *Discipline and Punish* and *The History of Sexuality*, Volume 1, Foucault's emphasis was on the production of the self by others and through the human sciences, in his later works he became interested in how "a human being turns him-or herself into a subject" (Foucault, 1982a: 208). Hence, while in *Madness and Civilisation* the problem was how madmen were controlled by outside forces, by *The History of Sexuality*, Volume 1 the problem had become how one controls oneself through a variety of inner mental techniques and with the aid of those who are experts in revealing the truth about oneself.

During the 1980s Foucault became increasingly interested in an aesthetics of self, resurrecting the Greek notion "to take care of oneself." Although the self is still seen as the outcome of discourses of the human sciences and of the institutional practices of political control, Foucault argued for an ethics of "caring for oneself" as a means of practicing freedom. He came to see the self, though constituted by power, as developing a new dimension of subjectivity which derived from power and knowledge but which was not dependent on them. Hence, although created by power in history, through interaction with others and by the necessity of reflection, a *rapport à soi* develops which constitutes an interior and creates its own unique aspect, (see Deleuze, 1988: 100–101)

Suggested here is that caring for oneself involved a notion of increasing maturity through processes such as problematization and reflection which could prevent one from being dominated by others or by aspects of oneself. In resurrecting the principle of "caring for oneself," Foucault is reversing the priority of Western culture as underpinned by the Delphic maxim "to know thyself" which supplanted the original Greek notion based on care. Originally in the Greco-Roman world, says Foucault, the care of the self through improving, surpassing, and mastering oneself was the manner in which individual liberty considered itself as ethical, and was basic to and prior to knowing oneself (Marshall, 1996a, 1996b).

FOUCAULT AND FEMINISM

Much of the significance of Foucault for an understanding of subjectivity can be seen in connection with the extensive feminist appropriation of his work. Diamond and Quinby (1988) note four convergences between feminism and Foucault. First, both recognize *the body* as the site of power, that is, as the locus of domination through which subjectivity is constituted. Second, both point to local and intermediate operations of power rather than focusing exclusively on the State or on the mode of production. Third, both highlight the crucial role of discourse in its capacity to produce and sustain hegemonic power. And fourth, both criticize Western humanism for having privileged the experience of Western masculine elites as they proclaim universals about truth. In this sense, both attempt to dismantle "existing but hithertofore unrecognised modes of domination" (1988: x).

Renate Holub also recognizes Foucault's significance for feminism:

[M]any feminist theorists have found much inspiration in the conceptual sophistication and methods of analysis of Foucault's work. In particular, his analysis of the operations of power, such as his critical studies of the institutions of medicine, prisons and science, which have identified the body as the site of power through which docility and submission are accomplished. . . . Moreover, Foucault's emphasis on the functional partiality of discourses and language in the production of domination and in the marginalization and silencing of counter-discourses has also been an important source of insight for feminist theory. Language, the symbolic sphere, the tools of our intercommunicative practices are indeed implicated in the production and reproduction of hegemonic domination. Furthermore, Foucault has called into question the legitimacy of ways of telling history, metanarratives which tell a linear story instead of a discontinuous one, and metanarratives which insist on telling the story from a western point of view, on telling the true story of how and why it all happened. . . . Indeed, objectivity and rationality itself were dismantled by Foucault as constructions designed to secure hegemony. These are but a few Foucauldian positions which feminists could easily [*sic*] incorporate into their theoretical work. (Holub, 1992: 200–201)

In relation to the issue of subjectivity, Foucault has influenced feminists such as Judith Butler (1990), Jana Sawicki (1991, 1995), and Susan Bordo (1988) in their rejection of identity-based politics rooted in the notion of an historical, pre-discursive "I." For Foucault "identities" are "self representations" or "fixations" that are neither fixed nor stable. The subject is not a "thing" outside of culture, and there is no pure "state of nature" to ground history either. The subject is not a substantive entity at all but rather a process of signification with an open system of discursive possibilities. The self is a regulated but not determined set of practices and possibilities.

This has led to moves within feminism to represent identity as politicized in the process of construction. The choice of experiences that constitute the self always have political effects for identity stands in a discursive relation to other discursive elements. Thus identity is always a bounded notion. In Butler's (1990) sense of "parodic repetition" or Haraway's (1990) sense of "the cyborg" forms of repetitive signification defy and exceed dominant cultural injunctions. Such examples might include the "lipstick lesbian" and "the effeminate man." Such an injunction that established identities are cultural means that their stability and coherence can be challenged prefiguring the establishment of other identities.

What has caused many feminists to turn away from Foucault, however, is that he sees, to cite Nancy Hartsock (1990), "no headquarters which set the direction" (Holub, 1992: 201); that is, he sees no structural source to power and thus is unable, finally, to answer the question "Who is it that has power?" It may be that a thinker like Gramsci is a corrective here, for while he, like Foucault, sees power relations as ubiquitous, "equally ubiquitous," as Holub expresses it, "are unequal relations of power" (1992: 200). For Gramsci more than Foucault, power relations are hierarchically structured and related to a source. This is a connection I will explore further in Chapter 7.

NOTE

1. Republished in 1962 as *Maladie Mentale et Psychologie* (Paris: Presses Universitaires de France). This was the revised edition with a different second part and conclusion. Translated by Alan Sheridan as *Mental Illness and Psychology* (New York: Harper and Row, 1976). It is this later, radically revised edition which is used in the 1987 University of California Press edition, from which all quotations used in this work are taken.

Part II

Considering Foucault
as Historical Materialist

Chapter 4

Foucault's Different Faces

In his book *Tropics of Discourse* (1978), Hayden White the points out that Foucault treats all phenomena as linguistic phenomena (White, 1978: 230). Such an interpretation appeared consistent with the way Foucault treated the subjects of madness and reason in his earlier studies, and was a common explanation of his work in general during the 1960s and 1970s. Such an interpretation was consistent with the emphasis given to language by writers such as Saussure, Lacan, and Barthes, and there was a tendency during the 1970s to see Foucault as another language theorist within the French tradition of social theory. Yet according to Mark Poster (1984), Dreyfus and Rabinow (1983), Barry Smart (1985), and Michèlle Barrett (1988), while in his earlier archaeological investigations Foucault held that the deep structures of human life and culture were explicable in relation to the structures of language, after 1968 he reorientated and reclassified his ideas, substantially altering the direction of his work. As Poster states, "after 1968 [the] structuralist concern with language and its autonomy that was paramount in *The Order of Things* . . . gave way to an ill-defined but suggestive category of discourse/practice in which the reciprocal interplay of reason and action was presumed. . . . This subtle yet ill-defined sense of the interplay of truth and power, theory and practice, became the central theme of Foucault's investigations" (1984: 9).

Whether this change in Foucault's views was as sudden as Poster suggests is controversial. Marshall (1990) and Donelly (1982) see a more gradual transition, with genealogy building on and extending archaeology. According to Michael Mahon (1992), it is highly debatable whether change took place at all in fact. Although Foucault may not have referred to the practices and institutions of the real world in any obvious sense, a careful reading reveals otherwise. As Mahon puts it,

There is more than a little difficulty . . . in reading *Histoire de la Folie*, Foucault's *archaeology* of madness's silence or *Naissance de la clinique: Une archéologie du regard médical* and still argue that Foucault in his early archaeological writings is simply concerned with autonomous discourse, independent of technologies of power, social practices and institutions. As Foucault insists with an interviewer, "there is only interest in describing this autonomous stratum of discourse to the measure in which one can put it in relation with other strata, of practices, of institutions, of social and political relations, etc. It is this relation which has always haunted me." (1992: 102–103)

Or again, as Mahon quotes Foucault,

The archaeology of the human sciences has to be established through studying the mechanisms of power which have invested human bodies, acts and forms of behaviour. . . . Archaeology examines the "archive", "that specific discursive configuration which permits a discourse to arise, to exist and to function within the framework of social relations and practices, within modes of institutionalized application and cultural usage." (Cited in Mahon, 1992: 103)

Dreyfus and Rabinow (1983) argue at great length that over time Foucault changed his emphasis, attempting to adopt a more realist position. They maintain that Foucault's continued dissatisfaction with the achievements of *The Archaeology of Knowledge* led him to shift emphasis from archaeology to Nietzsche's concept of genealogy as a dominant method. The idea of genealogy, claim Dreyfus and Rabinow, places a much greater emphasis on practices and social institutions and on the relations between discursive and extra-discursive dimensions of reality.

Michèle Barrett (1988) offers a similar thesis. According to Barrett, in his earlier works Foucault elaborated a view of the "production of 'things' by 'words,' " and she claims that Foucault as archaeologist was phenomenologically and epistemologically detached from the discursive formations studied (Barrett, 1988: 130). It is only Foucault's later works—*Discipline and Punish* and *The History of Sexuality*—where "practice is favoured over theory" and where "discourse is understood as a way of organising practices" (1988: 134). The shift from archaeology to genealogy means essentially that Foucault no longer regards himself as detached from the social practices he studies. Indicative of the transition, says Barrett, is the fact that Foucault "discovered the concept of power" (135). She cites Foucault to support her case:

When I think back now, I ask what else it was that I was talking about in *Madness and Civilization* or *The Birth of the Clinic* but power. Yet I am perfectly aware that I scarcely even used the word and never had such a field of analysis at my disposal. (cited in Barrett: 135)

Barry Smart (1985: 47–48) depicts a similar shift in Foucault's work, seeing the methodological approach of *The Archaeology of Knowledge* as significantly altered by Foucault's shift to genealogy. Although this

represented a change of emphasis and the development of new concepts . . . such shifts and transformations as are evident do not signify a rigid change of "break" between earlier and later writings, rather a re-ordering of analytic priorities from a structuralist-influenced preoccupation with discourse to a greater and more explicit consideration of institutions.

My own view also stresses the continuity between Foucault's earlier and later periods of writing. Although Foucault's later analysis adopts new methods and strategies, and explores new problems, there is no repudiation of the central theoretical insights of *The Archaeology of Knowledge*. There are shifts of emphasis as well in the problems of interest, and he becomes more manifestly materialist in the sense that he elaborates a theory of power, but there is no disqualification of his insights in *The Archaeology*. Moreover, *The Archaeology* can plausibly be read in a fundamentally materialist way. This view also accords with Foucault's own view that too much had been made of a supposed contrast between his earlier and his later writings: "I have said nothing different from what I was already saying" (cited in Racevskis, 1991: 28–29).

When he wrote *The Archaeology*, Foucault's primary object of investigation was the ontological nature of the discursive: how discourses arise; how they achieve their unity; how they define their objects. Hence, in the first chapters of *The Archaeology* he investigates how discourses such as psychiatry, grammar, economics, and medicine constitute their historical form: "on what kind of unity they could be based." He discovers that what accounts for the process of the formation of discourse is a "group of *rules* that are immanent in a practice, and define it in its specificity" (Foucault, 1972: 46). Hence, Foucault maintains that a discourse is not constituted according to the nature of the objects it subsumes in its gaze, that is, according to its referents. Thus, for example, he claims that "in the nineteenth century, psychiatric discourse is characterized not by privileged objects, but by the way in which it forms objects that are in fact highly dispersed" (1972: 44). While making this claim, he does not discard the existence of the referent, nor does he ontologically subordinate it to the discursive. In addition, he "has no wish . . . to exclude any effort to uncover and free these 'prediscursive' experiences from the tyranny of the text" (1972: 47). That, however, is not the aim of *his* analyses in *The Archaeology of Knowledge*. Rather, his aim, he states, is to

dispense with "things". To "depresentify" them. . . . To substitute for the enigmatic treasure of "things" anterior to discourse, the regular formation of objects that emerge only in discourse. To define these *objects* without reference to the *ground*, the *foundation of things*, but by relating them to the body of rules that enable them to form as objects of a discourse and thus constitute the conditions of their historical appearance. (Foucault, 1972: 47–48)

Here Foucault is asserting the ontological autonomy of the discursive, a claim which even as he moved to a more obviously realist position in his later works he was never to give up. He is pointing to the immediate ineradicable existence of the discursive through which life is made intelligible and which is always an obstacle to detecting anything beyond it. Thus our engagement with the world is always mediated by discourse that is constituted by "relations" as they "are established between institutions, economic and social processes, behavioural patterns, systems of norms, techniques, types of classification, modes of characterization [which] . . . enables it to appear . . . to define its difference, its irreducibility, and even perhaps its heterogeneity" (1972: 45). This "complex group of relations that function as a rule" constitutes the "system of formation" of discourse (74). In analyzing discourse, says Foucault, "one sees the loosening of the embrace . . . of words and things, and the emergence of a group of rules proper to discursive practice. These rules define not the dumb existence of reality, nor the canonical use of vocabulary, but the ordering of objects" (49). At the same time, Foucault stresses the *materiality* of the formative processes of discourse, noting that central to the theoretical choices and forms of exclusion that constitute them is an "authority . . . characterized . . . by the *function* that the discourse . . . must carry out *in a field of non-discursive practices*" (Foucault, 1972: 68).

Thus General Grammar played a role in pedagogic practice; in a much more obvious and much more important way, the Analysis of Wealth played a role not only in the political and economic decisions of governments, but in the scarcely conceptualized, scarcely theoretized, daily practice of emergent capitalism, and in the social and political struggles that characterized the Classical period. (1972: 68)

Foucault again reinforces the importance of the extra-discursive later in *The Archaeology*, where he claims that "archaeology also reveals relations between discursive and non-discursive domains" (Foucault, 1972: 162). Thus, taking the example of classical medicine, he compares archaeology as a form of analysis to Marxism:

A causal analysis . . . would try to discover to what extent political changes, or economic processes, could determine the consciousness of scientists—the horizon and direction of their interest, their system of values, their way of perceiving things, the style of their rationality. . . . Archaeology situates its analysis at another level. . . . It wishes to show not how political practice has determined the meaning and form of medical discourse, but *how and in what form* it takes part in its conditions of emergence, insertion and functioning. (1972: 163; emphasis added)

The unavoidability of discursive mediation is not changed in Foucault's post-1968 period, yet in his works of the 1970s—*Discipline and Punish* and *The History of Sexuality*, Volume 1—practice becomes increasingly *empha-sized* as that which exists independent of interpretation and as separate from discourse. This increasing recognition of material practice correlates with Foucault's shift in method from archaeology to genealogy. In focusing on archaeology, Foucault emphasizes the structure of the discursive, whereas in focusing on genealogy he gives greater weight to practices and institutions. Whereas archaeological investigations are directed to an analysis of the unconscious rules of formation which regulate the emergence of discourse, genealogical analysis focuses on the specific nature of the relations between discourse and practice, and the material conditions of emergence of the human sciences and of discursive systems of knowledge. Genealogical analysis is essentially a method of tracing the processes of *descent* and *emergence* in the search for antecedents. As a form of critical historical method, it seeks to identify links between the discursive and the extra-discursive, that is, between discourses and particular technologies of power located within social practices. In the shift from archaeology to genealogy, the major emphasis of the latter constitutes an expressed commitment to realism, to a form of historical materialism, and as Smart puts it, "a change in Foucault's value relationship to his subject matter" from the "relative detachment" of archaeology to a "commitment to critique" characteristic of genealogy (1985: 48).

What must be stressed, however, is that while there is a clear shift in Foucault's thought, and while that shift may express Foucault's dissatisfaction with his earlier works, the later methods should not be seen as excluding the earlier ones. Minson (1985: 115) argues that a full understanding of Foucault's later genealogies *requires* an understanding of archaeology. For Arnold Davidson (1986: 227), too, archaeology is quite consistent and compatible with genealogy and is in fact required to give genealogy its full expression. As Davidson states bluntly: "genealogy does not so much displace archaeology as widen the kind of analysis to be pursued. It is a question, as Foucault put it in his last writings, of different axes whose 'relative importance . . . is not always the same for all forms of experience' " (Davidson, 1986: 227).

Rabinow also sees Foucault's later works as consistent with his earlier ones: they simply *extend* the form of the analysis. He points out that Foucault continues to use the most important of the concepts and theoretical ideas of *The Archaeology of Knowledge* in his later works. In Rabinow's view:

Foucault has been consistently materialist. In asking, "How does discourse function?," his aim has been to isolate techniques of power exactly in those places where this kind of analysis is rarely done. But to achieve this, he at first overemphasized the inner articulations and seemingly self-enclosed nature of social scientific discourses.

Although Foucault has preserved the majority of his "archaeological" systematizations of the formation of concepts, objects, subjects, and strategies of discourse in the human sciences, he has now explicitly widened his analysis to show how these disciplines have played an effective part in a historical field that includes other types of nondiscursive practice. (1984: 10)

What also occurs between the earlier and the later works, as Thomas Flynn (1991a) has noted, is a shift from a *spatial* to a *temporal* motif in Foucault's work. That the different approaches are complementary, however, is established by Foucault himself when, after the publication of *Discipline and Punish*, he seeks to redefine the method of archaeology in genealogical terms:

The archaeology of the human sciences has to be established through studying the mechanisms of power which have invested human bodies, acts and forms of behaviour. And this investigation enables us to rediscover one of the conditions of the emergence of the human sciences: the great nineteenth-century effort in discipline and normalisation. (Foucault, 1980d: 61)

In his later works, Foucault introduced the concept of *problematization* as yet another theoretical device to supplement archaeology and genealogy. To study history in terms of problematization involves the choice of the material as a function of the givens of the problem and a focusing of analysis on elements capable of being resolved, together with the establishment of relations that permit a solution.

Characteristically, Foucault says that the concept of problematization has linked all his works since *Madness and Civilization*. In that work, it was a question of determining how and why at a particular moment madness was problematized via a certain institutional practice and a certain cognitive apparatus. Similarly, *Discipline and Punish* dealt with changes in the problematization of relations between personal practices and institutions at the end of the seventeenth century, while the question addressed in *The History of Sexuality*, Volumes 1 and 2, is how sexuality was problematized.

FOUCAULT AND THE LATER POST-STRUCTURALISTS

There seems little doubt that Foucault's form of analysis and methodological orientation changed to some degree, although there is some contention as to whether the change was sudden or gradual. There also appears to be a consensus that Foucault's analysis is compatible with a form of historical materialist analysis. It is, as Callinicos (1988: 68) has put it, summarizing Edward Said, "a worldly poststructuralism," a poststructuralism that articulates both "the said and the unsaid," the "discursive and the non-discursive." By referring to it in this way, it can be distinguished from the linguistic idealism of later versions of post-structuralism, especially the forms of textualism identified with writers such as Derrida, Lacan, and Lyotard. Barrett also makes this distinction between two forms of post-structuralism. Whereas Foucault's notion of discursivity is related to "context," the textualism of Derrida and the later post-structuralists is essentially "self-referential." As Foucault says, "the question posed by language analysis . . . is always: according to what rules has a particular statement been made, and consequently according to what rules could other similar statements be made? The description of the events of discourse poses a quite different question: *how is it that one particular statement appeared rather than another?*" (1972: 27; emphasis added).

One consequence of Foucault's more materialist position is that his own account is rendered incompatible with the Saussurean view of language where signification is represented as anterior to, and independent from, the world. Foucault does not prioritize the signifier in the classic Saussurean sense, either in the sense of bracketing the referent or abandoning it. Hence he avoids positing a world in which, as for Saussure and the later post-structuralists, there are only *words*, not *things*.[1]

For Derrida and the later post-structuralists, post-structuralism prioritizes the linguistic, places literature at the center of analysis, and treats all forms of discourse, including science, as literary genres. In addition, it is a form of anti-realism in that it privileges discourse over the world and denies the possibility of ever escaping the discursive and ever knowing reality independent of discourse. For Derrida, there is no escape from discourse. All is text. As he famously put it, "Il n'y a pas de hors-texte"—there is nothing outside the text (Derrida, 1976: 158).

The difference between textualism and Foucault's theoretical perspective is brought home forcefully in his definition of the *dispositif*, or *apparatus*, which constitutes the social body as a "thoroughly heterogeneous ensemble consisting of discourses, institutions, architectural forms, regulatory decisions, laws, administrative measures, scientific statements, philosophical, moral and philanthropic propositions—in short the said as much as the unsaid" (Foucault, 1980l: 194). While not disclaiming the importance of language, this statement entails a rejection of giving language priority. Rather, says Foucault, "I believe one's point of reference should not be to the great model of language . . . and signs but to that of war and battle. This history which bears and determines us has the form of a war rather than that of a language: relations of power, not relations of meaning" (Foucault, 1980b: 114).

For Foucault, the concept of *power-knowledge* is thus a pragmatic conceptualization. It is not a denial of the importance of practice or reality in relation to discourse, or a denial of the importance of discourse in relation to practice. Rather, says Foucault, "there is no power relation without the correlative constitution of a field of knowledge, nor at the same time any knowledge that does not presuppose and constitute at the same time power relations" (Foucault, 1977a: 27).

The difference between Foucault and Derrida could not be more marked. For Derrida, language is prioritized over the world in a sense reminiscent of Levi-Strauss, Lacan, and Lyotard. Although each discourse produces its own truth, the actual meaning of this truth is held to be uncertain, an uncertainty based on Derrida's conceptions of textual dispersal and deferral of meaning where meanings are never made clear because the constituent terms can never be pinned down (Derrida, 1976, 1981; Lacan, 1977; Lyotard, 1984). Moving beyond Saussure and Levi-Strauss, Derrida denies any systematicity to language at all, or any possibility of reference to a real world. In his critique of the "metaphysics of presence," for example, he critiques the doctrine that reality is directly given to the subject. Language, for Derrida, is "an infinite play of signifiers" where linguistic meaning "consists of the play of signifiers proliferating into infinity," and any attempt to halt the endless play and invoke a concept of reference to the real world must, says Derrida, involve postulations of a "transcendental signified" whereby the world is somehow assumed to be present to consciousness without any discursive mediation (Derrida, 1976: 148–153). Hence the idea that our discourses of science or knowledge provide a veridical insight into the nature of the world or of an independent reality is just a myth.

For Derrida, because we cannot secure the meaning of words in relation to their *referent*, we can never assume we are describing reality, and the assumptions entailed in the "metaphysics of presence," that the world is available to be understood through our discursive knowledge systems, must remain assumptions. The belief that the world has independent ontological status is the myth which for Derrida propels empiricism, positivism, rationalism, and historical materialism. Because it maintains that consciousness has direct access to reality with no requirement of discursive mediation, discourse cannot get in the way of apprehending reality. Derrida (1976: 143) introduces the concept of *différance* to emphasize that it is impossible to escape from the "metaphysics of presence." As Callinicos defines it, différance combines the meanings of two words—"to differ" and "to defer." It affirms a presence always deferred into the future or past but nevertheless constantly invoked (Callinicos, 1988: 75).

NOTE

1. In *The Order of Things* Foucault presents an historical materialism of signification. From the stoics to the seventeenth century, he says (1970: 42), the system of signs in the Western world had been a ternary one, for it was recognized as containing the significant, the signified, and the "conjuncture." From the seventeenth century, the arrangement of signs was to become binary, since it was defined, with Port-Royal, as the connection of a significant to a signified. From here, signi-

fication was reflected in the form of representation (p. 44). Foucault also comments that "Saussure, rediscovering the project of a general semiology, should have given the sign a definition that could seem "psychologistic" (the linking of a concept and an image): this is because he was in fact rediscovering the classical condition for conceiving of the binary nature of the sign" (67).

Chapter 5

Foucault and Marxism

If Foucault's worldly post-structuralism can be seen, as Poster, and Dreyfus and Rabinow suggest, as a form of historical materialist analysis, the important question is how does Foucault's form of historical materialism differ from that of Marx?

In the Marxist conception of historical materialism, discourse is represented as part of the superstructure that is split from material practice (the economic base) and subordinated to it. In the same way, the mental operations of consciousness are represented as derivative from the material base of society. The most famous expression of Marx's conception is from the Preface of *A Contribution to The Critique of Political Economy.*

In the social production which men carry on they enter into definite relations that are indispensable and independent of their will; these relations of production correspond to a definite stage of development of their material powers of production. The sum total of these relations of production constitutes the economic structure of society—the real foundation, on which rise legal and political superstructures and to which correspond definite forms of social consciousness. The mode of production in material life determines the general character of the social, political and spiritual processes of life. It is not the consciousness of men that determines their existence, but, on the contrary, their social existence determines their consciousness. At a certain stage of their development, the material forces of production in society come in conflict with the existing relations of production, or—what is but a legal expression for the same thing—with the property relations within which they had been at work before. From forms of development of the forces of production these relations turn into their fetters. Then comes a period of social revolution. With the change of the economic foundation the entire immense superstructure is more or less rapidly transformed. In considering such transformations the distinction should always be made between the material transformation of the economic conditions of production which can be determined with the precision of natural science, and the legal, political, religious, aesthetic, or philosophic—in short ideological forms in which men become conscious of this conflict and fight it out. . . . No social order ever disappears before all the productive forces, for which there is room in it, have been developed; and new higher relations of production never appear before the conditions of their existence have matured in the womb of the old society. Therefore, mankind always takes up only such problems as it can solve; since, looking at the matter more closely, we will always find that the problem itself arises only when the material conditions necessary for its solution already exist or are at least in the process of formation. (Marx, 1904: 11–12)

That Marx's formulation led to charges of economic determinism is evident from the political debates of his own day. Joseph Bloch had leveled such a charge, and in replying to Bloch's accusations in 1890 Engels sought to defend Marx's conception:

According to the materialist conception of history, the *ultimately* determining element in history is the production and reproduction of real life. More than this neither Marx nor I have ever asserted. Hence if somebody twists this into saying that the economic element is the *only* determining one, he transforms that proposition into a meaningless, abstract, senseless phrase. The economic situation is the basis, but the various elements of the superstructure: political forms of the class struggle and its results, to wit: constitutions established by the victorious class after a successful battle, etc., juridical forms, and then even the reflexes of all these actual struggles in the brains of the participants, political, juristic, philosophical theories, religious views and their further development into systems of dogmas, also exercise their influence upon the course of the historical struggles and in many cases preponderate in determining their *form*. There is an interaction of all these elements in which, amid all the endless host of accidents . . . the economic movement finally asserts itself as necessary. (Engels, 1978: 760–761)

In the twentieth century one of the central issues addressed by Western Marxists has been an attempted resolution and reconceptualization of the relation between the economic base and the cultural superstructure of society. In the classical Marxist model, both the character of a society's culture and institutions and the direction set for its future development are determined by the nature of the economic base, which can be defined as the mode of production at a certain stage of development (Williams, 1980: 33).

The simplest nature of this relation, as Williams tells us, was one of "the reflection, the imitation, or the reproduction of the reality of the base in the superstructure in a more or less direct way" (1980: 33)—that is, a relation in which the economic base and specifically the forces of production constituted the ultimate *cause* to which the social, legal, and political framework of the society can be traced back.

In the attempt to reformulate Marxism in the twentieth century, the economic determinist conception is challenged by those who see Marxism as granting rather more independence or autonomy to the superstructures of society. Hence a dialectical notion of the relation was stressed, suggesting a relation of reciprocal influence. It was argued that, although the base *conditions* and *affects* the superstructure, it is in turn *conditioned* and *affected* by it. In all cases, however, in order to remain as Marxists, the ultimate priority of the economic base as the causal determinant of the social character of a society was safeguarded by maintaining that the economic factor is "determining in the last instance." Hence, it was maintained that the superstructure had only a "relative autonomy," and the theory of "relative autonomy," as a short-hand designation of the base–superstructure relation, became a central concept of twentieth-century Marxism.

There were, of course, other attempted formulations of the process of determination and of the relations or mode of interaction between economic and cultural phenomena in a society. Some of these formulations sought to replace, or go beyond, the topographical metaphor of base and superstructure with its suggestion of a definite dichotomous spatial relationship and to conceptualize the issue of determination in altogether different ways. In his own summary of the qualifications and amendments introduced by twentieth-century Marxists, usually claiming to clarify Marx's true and original intentions, Williams points out that:

The first kind of qualification had to do with delays in time, with complications, and with certain indirect or relatively distant relationships. . . . The second stage was related but more fundamental, in that the process of the relationship itself was more substantially looked at. This was the kind of reconsideration which gave rise to the modern notion of "mediation", in which something more than simple reflection or reproduction—indeed something radically different from either reflection or reproduction—actively occurs. In the later twentieth century there is the notion of "homologous structures", where there may be no direct or easily apparent similarity, and certainly nothing like reflection or reproduction, between the superstructural process and the reality of the base, but in which there is an essential homology or correspondence of structures, which can be discovered by analysis. This is not the same notion as "mediation", but it is the same kind of amendment in that the relationship between the base and the superstructure is not supposed to be direct, nor simply operationally subject to lags and complications and indirectnesses, but that of its nature it is not direct reproduction. (1980: 32–33)

In his own attempted reformulations, Williams argues that

We have to revalue "determination" towards the setting of limits and the exertion of pressure, and away from a predicted, prefigured and controlled content. We have to revalue "superstructure" towards a related range of cultural practices, and away from a reflected, reproduced or specifically dependent content. And, crucially, we have to revalue "the base" away from the notion of a fixed economic or technological abstraction, and towards the specific activities of men in real social and economic relationships, containing fundamental contradictions and variations and therefore always in a state of dynamic process. (1980: 34)

Notions of "totality" (associated with Lukács), or of "hegemony" (associated with Gramsci), or of society as a "complex whole" (associated with Althusser), constitute attempts to move beyond simple dichotomous models of base and superstructure. In Althusser's conception, the social structure, represented as a "complex whole structured in dominance" is characterized by a series of *levels of practices,* including the level of science or theoretical practice, the level of ideological practice, the level of political practice, and the level of economic practice. Althusser argues for the *primacy of practice* "by showing that all the levels of social existence are the sites of distinct practices" (Althusser, 1970: 58) and claims that Marx's achievement was to found "a historico-dialectical materialism of praxis: that is . . . a theory of the different specific *levels* of *human practice*" (Althusser, 1969: 169).

The determination of events and processes was theorized using the concept of *overdetermination,* a concept that Althusser borrowed from Freud. It indicates a process of the *complex* and *multiple causation* of events whereby a causal contribution is made by all of the levels, the relative importance of any level in any particular instance varying according to time and place. Theorized in this way, Althusser argues that the non-economic practices have a *specific effectivity,* which means that they are determining as well as determined, just as economic practices are determining as well as determined. It also means that every aspect or part contributes in its own right to determining the character of the overall whole of which it is a part, as well as being shaped by it in turn. In the same way, rather than characterizing contradictions as singularly concerned with the economic forces and relations of production, there is in Althusser's conception a multiplicity of contradictions occurring at all levels of the social formation. In this sense, determination is never simple, but rather complex and multiple. Again, however, in order to retain his link to Marxism and to differentiate his own theory of social structure from non-Marxist theories of systems functionalism, Althusser argues that economic practice is fundamental and is "determining in the last instance." Although the economy is "determining in the last instance," it is not always the dominant structure. The apparent paradox is explained because the economy determines which of the other elements will be dominant. That is, it determines for the non-economic levels their respective degrees of autonomy or dependence in relation to each other and to itself, and thus the different degrees of effect that each will have. It can determine itself as dominant or non-dominant at any particular time. At a particular juncture one element may displace another to assume the dominant role. In addition, different elements can be dominant in different societies or at different times. Hence, this is what Althusser intends when he refers to the social formation as a *structure in dominance.*

Foucault rejects Marxist models of a determining economic base and a determined superstructure as well as refinements based on conceptions of totality by Marx's twentieth-century successors. Like Althusser, he retains a concept of *practice*, however. Also like Althusser, he utilizes a model of complex and multiple causation and determination within the social structure, although the specific elements and mechanisms of such processes, as elaborated by Foucault, differ in important respects.

After 1968, says Poster, Foucault attempted to come to grips with Marxist scholarship, and while the positions he adopted in some cases resembled those of Western Marxists, generally he went beyond those positions towards a new formulation of critical theory. Although Foucault rejects Marxism as a specific theory of the mode of production, as a critique of political economy, or as a dialectical method, he advances a critical view of domination which, like historical materialism, takes all social practices as transitory and all intellectual formations as indissociably connected with power and social relations (Poster, 1984: 39–40). Poster explains what he sees as Foucault's greater relevance than Marxism in terms of a shift from nineteenth- and early twentieth-century forms of capitalism based on the "mode of production" to new forms of later twentieth-century capitalism based on the "mode of information." These changes were associated, says Poster, with changes in the nature of the economy, an increase in the service and white-collar sectors, the increasing development of information technology, and developments in electronic communications, together with new possibilities that these developments generate for a decentralization of political power. Although Marxism's focus on labor and the central causal priority of the economy may have had heuristic value in the age of ascendant capitalism, in an era of "information capitalism" historical materialism finds its premise in power that is the effect of "discourse/practice." Thus, according to Poster, "the couplet discourse/practice . . . enables [Foucault] to search for the close connection between manifestations of reason and patterns of domination. . . . Foucault can study the way in which discourse is not innocent, but shaped by practice—without privileging any form of practice . . . such as class struggle. He can also study how discourse in turn shapes practice without privileging any form of discourse" (Poster, 1984: 12).[1] Foucault thus rejects Marx's conception of historical materialism as a mechanism by which discourse is split from material (non-discursive) practice and by which the former is then subordinated to the latter. By representing the mental operations of consciousness as derivative from the material base of society, Marx, for Foucault, remains firmly fixed within a traditional Enlightenment problematic (Poster, 1984: 16–18).

In Foucault's materialism, explaining the relations between discursive formations and non-discursive domains (institutions, political events, economic practices, and processes) is recognized as the ultimate objective, at least from the time of *The Archaeology of Knowledge*. For archaeology, in comparison to Marxism, however, "The *rapprochements* are not intended to uncover great cultural continuities, nor to isolate mechanisms of causality . . . nor does it seek to rediscover what is expressed in them . . . it tries to determine how the rules of formation that govern it . . . may be linked to non-discursive systems: it seeks to define specific forms of articulation" (Foucault, 1972: 162). Unlike Marxists, he sees no one set of factors as directing human destiny. Rather, the forms of articulation and determination may differ in relation to the relative importance of different non-discursive (material) factors in terms of both place and time. In the shift from a purely archaeological to a genealogical mode of enquiry, Foucault's concern with the relation between discursive and non-discursive domains is given a more historical and dynamic formulation, although, as argued above, the concern with synchronic analysis is not abandoned. Throughout, however, Foucault's central aim is to provide a version of critical theory in which the economic base is not the totalizing center of the social formation, whereby Hegel's evolutionary model of history is replaced by Nietzsche's concept of genealogy, and where causes and connections to an imputed center or foundation are rejected in favor of exposing the contingency and transitory nature of existing social practices. In Poster's view, this presents us with a crucial decision. In comparing Foucault and Althusser, he maintains that "the theoretical choice offered by these two theorists is dramatic and urgent. In my view Foucault's position in the present context is more valuable as an interpretive strategy. . . . Foucault's position opens up critical theory more than Althusser's both to the changing social formation and to the social locations where contestation actually occurs" (Poster, 1984: 39–40).

The essential point for Foucault is that he recognizes two levels of the real—the discursive and the extra-discursive. While he goes to great pain to insist that the material world has ontological status, he also insists that we grant a certain autonomy to discourse. Where he differs from Marxism as well as from empiricism, as Barry Smart points out, is that whereas those perspectives assume the possibility of an immediately pre-given correspondence between discourse and the world, Foucault, though not denying such a possibility, problematizes it (Smart, 1983: 94). Such a "non-correspondence" is described "as a routine feature of positive significance requiring analysis in each particular instance" (94). Or, as Gordon has put it, "our world does not follow a programme, but we live in a world of programmes, that is to say in a world traversed by the effects of discourses whose object . . . is the rendering rationalisable, transparent and programmable of the real" (Gordon, 1980, cited in Smart, 1983: 94). Margolis also supports the view that Foucault's approach is consistent with materialist analysis, at least on the criterion of realism. Foucault, says Margolis:

does not dismiss de re necessities of this or that episteme; they are rightly recognised *there* as the necessities they are. But they are also not enshrined as universal, change-less structures of any kind (regarding world or reason). (Rather) we are always invited to "test" for the "limits" that we may go beyond. That's to say: the invariances of any proposed transcendental limits of reason may be tested by exploring whether we can alter such a model of coherence convincingly, in a way that rests on historical change. (Margolis, 1993: 204)

For Foucault, then, historical materialism means that in any era or period the specific causal relations, as well as the priority of this or that structure, must be investigated *anew*. There are no universal, causally efficacious laws or mechanisms throughout history, just as there are no simple material cat-egories (e.g. class) that can explain everything. In addition, Foucault rejects classical forms of materialism that reject (or neglect) narrative structure, lan-guage, or interpretation. What Marx effected with classical historical mate-rialism was a "double manoeuvre," as Poster calls it, which splits discourse from practice and subordinates the former to the latter. In effect, it excludes mental operations and language from the domain of historical research, and privileges matter over ideas. While he thus recognizes the reality of the extra-discursive, Foucault actively opposes "the materialist mind-set that sees value only in the mute, grey world of the pre-discursive and treats with disregard the productive creations of discourse" (Barrett, 1988: 131). Since he does not allow for knowledge of a world independently of discourse, then forms of materialism claiming that knowledge is simply a *reflection* of material processes without remainder are rendered problematic and incom-patible with Foucault's position. At another level in relation to contempo-rary conceptions of historical materialism, there is a basic compatibility, however. This is the sense which holds that the objects of discourse are real structures themselves, independent of discourse, ontologically irreducible, and sometimes out of synchronization with the forms of their discursive representation.

While having a generally historicized view of the nature and development of knowledge, Foucault rejects the possibility of any absolute or transcen-dental conception of truth "outside of history" as well as of any conception of "objective" or "necessary" interests that could provide a necessary "ar-chimedean point" to ground either knowledge, morality, or politics. Read in this way, historical materialism is about the systematic character of society and how it might change. It is about the processes of change internal to social systems. It holds that societies are to varying extents integrated sys-tematically through their material practices and discursive coherences, and break down and change as the component elements of the system change.

CONSTRUCTIONISM

Attributing greater autonomy to the discursive, Foucault's approach affords a greater role to the constructionist dimension of knowledge. This is to say that under certain circumstances, and varying according to time and place, discourses may be instrumental in constructing the objects of which they speak. Foucault believed this to be the case with regard to the objective referents of psychiatric knowledge, and in his earlier works, as stated above, he tended to overgeneralize the view. In his later writings, however, while the constructionist theme is retained, it is qualified considerably in relation to the issue of realism. This gives Foucault's constructionism a dynamic quality (Hacking, 1986; Olssen, 1995). It is a constructionism that, while recognizing the generative potential of discourse in relation to the world, also recognizes the variations that might exist in relation to different domains of inquiry and different forms of knowledge. It also recognizes the existence of real-world structures and practices and the limits and boundaries within which discursive constructions are possible, and yet perceives the existence of numerous kinds of knowledge claim that are "not demarcated prior to the discourse but [come] into existence only contemporaneous with the discursive formation that made it possible to talk about them" (Rouse, 1994: 93).

The constructionist claims are stronger in relation to the social sciences than to the natural sciences. When Foucault compares medicine to psychiatry, for instance, he states that "medicine . . . has a much more solid scientific armature . . . but it too is profoundly enmeshed in social structures." The natural sciences such as theoretical physics or organic chemistry also have "solid scientific armatures." Although they are affected by the power relations in the larger society, Foucault recognizes that the relations between social structure and the discipline can be difficult to untangle. With respect to forms of knowledge like psychiatry, however, Foucault maintains that "the question . . . [is] much easier to resolve, since the epistemological profile is a low one and psychiatric practice is linked with a whole range of institutions, economic requirements and political issues of social regulation" (Foucault, 1980b: 109–110).

In relation to disciplines like psychiatry, Foucault maintains strong constructionist claims. Disciplines like psychiatry can, in Foucauldian terms, be represented as discourses which, rising in the nineteenth and early twentieth centuries, defined new ways of relating to the world, new means of administrative control, new ways of defining and talking about people. They produced new boxes to put people in, new labels, new categories and classifications that became inscribed in the practices of daily life and in the organizational and institutional structures of society. In addition, as new developments in technology produced new ways of addressing social problems, new patterns of normalization and new bases for social authority were established. The very emergence of the knowledge discipline, says Foucault, became implicated in producing the conceptions of normality they claimed to uncover. Hence, the human sciences formulate ways of organizing the world and in doing so position people in relation to the categorizations and classifications they construct. Foucault considers the human sciences "the dubious sciences" (Foucault, 1980b: 109) which, although contributing little knowledge about human beings, have attained massive importance and power in society, a fact that itself needs to be explained. In his conception they have become complex strategic constructs and forms of domination.

With relation to the constitution of subjectivity, Foucault advances a strong constructionist program that can be distinguished from the "weak" constructionist program of labeling theories and "social problem" perspectives. In his strong claims as they relate to the subject, Foucault takes objects like the body and focuses on how conceptions of subjectivity are created or invented in history: "We should try to discover how it is that subjects are gradually, progressively, really and materially constituted through a multiplicity of organisms, forces, energies, materials, desires, thoughts etc." (Foucault, 1980f: 97).

None of Foucault's constructionist claims cancels out or nullifies his right to be called a *materialist*, however, for although discourse has a constructive potential, its grammar is determined in turn by neighboring practices. Hence, as Foucault's long-time friend Paul Veyne says, Foucault's method seeks to understand the discursive only as the "objectivizations of determined practices," determinations that themselves must be brought to light (1997: 159). Veyne labels this approach as "rarefaction," which explicates how Foucault sees discursive systems as constituted by historical practices "just as pear trees produce pears and apple trees bear apples" (1997: 160). Micro-analysis reveals, however, that the heterogeneity of practices does not "trace a vector we can call progress," nor is it pushed or directed by forces such as "reason, desire or consciousness" (167). As Veyne makes clear, for Foucault, the truth of history resides ultimately in practices, not discourses. Hence "it is a 'wholly *material* universe' made up of prediscursive referents that remain faceless potentialities; in this universe practices that are never the same engender, at varying points, objectivizations that are never the same, ever-changing faces. Each practice depends on all the others and on their transformations. Everything is historical, and everything depends on everything else" (171).

Foucault's constructionism is thus similar to what Ian Hacking (1986) calls "dynamic nominalism," which expresses the thesis that the basis of classification varies and may derive its justification from both the occurring phenomena and the particular ways of grouping and classifying phenomena in different societies. For Foucault, then, although the idea of social construction refers to material, historical constitution, it also attests to the view that certain phenomena are constructed in the realm of the discursive. In addition, Foucault recognizes that different forms of categorization are based on different forms of kindhood. Some categories ("the Devil") may exist because of a moral or religious discourse; others ("Intelligence Quotients") may exist because of an historically constituted discipline of knowledge (Individual Difference Psychology); yet others ("tigers") would exist as kinds with physical extension and an historically evolved form. While the latter would exist independent of the category naming it, this is not obviously the case with regard to the Devil or to Intelligence Quotients, and there is a very real sense in which these latter objects *depend on* the discursive formation that names them. Hence, the constructionist thesis applies differently to different forms of kindhood. Yet, even to tigers, or any other phenomenon with physical extension, it is not clear that there is not a constructionist dimension in that such phenomena can be classified and grouped differently. Gender constitutes a good example, for, while it is now widely recognized that gender characteristics are not inevitable effects of physical sexual characteristics, they are not unrelated to them.

Hence, with reference to Foucault, although there is a sense in which his work utilizes a *constructionist dimension*, it is not clear that he can be termed a *social constructionist* if by this term we mean, as is often intended (Craib, 1997; Burr, 1995), a form of anti-realism or discursive idealism whereby objects in the world are posited in the process of naming them.[2] This is clearly the case for some types of objects, but it is not for others. Although Foucault grants a degree of autonomy to discourse and the relations of signification are not direct, they are nevertheless set in play by the constraints of a wholly material universe.

In relation to Marxism, although discursive systems are related to material practices, the extent to which they reflect or depend on such material practices varies from time to time and from society to society. While in both *The Order of Things* and *The Archaeology of Knowledge* discourse is bracketed off from the social practices and institutions in which it is embedded, thus creating the sense of a linguistic or discursive idealism, it is in fact the case, as Rabinow points out, that Foucault "never intended to isolate discourse from the social practices that surround it. Rather, he was experimenting to see how much autonomy could legitimately be claimed for discursive formations. His aim, then as now, was to avoid analyses of discourse (or ideology) as reflections, no matter how sophisticatedly mediated, of something supposedly 'deeper' and more 'real' " (Rabinow, 1984: 10).

AGAINST TOTALITY

The central element of Foucault's critique of Marxism relates to the notion of *totalization*. Essentially, for Foucault, Marxism was not just a deterministic but a deductivistic approach. That is, it directs attention not just to the primacy of the economy but it seeks to explain the parts of a culture as explicable and decodable parts of the whole totality or system. Marxism, claims Foucault, seeks to ascertain "the principle that binds the whole, the code that unlocks the system, and the elements that can be explained by deduction" (Thompson, 1986: 106). This was the approach of Hegel, as well as Marx, which seeks to analyze history and society in terms of "totality," where the parts are an "expression" of the whole—hence the notion of an "expressive totality." In this respect, Foucault draws a distinction between "total history" and "general history." The central differences are:

The project of total history is one that seeks to reconstitute the overall form of a civilization, the principle—material or spiritual—of a society, the significance common to all the phenomena of a period, the law that accounts for their cohesion. . . . A total description draws all phenomena around a single centre—a principle, a meaning, a spirit, a world-view, an overall shape . . . it is supposed that between all the events of a well-defined spatio-temporal area, between all the phenomena of which traces have been found, it must be possible to establish a system of homogeneous relations: a network of causality that makes it possible to derive each of them, relations of analogy that show how they symbolize one another, or how they all express one and the same central core; it is also supposed that one and the same form of historicity operates upon economic structures, social institutions and customs . . . and subjects them all to the same type of transformation; lastly, it is supposed that history itself may be articulated into great units—stages or phases—which contain within themselves their own principle of cohesion. . . . [G]eneral history, on the contrary, would deploy the space of dispersion . . . it speaks of series, divisions, limits, differences of level, shifts, chronological specificities, particular forms of rehandling, possible types of relation. . . . The problem . . . which defines the task of general history is to determine what form of relation may be legitimately described between these different series. (Foucault, 1972: 9–10)

Whereas total history seeks to explain all phenomena in relation to a single center, general history employs the space of dispersion. For Foucault, the explanatory quest is not to search for the organizing principle of a cultural formation—whether the "economy," or the "human subject," or the "proletariat." Rather, Foucault is interested in advancing a polymorphous conception of determination in order to reveal the "play of dependencies" in the social and historical process. As he puts it in an article written in 1968 and translated and printed in English in 1978, "I would like to substitute this whole play of dependencies for the uniform, simple notion of assigning a causality; and by suspending the indefinitely extended privilege of the cause, in order to render apparent the polymorphous cluster of correlations" (Foucault, 1978b: 13).

For Foucault the play of dependencies had three aspects: first, the *intra-discursive*, which concerns relations between objects, operations, and concepts within the discursive formation; second, the *inter-discursive*, which concerns relations between different discursive formations; and, third, the *extra-discursive*, which concerns the relations between a discourse and the whole play of economic, political, and social practices. Rather than seek to find the articulating principle of a cultural complex, Foucault was interested in discerning how cultural formations were made to appear "rational" and "unified," how particular discourses came to be formed, and what rules lay behind the process of formation. In doing so, he sought to produce accounts of how discursive formations like nineteenth-century psychopathology came to be formed, how it constituted its scientific legitimacy and shaped the thinking of a particular period. Thus, in the case of nineteenth-century psychiatry and psychopathology, Foucault shows how the term *madness* came to be applied to certain types of behavior, and how, in its very designation by what it wasn't, it helped establish our conceptions of "the rational" and "the sane."

In all of these studies, however, Foucault resists the temptation to try to explain the development of particular discursive formations as a result of any single cause or principle. In opposition to the themes of totalizing history with its notions of "the progress of reason" and "the spirit of a century" Foucault substitutes what he calls a differentiated analysis:

Nothing, you see, is more foreign to me than the quest for a sovereign, unique and constraining form. I do not seek to detect, starting from diverse signs, the unitary spirit of an epoch, the general form of its consciousness: something like a *Weltanschauung*. Nor have I described either the emergence and eclipse of formal structure which might reign for a time over all the manifestations of thought: I have not written the history of a syncopated transcendental. Nor, finally, have I described thoughts or century-old sensitivities coming to life, stuttering, struggling and dying out like great phantoms—ghosts playing out their shadow theatre against the backdrop of history. I have studied, one after another, ensembles of discourse; I have characterised them; I have defined the play of rules, of transformations, of thresholds, of remanences. I have established and I have described their clusters of relations. Whenever I have deemed it necessary I have allowed the *systems* to proliferate. (Foucault, 1978b: 10)

It is the attempt to "individualize" discourses that defines Foucault's methodological imperative: specifying their systematic and specific character; searching for the rules of formation for all of its concepts, methods, and theoretical postulates; examining the conditions of its transformation which are effective, at a precise time, for its operations, concepts, and theories to be formed, or discarded, or modified; and ascertaining its specific existence in relation to other types of discourse (Foucault, 1978b: 8–10).

In seeking to characterize the nature of his "pluralism" and how it affects the analysis of discourse, Foucault explains how he "substitute[s] the analysis of *different types of transformation* for the abstract, general, and monotonous form of 'change' in which one so willingly thinks in terms of succession" (Foucault, 1978b: 11). In this, he seeks to define with the greatest care the transformations that have constituted the change, replacing the general theme of *becoming* ("general form, abstract element, primary cause, and universal effect") by the analysis of the transformations in their specificity, an examination of "the diversity of *systems* and the play of discontinuities into the history of *discourses*" (1978b: 15). This involves, says Foucault, within a given discursive formation (1) detecting the changes that affect the operations, objects, theoretical choices, and so on; (2) detecting the changes that affect the discursive formations themselves (e.g., changes in the boundaries that define the field); (3) detecting the changes that simultaneously affect several discursive formations (e.g., reversal of the hierarchy of importance, as happened, for instance, in the Classical period when the analysis of language lost the "directing role" that it had in the first years of the nineteenth century to biology, which in turn led to the development of new concepts such as "organism," "function," and "organization," which in turn affected other sciences). All of these types of changes, says Foucault, characterize changes in individual discourses and affect modifications in the episteme itself: its "redistributions," that is, "the different transformations which it is possible to describe concerning ... states of discourse" (Foucault, 1978b: 11–12).

In opposition to totalizing models, Foucault sees his own analysis as more limited: to searching for the empirical historical grounds for discursive consistency or coherence; to recognizing in discourse its empirical worldly features—"the work of the author, and why not?—his juvenilia or his mature work ... the patterns of a linguistic or rhetorical model (a genre, a style)"; and acknowledging that all the transformatory operations are carried out "prior to discourse and outside of it" (1978b: 17).

In his later studies, Foucault asserts the "pluralist" nature of his project through his use of concepts like "eventalization"; he observes that specific events (*événéments singuliers*) cannot be integrated or decoded simply as an application of a uniform and universal regularity. In this non-unified sense, the analytic of discourse effects a non-unified perspective. As Foucault explains it:

It has led to the *individualization* of different series, which are juxtaposed to one another, follow one another, overlap and intersect, without one being able to reduce them to a linear schema. Thus, in place of the continuous chronology of reason, which was invariably traced back to some inaccessible origin, there have appeared scales that are sometimes very brief, distinct from one another, *irreducible to a single law*, scales that bear a type of history peculiar to each one, and which cannot be reduced to the general model of a consciousness that acquires, progresses, and remembers. (Foucault, 1972: 8; emphasis added)

The notion of "eventalization" itself contains a number of elements. First it treats all objects of knowledge as historical *events*. Second, it refers to a "pluralization of causes":

Causal multiplication consists in analysing an event according to the multiple processes that constitute it. . . . "[E]ventalization" thus works by constructing around the singular event analysed as process a "polygon" or rather a "polyhedron" of intelligibility, the number of whose faces is not given in advance and can never properly be taken as finite. One has to proceed by progressive, necessarily incomplete saturation. And one has to bear in mind that the further one decomposes the processes under analysis, the more one is enabled, and indeed obliged to construct their external relations of intelligibility. (Foucault, 1987a: 104–105)

In addition, says Foucault, eventalization refers to the rediscovery of the "connections, encounters, supports, blockages, plays of forces, strategies, and so on that at a given moment establish what subsequently comes to count as being self-evident, universal and necessary." Finally, it constitutes a "breach of self evidence"; that is, "it means making visible a *singularity* at places where there is a temptation to invoke historical constants, an immediate anthropological trait, or an obviousness that imposes itself uniformly on all." In this sense, the theoretical function of eventalization seeks to breach the self-evidence of historical phenomena; "to show that things 'weren't as necessary as all that'; it wasn't a matter of course that mad people came to be regarded as mentally ill; it wasn't self-evident that the only things to be done to a criminal was to lock him up, it wasn't self-evident that the causes of illness were to be sought through the individual examination of bodies; and so on" (Foucault, 1987a: 104). Eventalization thus opposes the evidence on which knowledge sequences and practices rest.

Alongside the concept of *singular events* is that of *exteriority*. What Foucault means by "exteriority" is that each individual element is irreducible "to the unified discursive principle, or to an internal core of meaning to be found in the discourse." As Frank defines it:

What the rule of exteriority of discourse means, then, is: "not moving from the discourse towards its internal, hidden core, towards the heart of the thought or the meaning, which is manifest in it". So the procedure of the analytic of discourse is external because it wishes to leave the series (*série*) of single events, mutually irreducible (in terms of a deductive or teleological principle), just as they are "external" to any totalizing general concept. (1992: 108)

In that events and instances are individualized, "individualized" means here, as Frank states it, "not predictable from the point of view of their structure, and contingent with respect to the way they happen to be" (1992: 110). What is important to Foucault in this instance is the avoidance of subsuming the single elemental event or statement as an echo or a reflection of the discursive formation. Again this is *but another aspect* of his opposition to the determined notion of causality embodied in the Hegelian conception of an "expressive totality" and, by derivation, also embodied in the notion of a primary causal necessity (*un causalisme primaire*), which he sees as central to Marxism. What concerns Foucault is the "uniqueness" and "unpredict-ability" of the singular historical instance, an issue that he describes in *The Archaeology of Knowledge* (1972) as a "central theme" (114). What he seeks to do is introduce conceptions of *indeterminacy, irregularity, openness,* and *complexity* as integral to his conception of the historical process. In *The Archaeology of Knowledge* this takes the form of establishing the spatio-temporal coordinates that ensure the *novel aspect* of the "statement" (*énoncé*): "The enunciation is an unrepeatable event; it has situated and dated uniqueness that is irreducible. Yet this uniqueness allows of a number of constants—grammatical, semantic, logical—by which one can, by neutral-izing the moment of enunciation and the coordinates that individualize it, recognise the general form" (Foucault, 1972: 101). Or again, "every state-ment belongs to a certain regularity—that consequently none can be re-garded as pure creation, as the marvellous disorder of genius. But we have also seen that no statement can be regarded as inactive, and be valid as the scarcely real shadow or transfer of the initial statement. The whole enunci-ative field is both regular and alerted: it never sleeps" (146–147).

In terms of the sociological implications of the principle of totality as utilized by Marxism, Balibar notes that it conveys "the idea that, in the social . . . 'whole,' the 'parts' or the 'cells' are necessarily *similar* to the whole itself" (1992: 44). Foucault's objection to this principle on a practical level, that is, in terms of its implications for actual historical and social re-search, can be seen in regard to any number of institutional sectors. Balibar gives the example of the family which Foucault analyzes in *The History of Sexuality*, Volume 1. While typically Marxists had considered the family re-ductively as the consumption-hub of bourgeois society (i.e., as purely re-productive of capitalist class relations), for Foucault, the family has more positive functions. As Balibar points out:

Foucault stresses the strategic role of the family (its moralisation and its medicalisa-tion) in the apparatus of the regulation of populations which forms one of the es-sential powers of the "bourgeois" State; also it is important for him to show that the family is simultaneously the locus of institutional perversion . . . the hysterisation of the women's body . . . the space which is the opposite to psychiatric space . . . the central concern in the competition between holders of professional knowledge about man . . . the means of socialising reproductive activity and, in particular, the locus of the juridical "recoding" of bodily techniques in general into forms of alliance or kinship. . . . It is for all these reasons that the family *cannot* be considered as the reduced *image* of the global society. (1992: 44)

Hence, the family does not reproduce society and the society does not im-itate the family. As Balibar states, it is "not a monad *pars totalis* of 'the society' " (1992: 44), and its strategic importance lies not in its resemblance but in the specific nature of its difference. Foucault's criticisms of the Marxist use of the concept of power is also related to totalism in that the power of dominant groups is seen in Marxism to echo through "successive amplifications . . . through the whole social body" (see Foucault, 1978a: 121; Balibar, 1992: 44).

In a more philosophical vein, Foucault opposes totality in order to reintroduce the category of *chance* back into the historical process. It is against the kinds of chance that had been excluded by the Age of Reason. Against the dominant Enlightenment norm of "determined necessity" he counterposes "pure irregularity" (Hacking, 1990: 10). As Hacking explains, "it harked back, in part, to something ancient or vestigial. It also looked into the future, to new and often darker visions of the person. . . . Its most passionate spokesman was Nietzsche" (Hacking, 1990: 10).

Foucault's rejection of Marxist and Enlightenment conceptions of causality explicitly reflects his Nietzschean heritage and his belief that Marxism had outlived its usefulness (Sheridan, 1980: 70; Barrett, 1988: 130). Following Nietzsche, and based on his condemnation of the postulates of identity, Foucault counterposes the "logic of identity," which characterizes modernist forms of thought, including Marxism, to the "logic of difference" which characterizes his. On the epistemological difference between the two, the feminist writer Elizabeth Grosz writes: "identity, in which A = A, is the most basic axiom in Aristotelian logic; it underlies our received notions of personal identity as well as the foundations of western ontology and epistemology. In opposing a logic of identity, a logic of Being, and in advocating a 'logic' of difference or becoming, Nietzsche initiated a major critical trajectory in contemporary theory" (1989: ix).

In linguistics, Saussure uses a philosophy of difference to explain the complexity and functioning of language and representation. He claims that "language itself undermines and problematises the very identities it establishes. A sign is self identical (A = A), but it is also always something else, something more, another sign, dependent on a whole network of signs" (Grosz, 1989: ix).

The ontological objection to identity underpins the post-structuralist rejection of totality and establishes *difference* as a central post-structuralist principle. What difference entails in this context is that an object's essential identity is not fixed within it but is established by its relations or connections to other objects. The difference that an object has with other objects in terms of the overall matrix of relations establishes the contrasts that count in establishing its identity. In this process, however, there is no final resolution or settlement as to what an object finally is since any attempted conclusion as to an object's identity introduces further changes and new differences in its matrix of relations to other objects. This opposition to totality, which rejects the idea that an object has any essential identity or unity, maintains that any apparent unity exists only through an object's relations to other objects. These relations are constitutive of a multiplicity revealing that any unity or essential identity is only an illusion. Hence it is argued that an analytic of difference consistently applied reveals the falsity of any supposed unity or totality.

At a political level, the post-structuralist claims that the search for totality or unity results in totalitarianism. This is because the search for unity entails a limitation of discourse within a predefined range of possibilities, a range defined by the supposed real nature of the totality to be discovered. Such assumptions thus prevent freedom of expression in that the very attempt to achieve unity in the light of a predefined totality forces a reduction and delimitation of the differences that exist to a single theoretical idea or supposed material state of the real. For the post-structuralist this implies totalitarianism in that thought is directed along a single channel where differences and oppositional elements are suppressed.

It was in terms of the philosophy of difference and the debt to Nietzsche that Foucault enunciates a theory of discursive formations and rejects Marxist and Hegelian conceptions of history. Although Foucault's work can be broadly located within a tradition of thought beginning with Hegel, it is the rejection of the Hegelian dialectic, with its beliefs in progress, Enlightenment, and optimism concerning human ability to understand reality, that characterizes Foucault's Nietzschean method. Whereas Marxists like Althusser adopted a structuralist program of seeking to explain the whole by understanding the interrelations between its component parts, for Foucault the totality always eluded analysis or understanding in terms of "necessity," and hence the ability to predict any future course of events, but rather was characterized by *incompleteness, indeterminacy, complexity,* and *chance.* As Foucault says, "though it is true that these discontinuous discursive series each have within certain limits, their regularity, it is undoubtedly no longer possible to establish links of mechanical causality, or of ideal necessity between the elements which constitute them. We must accept the introduction of *alea* (chance) as a category in the production of events" (Foucault, 1981a: 69).

In relation to this conception it can be observed that Foucault's model is analogous to Roy Bhaskar's thesis concerning "open systems" and causal complexity. For Bhaskar (1978), "open systems" are inevitably characterized by a multiplicity of generative (causal) mechanisms. As a result, the achievement of scientific closure, in the sense of deduction or predictability, is impossible. Although Foucault would concur with Bhaskar on this, he does not appear to share Bhaskar's faith in the possibility of a science of genuinely universal generative mechanisms. While Foucault doesn't explicitly deny the existence of universal regularities or mechanisms (see Foucault, 1984a: 48), he avoids the use of universal categories of analysis, or the search for universal truths or regularities in the world. In this sense, it could be conjectured that Foucault advances a more radical thesis than Bhaskar as to the openness of social systems and of the limitations of science entailed as a consequence of such.

Foucault's project thus marks a break with Marxism's central postulates; yet as Balibar (1992: 56) observes, there is a partial usage of Marxist tenets as well. Like Marx, Foucault asks questions of the same order, concerning philosophy and philosophy of history, and concerning the nature of historical investigations. Moreover, both writers can be represented as "historical materialists." As Balibar notes:

Inasmuch as it is true that the *shift* in philosophy as practised by Marx and by Foucault involves, in a nutshell, the need which has existed for a century to move from a philosophy *of* history to a philosophy *in* history, it is necessary, in the rigorous form of a series of dilemmas (*either* Marx, *or* Foucault), that the main lines of tension of a theoretical field should become apparent and, eventually, definable. This field must, in some form, *already exist*, and it must already have been traversed and particularised. Nonetheless it must remain to a large extent *to be discovered* and defined cartographically. Perhaps it could be referred to as the field of "historical materialism." . . . Central to this . . . is the concept of "social relations" or, contradiction as a structure internal to power relations. This is what sustains the Marxian notion of historical materialism. This then is what, more and more explicitly, Foucault questions. At the (provisional) point of his evolution on this question . . . he developed ideas which it would not be wrong to refer to by the name of "historical materialism," but in a way which is opposed, in each of the ways in which it is meant, to Marx: *materiality* is seen not as the materiality of "social relations" but as the materiality of the apparatus and practice of power, inasmuch as it affects *bodies; historicity* is seen not as the historicity of contradiction (whether this be viewed as an instance of the totalisation of different forms of struggle or as an instance of the interiorisation of their necessity) but in terms of the historicity of the *event*; the improbable outcome of various strategies of repression and of multiple and partially uncontrollable forms of subjugation. (Balibar, 1992: 54–55)

A KIND OF NOMINALISM

As part of his general opposition to Marxism, Foucault draws on nominalism as a means of preventing materialism "from turning back into metaphysics" (Balibar, 1992: 56). In this way, he avoids the reification and idealization of particular concepts and theoretical terms as entities or abstractions that are claimed to have solid transhistorical existence. The doctrine of nominalism, although it does not deny the existence of the material world, denies that it is sorted in any particular way in any transhistorical sense. Thus, it disputes the existence of "natural categories" (kinds). While if taken to an extreme and applied to the objects of the physical world it becomes absurd, applied to the social and historical world it becomes a thesis about the unreality of abstractions and collective representations (e.g., social class) applied in a similar way in different historical periods. It thus assists as a general philosophical strategy in prioritizing the uniqueness of historical events over the universality of historical laws and categorizations. Nominalism concerns the great question started by Plato about the nature of generalizations and definitions and is based on a distrust of essences and natures.

Foucault's appropriation of nominalism must be distinguished as regards the claims concerning realism. Realism, as I am using this term, stands in opposition to idealism. Idealism, as Hacking tells us, is a thesis about existence. "In its extreme form it says that all that exists is mental, a production of the human spirit." Nominalism, on the other hand, though seen as the opposite of realism "prior to Kant," does not in fact deny the real existence of matter, or of its ontological privileging in relation to mind. As Hacking says:

Nominalism is about *classification*. It says that only our modes of thinking make us sort grass from straw, flesh from foliage. The world does not have to be sorted that way; it does not come wrapped up in "natural kinds". In contrast the Aristotelian realist (the anti-nominalist) says that the world just comes in certain kinds . . . the nominalist does not deny that there is real stuff, existing independent of mind. He denies only that it is naturally and intrinsically sorted in any particular way. (1983, 108)

Although Foucault explicitly calls upon nominalism, it is arguable as to whether the concept has a stable enough meaning in the history of its usage to warrant claims concerning affinities between nominalism and anti-realism. As Hacking notes, the two doctrines—nominalism and realism—are "logically distinct." Certainly, too, Foucault is not an "old-fashioned nominalist . . . [who sees] systems of classification as products of the human mind," for he theorizes intellectual production in relation to historically elaborated discourses rather than in terms of the human subject. In addition, whereas the "old-fashioned nominalist" saw the human mind as unalterable, Foucault sees discursive systems as transformable (Hacking, 1983: 110).

In this sense, Foucault's form of nominalism is more akin to T. S. Kuhn's, whose work Hacking classifies as "revolutionary nominalism." Hacking explains this notion with respect to Kuhn's views on scientific revolutions:

[It] produces a new way of addressing some aspect of nature. It provides models, conjectured laws, classes of entities, causal powers which did not enter into the predecessor science. In a completely uncontroversial sense we may now live in a different world from the nineteenth century age of steam—a world in which aeroplanes are everywhere and railways are going bankrupt. More philosophically . . . it is a different world, in that it is categorized in new ways, thought of as filled with new potentialities, new causes, new effects. But this novelty is not the production of new entities in the mind. It is the imposition of a new system of categories upon phenomena, including newly created phenomena. That is why I call it a kind of nominalism. (1983: 109).

Hacking clarifies the concept further by citing Kuhn (1981: 25):

What characterizes revolutions is, thus, change in several of the taxonomic categories prerequisite to scientific descriptions and generalizations. That change, furthermore, is an adjustment not only of criteria relevant to categorization, but also of the way in which given objects and situations are distributed among pre-existing categories. Since such redistribution always involves more than one category and since those categories are interdefined, this sort of alteration is necessarily holistic. (Hacking, 1983: 109)

Any comparison between Kuhn and Foucault must be qualified in that while Kuhn wrote in relation to the physical sciences in *The Structure of Scientific Revolutions*, Foucault's central interest is in the human sciences, the "immature sciences," as Hacking (1979) calls them, which Foucault depicts as "groups of statements that borrow their organization from scientific models" (1972: 178). Yet, on the issue of nominalism, Foucault's brand, like Kuhn's, is able to theorize the possibility of revolutionary change and yet not deny the ontological existence of the material world. Hence, Foucault would hold that given certain changes in the structure of society, or of our schemes of discursive representation, certain (but not necessarily all) of our classifications systems and categorizations could change. One of Foucault's central theses concerning science is that while we may think we are categorizing the world in terms of fixed, immovable, natural categories, such classificatory schemes are more contingent than we think. While he sees important differences between the physical and the human sciences in their claims to adequately represent the world, in both cases the schemas of our classifications must themselves be seen as historical episodes. In addition, there is no final way to classify or represent the world that we can be certain of. Like Kant he sees no means of escaping conceptualism. Unlike Kant, he sees no way of salvaging objectivism, but accepts the implications of a radical historicism. His empirical studies are attempts to describe the ways that our schemes of reality change.

NOTES

   1. Poster makes a telling point here, but his language is mistaken. The distinction is not between discourse/practice, as Foucault refers frequently to discursive practices (see Foucault, 1972: 162; 1997g: 12). The distinction Poster intends is between discursive practices and pre-discursive or non-discursive practices, and as this is true to Foucault's usage of these concepts, it is the way I will be representing the distinction in the remainder of this book.
   2. One difficulty associated with "social constructionism" as a theory is that there

are several variations. It can be traced through Symbolic Interactionism and can include ethnomethodology, "postmodern" and various "post-structuralist" approaches. It is also a term used to include approaches in psychology such as Kenneth Gergen's (1985). Burr (1995) traces the roots of contemporary constructionism back to Mead's Symbolic Interactionism (although the "I," in representing the non-socialized source of creativity and originality, is not compatible with modern versions of constructionism). Burr (cited in Craib, 1997: 4) lists four factors as essential to constructionism: (1) a critical stance toward taken-for-granted knowledge, (2) a belief in the cultural and historical specificity of knowledge, (3) a belief that knowledge is sustained by social processes, and (4) a belief that knowledge and social action go together. However, as Ian Craib points out, such a definition "would appropriate the whole of sociology to social constructionism," and Burr's definition leaves enough out to make it not worthwhile from the point of view of this analysis anyway. Craib defines it as including two aspects: (1) anti-essentialism—essentialism is the view that sees "the person as having some definable and discoverable nature, whether given by biology or by environment" and (2) anti-realism. "Social constructionism," says Craib, implies that (a) there is something constructed, (b) something doing the construction, but "there is no raw material out of which the finished product is formed" (1997: 4). In this sense, Foucault is not a social constructionist, although he is an anti-essentialist. He is not an anti-realist, however. While he denies a direct perception of reality, he allows an indirect relation to reality, and he does not see the world as an element of discursive practice. For Foucault, our relation to the world is mediated through discourse. In that "social constructionism" typically represents an anti-realist thesis, it is not accurate to apply the tag to Foucault. All that can be said is that he exemplifies some constructionist themes (e.g., he is skeptical of foundationalist warrants for the sciences; he replaces foundationalist philosophies of science with a predominantly social and historical account of theoretical advances. Unlike many so-called social constructionists (Gergen, Mead, Vygotsky, Schutz, Berger and Luckman), Foucault places less weight on cognitive dimensions such as "subjectivity," "consciousness," or "mental processes." Unlike others, he does not deny ontological status to the world or to thought. None of this makes it useful to call him a "social constructionist," however.

Chapter 6

Relativism

In *The Philosophical Discourses of Modernity* (1987), Jürgen Habermas accuses Foucault of three forms of skepticism which derive, he tells us, from his dependence on Nietzsche. These forms of skepticism all relate to Foucault's theory of power, which he sees Foucault as developing "from the late 1960s" (1987: 241) and which generate a "systematic ambiguity" (1987: 270) in relation to (1) *presentism*, (2) *relativism*, and (3) *arbitrary partisanship* (1987: 276).

By *presentism* Habermas means "a historiography . . . hermeneutically stuck in its own starting position" (1987:276), which entails a methodological opposition to something Foucault can't himself eliminate: that is, a tendency to filter the past through the lens of the present. As a radical historicist, Foucault has no standpoint (such as an origin) from which assessments can be established, and, in the absence of any objective standard, he has no option but to fall back on a subjective standard. In other words, he "can only explain the technologies of power and practices of domination by comparing them with one another. . . . In doing so, one inevitably connects the viewpoints under which the comparison is proposed with his own hermeneutic point of departure" (1987: 277).

By *relativism* Habermas means "an analysis . . . that can understand itself only as a context-dependent practical exercise" (1987: 276). Whereas presentism refers to the order of signification, relativism concerns the order of truth. In this regard, says Habermas, Foucault's historicism is inevitably caught in its own trap of being able to follow practices that are caught in the endless play of power. This produces a "self-referentiality" which cannot be escaped. "Not only are truth claims confined to the discourses within which they arise; they exhaust their entire significance in the functional con-

tribution they make to the self-maintenance of a given totality of discourse
. . . this basic assumption of the theory of power is self-referential; if it is
correct, it must destroy the foundations of research inspired by it as well"
(1987: 279).

As Habermas admits, Foucault gives answers of sorts claiming that the
superiority of genealogical enquiry will establish its preeminence above all
the other human sciences in its own performance, linked as it is in its positive
moments to the disqualified, "subjugated" knowledges "beneath the required level of cognition or scientificity" in which there slumbers "a historical
knowledge of struggles" (Habermas, 1987: 279–280). Yet genealogical historiography falls short of escaping self-referentiality, claims Habermas. The
validity claims of subjugated knowledges count no more and no less than
those of the dominant discourses of power that they attack, for "they, too,
are nothing else than the effects of power they unleash" (281).

Arbitrary partisanship refers to "a criticism that cannot account for its
[own] normative foundations" (276). As such, it is a form of "cryptonor-
mativism" of the sort Foucault attacks in the human sciences and which he
claims in his own work not to manifest. Foucault's "grounding of a second-
order value freedom is already by no means value free," says Habermas. In
addition, it is not clear why we should undertake analysis in the first place:
"Why should we muster any resistance at all-against this all-pervasive power
circulating in the bloodstream of the body of modern society, instead of
just adapting ourselves to it . . . why fight at all?" (Habermas, 1987: 284).

Habermas attributes these errors to Foucault's theory of power present
in his work all along but intensified after his turn to Nietzsche from the late
1960s. In this, Habermas attributes to Foucault a particular reading of Nietzsche where the will to knowledge is seen as but one aspect of the will to
power. Dominique Janicaud (1992: 292) explains that "behind apparently
universal truth claims are hidden the subjective claims to power of value
judgements." Hence, for Habermas, says Janicaud, "the will to power becomes . . . the *truth* of the claim to truth." It is, indeed, "a continuation of
the confrontation between Socrates and Callicles . . . the rationalist affirms
the universal validity of his judgements; the Nietzschean unmasks this latter
as a form of the will to power." Hence, Habermas reads Nietzsche as offering an "anti-rational, anti-universal *thesis* in favour of a subjective imposition of strength" (292), and he sees Foucault as following in this mode
where power and reason are inextricably linked.

Hilary Putnam's objections are similar to Habermas's, although the central error identified is that of "relativism." Noting that while Hegel taught
us to see all our ideas, forms of rationality, images of knowledge, and so on
as historically conditioned, he also posited an *objective* notion of rationality
which we (or Absolute Mind) were coming to possess, "Thinkers who accept the first Hegelian idea, that our conceptions of rationality are all historically conditioned while rejecting the idea of an end (or even an ideal
limit) to the process, tend to become historical or cultural relativists" (Put-

nam, 1983: 287–288). And relativism, says Putnam, is "self-defeating," "in-coherent," and "self-contradictory" (288). Arguments similar to this one have been offered by Charles Taylor (1986), Michael Walzer (1986), and Christopher Norris (1993). According to Norris, Foucault offers "no secure vantage point," no "sky hook," in Rorty's sense, on which to base either arguments or judgments. Thus, there is "no standard of right reading, no ethical criterion, no critical court of appeal. . . . few writers have done more to undermine the claims of authorial intent, to dislodge the knowing and willing subject from its erstwhile privileged status and to promulgate an 'ethics' of reading indifferent to issues of interpretative truth or falsehood" (Norris, 1993: 50).

Joseph Margolis (1993) presents an interesting defense of Foucault against the kind of charges made by Habermas, Putnam, and Norris. According to Margolis, Foucault's historicism is neither "self-refuting" nor "self-referential," and charges from Kantian or Anglo-American philosophical quarters based on assumptions and perspectives that Foucault does not accept are hardly satisfactory. Neither Habermas nor Putnam, says Margolis, are prepared to consider that any form of relativism could be coherent. Although some versions of historicism (e.g., Ranke's) do entail self-referential paradoxes, Foucault's version is free from such inconsistencies "either cross-culturally or diachronically" (Margolis, 1993: 197). What is centrally at stake, says Margolis, is the meaning of objectivity under historicist conditions. For Foucault, there is no "fixed origin" or no "secure exit" from history in terms of which Habermas's, Putnam's, or Norris's charges could be addressed. And since when did *rationality* dictate that we have to posit some objective "archimedean point" in terms of which all of history can be grounded? For Foucault, "genealogy . . . rejects the metahistorical deployment of ideal significations and indefinite teleologies. It opposes itself to the search for origins" (Foucault, 1977b: 140). Thus Foucault opposes the notions of *constants, origins, rules of enquiry, absolutes, continuities,* or the like. Opposing any attempt to apply *objective* methods of the study of man (as intended by Kant or Marx, for instance), rather it is the *constitution of man* whose history Foucault seeks to trace. On this, he is in fact explicit:

Criticism is no longer going to be practised in the search for formal structures with universal value, but rather as a historical investigation into the events that have led us to constitute ourselves and to recognize ourselves as subjects of what we are doing, thinking, saying. In this sense this criticism is not transcendental, and its goal is not that of making a metaphysics possible: it is genealogical in its design and archaeological in its method. (Foucault, 1984a: 46, cited in Margolis, 1993: 203)

In short, says Margolis, the objections raised by Habermas and Putnam are not questions Foucault *can* address within the scope of his analysis. Although both Habermas and Putnam fundamentally believe that "the horizon of the understanding of meaning . . . is not prior to, but subordinate to the question of truth," and accuse Foucault for not upholding this maxim, the real issue, says Margolis, is that "it is not that the horizon of the understanding of meaning is 'prior' or 'subordinate' to truth but that meaning and truth (reference and identity) are conceptually inseparable, on a par with one another—and taken together, are (now) (with Foucault) being irresistibly historicized. There's the lesson stretching from Hegel to Foucault" (Margolis, 1993: 203).

For Foucault, then, historical materialism means that in any era or period the specific causal relations, as well as the priority of this or that structure, must be investigated *anew*. There are no universal, causally efficacious laws or mechanisms throughout history, just as there are no simple material categories (e.g., class) that can explain everything. What Foucault stresses is that the act of justification, and the norms we appeal to, will always be internal to the practices we are criticizing. Our judgments will involve comparative historical and social evaluations not on the basis of transhistorical universals but in terms of "local" comparisons.

As an historicist, Foucault's method is a combination of critical analysis and rigorous empirical research: an attempt both to describe history and to penetrate its "inner core" while denying the existence of historical laws. While "necessity" operates, almost in Ranke's sense, as that which has already been formed and cannot be overturned, Foucault denies the existence of historical laws, of a constant human nature, or any claims to transhistorical values. The notion of *transience* is thus central to Foucault's historicism. All discursive forms are part of the process of history, and there is no foundational sense in terms of which claims to knowledge can be grounded. On this point, then, Foucault could agree with Marx's statement in Volume 1 of *Capital* that "every historically developed social form is in fluid movement, and therefore takes into account its transient nature no less than its momentary existence" (Marx, 1917: 29).

If we are to make any progress in discussing Foucault and the problem of historical relativism, it is important to distinguish types of relativism. Roy Bhaskar (1986) has distinguished two types: (1) *epistemic relativism* which holds that all beliefs are socially constructed so that knowledge is *transient* and that neither truth values nor criteria or rationality exist outside historical time, and (2) *judgmental relativism*, which claims that all beliefs are equally valid in the sense that there are no rational grounds for preferring one to the other. It is "epistemic relativism" that Foucault asserts, and "judgmental relativism" that he is sometimes charged with. "Judgmental relativism" is usually associated with the Incommensurability Thesis. We accept Ian Hacking's point that incommensurability is not a problem; that "as a matter of brute fact all human languages are fairly easily partially translatable" (1985: 157–159). In addition, we accept Bhaskar's (1986: 72–76) point that if theories are completely incommensurable, then they are not incommensurable, for they do not relate to the same domain of analysis. If on the other hand they offer competing explanations of an object, then there is some common basis for their independent assessment.

"Epistemic relativism" presents potential problems for Foucault relating to (1) the thesis that there are no facts independent of interpretation, or real-world structures independent of discursive mediation, (2) the claim that different periods of Western thought have been ruled by radically different epistemes, (3) the claim that all knowledge is essentially "power-knowledge" and is tied to non-discursive social structures, and (4) claims relating to the explicitly local and regional nature of Foucault's analysis which pertain also to the issue of the universality of knowledge.

The problems for Foucault—and unquestionably there are remaining problems with such a thoroughly historicized version of historical materialism—relate not to ontology but to epistemology. They are issues relating to the question of how we *know* the truth. Is there any discourse which has, or can have, a privileged access to the real? For if reason and knowledge are historicized, but "the real" and "truth" are not, then the conditions under which we can ever gain any secure knowledge are rendered problematic. It needs to be resolved, as Margolis concludes, if Foucault's "Hegelian project is ever to seriously advance" (Margolis, 1993: 203). Although I am not claiming to have resolved the issue, once and for all, a number of resolutions have been attempted, which can be discussed briefly in the following sections.

HISTORICAL NECESSITY: CONGRUENCE BETWEEN DISCOURSE AND PRACTICE, AND DISCOURSE AND DISCOURSE

There are no absolute ways that Foucault can be saved from the problems associated with skepticism that confront him, and, in this sense, most of the suggestions made later in this chapter are pragmatic attempts if not to resolve the issues, at least to moderate them. Foucault himself, in *The Archaeology of Knowledge*, admits he is "avoiding the ground upon which [his studies] could find support" (1972: 205). Also, as Janicaud (1992: 29) points out, the source of most of what Habermas says is Foucault himself who made various admissions and criticisms of his own work in the Introduction to *The History of Sexuality*, Volume 2. In addition, Foucault fully understands the complications and consequences of his rejection of the Kantian *transcendental subject* as a condition for the possibility of any knowledge. As he says to Giulio Pretic in an interview published first in 1972 in *Il Bimestrein*:

When I say that I strive to avoid it, I don't mean that I am sure of succeeding. My procedure at this moment is of a regressive sort, I would say: I try to assume a greater and greater detachment in order to define the historical conditions and transformations of our knowledge. I try to historicize to the utmost in order to leave as little space as possible to the transcendental. I cannot exclude the possibility that one day I will have to confront an irreducible *residium* which will be, in fact, the transcendental. (Foucault, 1989c: 79)

Although the assuredness given to knowledge by Kant is replaced by doubt and uncertainty given the absence of transcendental foundations, it is not true, as Christopher Norris (1993: 86) says, that all judgments are equally arbitrary or that no evaluations can be made. What it does mean, however, is that the basis for such judgments is more practical and concrete, and, admittedly, less certain. This, however, was a central correction that Foucault seeks to introduce in his critique of the Enlightenment. As Dreyfus and Rabinow maintain:

The archaeological step back that Foucault takes in order to see the strangeness of our society's practices does not mean that he considers these practices meaningless. Since we share cultural practices with others, and since these practices have made us what we are, we have, perforce, some common footing from which to proceed, to understand, to act. But that foothold is no longer one which is universal, guaranteed, verified, or grounded. (1986: 115)

It is not, then, that nothing counts as valid criteria. Just as Kant's conception of "practical reason" involves a form of thinking "whose autonomy consists in its reflective distance from matters of phenomenal self-evidence or straightforward empirical truth, but which nonetheless cannot be conceived . . . as existing in a separate realm" (Norris, 1993: 85), so Foucault's conception of "practical critical interrogation" cannot be and should not be divorced from the interests of, to use Norris's phrase, "veridical warrant." Such a warrant would include both correspondence with the facts as well as coherence with "mature" discursive systems, or rules of cognitive enquiry.

Writers like Morea (1990), Hacking (1985), and Flynn (1994) suggest a sense of objectivity *as being in accord with historical necessity*, necessity being recognized in that Foucault recognizes the existence of "de re" structures and practices. In this sense, what could be suggested is an historicist conception of rationality and objectivity operating in relation to values that "correspond to" the "movement of history." Ian Hacking (1985) offers such a suggested resolution when he asks how discursive formations relate to the real world, and whether they survive or die depending on their usefulness to particular societies at particular times. This doesn't necessarily license a conception of history in the sense that whatever has survived must have done so because it is useful and therefore better, for it may not be useful tomorrow, or it may have already outlived its functional importance and thus constitute a residual and disappearing category. What Hacking is suggesting, rather, is that discourses are in a constant process of testing themselves in terms of practice in history and, further, that the fact that real-world structures and practices are always discursively mediated does not necessarily therefore suggest relativism. As Hacking states, "it has taken millennia to evolve systems of reasoning. . . . Some of our once favoured styles of reasoning have turned out to be dead ends and others are probably on their way. However, new styles of reasoning will continue to evolve" (1985: 150).

Looked at in this way, the historicity of our styles of reasoning in no way makes them less objective or less rational. Rationality and objectivity are related to context. Discursive systems have histories. Some work better than others, are more useful, or continue "to deliver the goods." While the truth claims associated with any particular discourse may be internal to the formalized structure, this does not mean that human beings cannot *also* exercise rational judgment related to their being in the world. Hacking believes this when he says "there are good and bad reasons for propositions about nature. They are not relative to anything. They do not depend on context" (1985: 151). Thus, Hacking sees two sorts of knowledge claim: one where claims are relative to a "style of reasoning" (or discourse) and another, involving more trivial types of knowledge, where they are not. In this sense he sees a common stock of non-relativized observational truths that serve to anchor communication.

Gramsci makes a similar distinction when he distinguishes between "good sense" and "folklore" as being the two elements of "common sense." By such a distinction, Gramsci attempted to resolve the impasse of relativism in the context of historicist and anti-foundational conceptions of the emergence and development of knowledge. For Gramsci, good sense was the criterion of evaluation generated by experience, whereas folklore was knowledge handed down from generation to generation simply on the basis of custom or tradition. The task of educators was to instill good sense and eradicate folklore.

THE PERVASIVENESS OF INTERPRETATION

For Foucault, there are no "simply given facts" or sense impressions. Similar to Bachelard, Canguilhem, and Kant, Foucault believed that facts always have to be interpreted. In Donald Davidson's (1985) sense, Foucault invokes a dualism of "scheme and reality." The idea of uninterpreted experience or of experience uncontaminated by interpretation is just another "dogma of empiricism." However, this does not entail the relativistic position that there are no genuinely objective facts. Rather, like Kant, Foucault adopts the view that explanation in terms of a categorical scheme is a condition of objectivity. It is through archaeological/genealogical analysis that the successive layers of the world can be uncovered. Like Bachelard and

Canguilhem, Foucault came to reject the hermeneutic position that there is nothing but interpretation, that all description is interpretation, in Nietzsche's sense, "all the way down," in preference to a method designed to describe discursive formations as objective structures quite apart from the meanings that subjects may give them.

The charge that relativism arises due to the pervasiveness of interpretation has led some to accuse Foucault of Nietzschean perspectivism—that there is no reality but only differing perspectives that are infinite. Gary Gutting notes that some commentators have viewed Foucault's essay "Nietzsche, Freud, Marx" (Foucault, 1986b) as offering such a perspectival position. Yet, as Gutting observes, correctly in my view, Foucault is merely describing Nietzsche's own position here in the context of his general thesis as to how structures of signification vary in different historical periods. In his own words Foucault made it clear in *Birth of the Clinic* and *The Archaeology of Knowledge* that archaeology rejects hermeneutics or interpretivism for archaeology seeks to describe objective structures independent of any interpretation or perspective. This would also square with archaeology's close affinity to semiology when Foucault points out in the last paragraph of "Nietzsche, Freud, Marx" that "hermeneutics and semiology are two fierce enemies since semiology denies the infinity of interpretations, believing in the absolute existence of signs" (Foucault, 1986b: 5). This essay shows that Foucault is offering an historical materialism of signification consistent with his general position in *The Order of Things* where he describes (1970: 42) the differences in systems of signification between the age of resemblance and the age of representation.

While Foucault maintains that historically generated interpretivist categories are essential to the production of knowledge, and that in this sense there are no uninterpreted facts or data, this does not gainsay the existence of facts or data or truths. Only "getting at them" is seen to be problematic.

Foucault can also be charged with relativism on a particular reading of his thesis concerning the insularity of *epistemes*. Although *epistemes* constitute a structural basis for the generation and meaning of discursive systems, Foucault does not represent them as being completely insulated or separate and it is not acceptable to accuse Foucault of relativism on the basis that statements made under one episteme are incomprehensible or meaningless from the point of view of another. On this issue Foucault follows Canguilhem. In *The Order of Things* and *The Archaeology of Knowledge*, as Gutting points out, he does not deny all continuity in changes between epistemes, acknowledging "transitional" modalities of expression, as well as "transitional theories," which enable a "bridge" between one episteme and another. In addition, as Gutting also notes, the notion of "discontinuity" that operates between one episteme and another does not necessarily preclude a conception of social progress (1989: 275).

Foucault believes that constraints on discourse operate in several ways and that they allow for the gradual "excavation" of the real. One is that the existence of discourses arises from events in history, that is, from "practices" that enable statements to be assessed as true or false, as valid or invalid, and as authoritative. This provides a check on the autonomy of discourse within limits. Foucault's concept of *practice* refers to "a pre-conceptual, anonymous, socially-sanctioned body of rules that govern one's manner of perceiving, judging, imagining and acting" (Flynn, 1989: 135). Pre-discursive practices are linked (enchainment) to discourses. Such a practice thus forms the intelligible background for actions by its twofold character as both judicative and veridicative. On the one hand, pre-discursive practices establish and imply norms, controls, and exclusions. On the other hand, they render true/false discourse possible. Thus the practice of legal punishment, for example, entails an interplay between a code that regulates ways of acting—how to discipline an inmate—and the production of true discourse which legitimates these ways of acting (Flynn, 1989: 134–147). While such practices thus act as constraints on discourse, they are unable to totally explain the discursive context of explanation and belief, which is to say, with Duhem and Quine, that practices underdetermine the discursive context of their explanation.

In this sense, Foucault's critical social science is characterized by the same sense of indeterminacy as other forms of social science. Because the idea of practice is historicized, Kant's finite and grounded concept of objectivity is overturned, as Hegel's Geist is eliminated. As a consequence, reasons and explanations for events and occurrences are relative to an overall context or period, discourse, or episteme. The whole point of Foucault's analysis is to reveal the contextualization and radical contingency of our most prized certainties. One key problem for Foucault is how to derive standards of assessment, comparison, and evaluation, without falling headlong into an ahistorical and essentialist epistemology. There can be no assuredness in terms of foundations. All that provides security or assuredness of belief is not any timeless conception of truth but a simple *correspondence* between discourse and practice, and a *coherence* between discourse and other (more mature) discursive systems. Although these processes provide a check on discursive meaning within any particular historical context, they are quite compatible with a coalescence of truth and ideology, which is to say that Foucault believes that the attainment of truth within limits is compatible with a strong ideological bias. In this sense, the criterion of validity and assessment of the adequacy of statements depends on, or is relative to, the circumstances of users, and the rules of agreement and criteria of truth are internal to a discursive system and a given society. Explanations accept the burden of a pragmatic and normative criteria of adequacy. Explanation stops at the point where questioning by the relevant local consensus ceases and there is no sense attached to the idea that some standards or beliefs are truly rational as distinct from merely being accepted as such within a given historical period, except on pragmatic grounds.

POWER AND KNOWLEDGE

Perhaps the most common accusation of relativism is that Foucault sees knowledge as originating from non-discursive social structures. Much of the basis for those who criticize Foucault for being a relativist in this sense of linking knowledge to power derives from a particular Nietzschean reading of Foucault as seeing the "will to truth" as but an aspect of the "will to power." This is one of Habermas's central criticisms, as stated above. A number of possible responses can be made to Habermas in order to defend Foucault here. One is to defend Nietzsche against such a view. A second is to establish that Foucault, though influenced by Nietzsche, cannot be saddled with the deficiencies of Nietzsche's approach. A third is to represent Foucault's own approach to *power-knowledge* in a way that resolves the issue of relativism.

In relation to the first, Janicaud (1992) denies that Nietzsche's thought can be reduced to such an anti-rationalist thesis. What is more, he says,

it would be easily refuted: not only because a subject's will to power could be denied from one instant to another by another subject in the most arbitrary way, but also because it contradicts itself; for by denying truth (in general terms) it affirms (in general terms) non-truth, which boils down to affirming the truth of this non-truth called the will to power. The Nietzschean (just like Callicles) is caught in the trap of an implicit truth judgement which cannot subtend its own negation: "I affirm (I put forward as truth) that there is no truth." (292–293)

Janicaud then proceeds to defend such a reading of Nietzsche:

In Nietzsche the questioning of rationality can by no means be reduced to a naive dispute on the surface level between the intrinsic and formal validity of truth judgements. Nietzsche never contested either the coherence or the interest of the logical, mathematical or scientific *corpus*. Rather, he affirmed the eminent *disciplinary* value of the spirit of analysis and observation and the critical value of the exercise of reason in sciences. It is well known that he dedicated *Humain trop humain* to Voltaire, that he admired the Encyclopédistes and that he made plans to pursue scientific studies in Paris. Even if this leaning towards positivity grew less marked during the latter years of his lucidity, it would be an untenable misinterpretation to reduce Nietzsche's thought to a challenge to rationality made by life or to the destruction of objectivity by the *pathos* of subjectivity. (1992: 293)

In relation to the second argument there are some grounds for minimizing Foucault's dependence on Nietzsche. While Foucault was influenced by Nietzsche to a marked extent in the 1970s, Foucault himself has cautioned us not to exaggerate the extent to which he follows in Nietzsche's footsteps. As he said to Gérard Raulet, "I do not believe there is a single Nietzscheanism. There are no grounds for believing that there is a true Nietzscheanism, or that ours is any truer than others." Foucault then proceeds to admit that he "found in Nietzsche . . . a means of displacing [himself] in terms of a philosophical horizon dominated by phenomenology and Marxism" (Foucault, 1988a: 31). Although he admits he took Nietzsche seriously and that his debt is largely to the texts Nietzsche wrote around the 1880s where the question of truth and the history of truth were central to his work, Foucault downplays his dependence on Nietzsche, denying for himself, as for Deleuze, that there is any "deafening reference" (32). When confronted by Raulet that "Nietzsche makes no fundamental distinction between will to knowledge and will to power," Foucault responds by indicating that he thinks "there is a perceptible displacement in Nietzsche's texts between those which are broadly preoccupied with the question of the will to knowledge and those which are preoccupied with the will to power," but adds "I do not want to get into this argument for the very simple reason that it is years since I have read Nietzsche" (33).

The point of exploring these comments is to indicate that Nietzsche cannot be seen as determining the outcome of Foucault's approach in any overall sense. This constitutes important background in order to understand the third point, that Foucault does not see power and knowledge as inextricably tied in any final or absolute sense. Although he does see power as always *associated* with knowledge, a plausible case can be made to suggest that he is not trying to situate all knowledge as a mere product, that is, as *reducible* to power. Rather, the nature of the relation is one where the respective effects of *power-knowledge* can be "separated out," a conception that would seem to be implied when Foucault speaks of "untangling" the interrelations between medicine and social structure, or physics, organic chemistry, psychiatry, and so on, and social structure (Foucault, 1980b: 109; 1984g: 386–387). Hence, although constituted by *power-knowledge* relations, it is possible to establish an authority, in some cases to "wrench free" from the immediacies of the historical present. Gutting makes a similar point when he notes that "even though Foucault sees bodies of knowledge as *originating* from non-discursive practices of social control, he also allows that some disciplines have been able to free themselves effectively from this connection" (1989: 275; emphasis added). As Gutting says, Foucault gives this explanation in relation to his account of the emergence of the physical sciences, which he saw as arising from the methods of judicial investigation employed by the Inquisition. "In becoming a technique for the empirical sciences, the investigation has detached itself from the inquisitorial procedure in which it was historically rooted" (Foucault, 1977a: 226, cited in Gutting, 1989: 276).

Thus a particular conception of objectivity is present in Foucault's work with regard to the judgments he makes about the epistemological status in relation to the discourses of the sciences. While constituted in relation to *power-knowledge*, Foucault suggests that the sciences are not inexorably bound by the same distorting effects in all times and places, but can establish relative degrees of freedom at various stages of their development. Foucault clearly makes this type of judgment in his comparisons between the physical and social sciences in terms of the "solidness" of their "epistemological armatures" (Foucault, 1980b: 109). The appropriate epistemological conceptions in this regard are those of "degrees of detachment," "developing maturity," or "having stood the test of time." Such might be the basis, for example, for comparing the authoritativeness of "mathematics" compared to "craniometry," or as Foucault does, of comparing "theoretical physics" to "psychiatry" (109). This, then, offers some basis for establishing the authoritativeness of particular discourses.

Part of what is involved in the notion of *power-knowledge* is that knowledge is inevitably dependent on context. Yet this does not necessarily entail a skeptical position. While contextualism entails that knowledge occurs only against a background and further, that all knowledge is conditioned by that background, it is not necessary to see these forms of entailment as vicious, for several reasons. First, the fact that shared practices and beliefs evolve in a context does not mean that the links are so strong that some form of distance cannot, with effort, be obtained. Second, the context dependence of knowledge, though transient in terms of its production, does not mean that truth is merely contingent. What is revealed may be contingent. Then, again, it may not be. Historicism entails claims about knowing the world, not about the world itself. Third, the fact that knowledge is conditioned does not mean that what is revealed does not have objective status. The context, in this sense, is a constraint, but not a limitation, in a way similar to language. Just as language is a constraining condition on communication, it is not a fixed limit on our capacity to communicate. Language use presents a series of flexible constraints rather than fixed limits on interpretation and understanding. A fitting example of this point is provided by Gutting (1989: 276) when he notes that the existence of an essential connection between power and knowledge may not necessarily impair the validity of the discipline. In one of his last interviews, as Gutting reports, Foucault claims that even "mathematics is linked, in a certain way, and *without impairing its validity*, to games and institutions of power" (276; emphasis added). Fourth, Foucault's critical orientation is itself based on norms of correctness, coherence, and correspondence. Hence, contextual historical knowledge may produce revisable publicly warranted knowledge. The fact that science is a social practice that takes place within a broader social and historical context does not therefore necessarily mean that knowledge lacks objectivity or representational status.

This conception, which is of course crucial to resolving the paradox of relativism in Foucault's work, also finds textual support in his writings and interviews. In *What Is Enlightenment?* (1984a: 48), while commenting on the nature of critical method, Foucault asks, "How can the growth of capabilities be disconnected from the intensification of power relations?", in order to answer the question that his critical historicist method means "that no work can be done except in disorder and contingency" (47). In addition, in response to a question by François Ewald in 1984, Foucault confronts the criticism directly, showing a certain degree of irritation:

If I had said, or wanted to say, that knowledge was power I would have said it, and having said it, I would no longer have anything to say, since in identifying them I would have had no reason to try to show their different relationships. I directed my attention specifically to see how certain forms of power which were of the same type could give place to forms of knowledge extremely different in their object and structure. Let's take the problem of the hospital's structure: it yielded to a psychiatric type of inclosure to which corresponded the formation of a psychiatric knowledge whose epistemological structure could remain rather special. But in another book, *The Birth of the Clinic*, I tried to show how this same hospital structure had developed an anatomic-pathological knowledge which was the foundation of a medicine with a completely different scientific fecundity. Thus one has structures of power, two neighbouring institutional forms—psychiatric inclosure, medical hospitalization—to which different forms of knowledge are linked, between which one can establish relationships, conditional connections, but not of cause and effect, nor *a fortiori* of identity. Those who say that for me knowledge is the mask of power don't seem to have the capacity to understand. There's hardly any point in responding to them. (Foucault, 1989q: 304–305)

Or, again, as he explained to Gérard Raulet, "when I read—and I know it has been attributed to me—the thesis, 'knowledge is power', or 'power is knowledge', I begin to laugh, since studying their *relation* is precisely my problem. If they were identical, I would not have to study them. . . . The very fact that I pose the question of their relation proves clearly that I do not *identify* them" (1988a: 43).

UNIVERSALITY

Are there any universal truths? The issue of universality is also more problematic in Foucault than has often been thought by those who charge Foucault with naive nihilism or relativism. It is frequently claimed that Foucault advocates "local and regional" forms of analysis and denies the possibility of universal truth. There are several instances in his interviews where he explicitly claims that he is not denying the possibility of universal structures, however. In *The Foucault Reader*, for instance, Foucault speaks of possible "universalising tendencies" at the root of Western civilization—"the acquisition of capabilities and the struggle for freedom"—as, in his opinion, "permanent elements" (1984a: 47–48). Again, in the Preface to *The History of Sexuality*, Volume 2, Foucault says that "singular forms of experience may very well harbour *universal structures*; they may well not be independent from the concrete determinations of social existence . . . this thought has a historicity which is proper to it. That it should have this historicity does not mean that it is deprived of all *universal form*, but instead that the putting into play of these universal forms is itself historical" (1984e: 335; emphasis added).

We must also consider that in some interviews (with Gérard Raulet, for instance) Foucault seems to echo genuine incredulity of the interpretations of his work which see him as representing reason or science as coming to an end, or as representing a break between modernism/postmodernism (1988a: 35). What he asserts, however, is the not altogether unsupportable claim that knowledge is always related to social context, that social life is conditioned by the structures inherited from the past, and that all phenomena must be understood in their historical circumstances. This makes the achievement of certain knowledge an even more difficult affair than has been presumed in the dominant Anglo-American empiricist traditions.

THE AUTONOMY OF THE CONCEPTUAL

Todd May makes a parallel attempt to resolve the relativistic implication of Foucault's thesis in distinguishing the conceptual status of Foucault's propositions from their historical and social contingency. According to May, "that conceptual thought can recognise its own rootedness in history, society, and politics does not imply any reduction to the latter." In this sense, May seeks to argue for the non-reducibility and autonomy of the conceptual. Hence, while the conceptual may be "inconceivable outside a socially and politically situated normative framework is not to claim that the conceptual just is the social and political forces of such a framework" (1995: 46). Such a situation would only arise, says May, if Foucault's analysis committed him to a denial of the mental: which it does not.

This contention is supported by Foucault's many comments on the autonomy and separatedness of thought: "Thought is freedom in relation to what one does, the motion by which one detaches oneself from it, establishes it as an object and reflects on it as a problem" (1984g: 388). Or: "We must free ourselves from the sacrilization of the social as the only reality and stop regarding as superfluous something so essential in human life and in human relations as thought. Thought exists independently of systems and structures of discourse. It is something that is often hidden, but which always animates everyday behaviour" (1988i: 155). Or: "When thought intervenes, it doesn't assume a unique form that is the direct result or the necessary expression of these difficulties; it is an original or specific response—often taking many forms, sometimes even contradictory in its different aspects" (1984a: 388–389). Hence, judgment is always autonomous and freely willed, always underdetermined by circumstances, and thought becomes possible in that the thinker can "step back from [a certain] way of acting or reacting, to present it to oneself as an object of thought and question it as to its meanings, its conditions, and its goals" (388). Thought is free to the extent that it permits a problematization of the grounds of taken-for-granted attitudes and beliefs (Norris, 1993: 91), and "the work of philosophical and historical reflection is put back into the field of the work of thought only on conditions that one clearly grasps problematization not as an arrangement of representations but as a work of thought" (1984: 390, cited in Norris, 1993: 91).

THE TURN TO SUBJECTIVITY

The issue of relativism in a specifically moral sense is frequently raised against Foucault, and while Foucault may not present us with formally stated and explicit criteria to support one form of moral conduct over another, it is not evident that the basis of such a justification could not be elaborated, especially, as we will see, in relation to Foucault's theoretical articulation of the relations between self and others. Ethical work, for Foucault, is the work that one performs in order to attempt to transform one's self into an ethical subject of one's own behavior. Such work of self upon self involves "practices of freedom," which involves challenging normalized conceptions of behavior. It is in this sense that the theme of "care of the self" as an ethical action involved a relationship to both self and others (see chapter 9). In the Greek and Roman worlds, individual and civic liberty considered themselves as ethical, and from Plato to Descartes the theme of the care of the self permeates all ethical thought.

Some writers, notably Arnold Davidson (1986) and Gilles Deleuze (1988), believe that Foucault's "turn to subjectivity" constitutes a new and, in Davidson's sense, "primary domain of analysis," and that Foucault's notion of *rapport à soi* offers a new line of defense against nihilism and relativism. Even Christopher Norris believes it constitutes "an escape route of kinds" (1993: 30).

In his final period, in the 1980s, Foucault turned to the issue of subjectivity as an attempt to confront the arbitrariness of historicity. During this period he argues for an aesthetic view of the person as moral agent in which "care of oneself" through "inner dialogue" is seen as a "way out" of the absence of moral or epistemological grounds and in the face of the political domination of discursive construction of self. This process requires the development of an ethics of the self (Foucault, 1989a).

The emphasis on the "turn to subjectivity" that is central to Deleuze's reading of Foucault sees the self, although constituted by power, as being

able to forge a new dimension which can be distinguished from both relations of knowledge and of power. For Deleuze, Foucault's idea is "that of
a dimension of subjectivity derived from power and knowledge without being dependent on them" (Deleuze, 1988: 101). The subject comes into
being when the forces that constitute power fold back on themselves, thus
creating the conditions for self-mastery. As Deleuze says, "it is as if the
relations of the outside folded back to create a doubling, allow a relation to
oneself to emerge, and constitute an inside which is hollowed out and develops its own unique dimension . . . [t]his is the Greek version of the snag
and the doubling: a differentiation that leads to a folding, a reflection"
(100).

The way of freeing oneself from the effects of *power-knowledge* counterposes itself to the fact that power insinuates itself in the constitution of
rational self-identity. While it is still impossible in any absolute sense to know
rationally one's true humanity independent of power's distorting effects, the
possibility of maturity is constituted through acts of self-creation in a way
reminiscent of Sartre's conception of "free choice," constrained by others
and the world. Whether this Nietzschean theme of life as a work of art
satisfies the requirements of an adequate justification of moral action for
Foucault is perhaps more problematic. While notions of pragmatics and maturity may suffice in relation to truth, many may be dissatisfied with Foucault's unwillingness or inability to provide a firm ground on which he
stands from which he can defend one moral viewpoint against another.
Hence, Dreyfus and Rabinow (1982: 264) state that Foucault "owes us a
criterion of what makes one kind of danger more dangerous than another."
Yet Foucault, in his own writing and interviews, implicitly advocates a theory
of the good, albeit one that opposes totalization and supports pluralism, and
that enables self-creation in a democratic context where others can act similarly as well as challenge dominant structures. What he wants to avoid is
promoting a theory of the good as a substantive ideal which promotes a
universal ethic and is totalizing and oppressive. Thus, when fully extended,
if we were to ascertain the conditions of possibility for self-creation as everyone's right, it is not clear that Foucault's approach would not contain a
moral and political standpoint.

Even so, our judgments will always involve comparative historical and
social judgments, and there are no transhistorical universals to ground our
critiques and to guide change. Such judgments may well appeal to democratic discourses that are immanent in the historical struggles of existence
and that have engraved their memory upon us. Such a possibility would not
lack contingency, but, at the same time, it would not lack value because of
that. Hence, it would seem that the justifications and norms we appeal to
will always be internal to the practices we are criticizing. Hence the constitution of rights in history does not derive from a hypothetical thought process or a conceptual archimedean point outside of experiences but from an

actual dialogical situation in which agents communicate with each other in terms of "situated knowledges," as Haraway (1990) calls them, located in historically evolving conceptions of justice negotiated in complex struggles and debates. Perhaps the fact that Foucault never debated the issue of relativism but frequently avoided the grounds on which he could find support may have led him to support Rorty's claim that "the ritual invocation of the 'need to avoid relativism' is most comprehensible as an expression of the need to preserve certain habits of contemporary European life" (Foucault 1972: 205).

Yet while Foucault may well agree with this, he does not himself think it "useless to revolt" or to "protest" or take a stand. As he says in his article "Is It Useless to Revolt?":

It is through revolt that subjectivity (not that of great men but that of whomever) introduces itself into history and gives it the breath of life. A delinquent puts his life into the balance against absurd punishments; a madman can no longer accept confinement and the forfeiture of his rights; a people refuses the regime which oppresses it. This does not make the rebel in the first case innocent, nor does it cure in the second, and it does not assure the third rebel of the promised tomorrow. One does not have to be in solidarity with them. One does not have to maintain that these confused voices sound better than the others and express the ultimate truth. For there to be a sense in listening to them and in searching for what they want to say, it is sufficient that they exist and that they have against them so much which is set up to silence them. A question of morality? Perhaps. A question of reality? Certainly. All the disenchantments of history amount to nothing; it is due to such voices that the time of men does not have the form of an evolution, but precisely that of a history. (Foucault, 1981e: 8)

Finally, Foucault also gives a moral priority to difference and pluralism. Thus Taylor's criticism that Foucault relinquishes any critical power that his historical analysis might have, because there is for him "no order of human life, or way we are, or human nature, that one can appeal to in order to judge or evaluate between ways of life" (1986: 93), displays a peculiar criterial finality that Foucault would wish to be without. Many possible styles of existence have value, and there are many ways of assessing them, but all depend for their validity on supports and guides which are not as grounded as some, like Taylor, might believe exist, or hope for.

Chapter 7

Foucault and Gramsci:
Is There a Basis for Convergence?

It is commonplace today for authors to cite Foucault on one page and Gramsci on the next without mention of the fact that the work of these two authors belong to fundamentally different theoretical traditions. This chapter examines whether a synthesis between their different projects is possible. The convergence thesis was initially proposed by Chantal Mouffe in 1979 when she suggested that substantial elements of Foucault's work are compatible with much of Gramsci's and that particular aspects of Gramsci's work converge with Foucault's (Mouffe, 1979: 201). Since then various attempts have been made to link the two thinkers in a common frame of reference (Laclau & Mouffe, 1985; Smart, 1986; Kenway, 1990; Cocks, 1989). This chapter considers the feasibility of such a convergence by comparing Foucault and Gramsci in respect to their different views on social structure, materialism, the role of intellectuals, history, collective politics, power, and the State. In addition to this direct comparison, consideration is given to more recent twentieth-century attempts to link Marxism and post-structuralism, with specific attention to the writings of Laclau and Mouffe, and to possible objections to such a convergence. The chapter concludes by arguing that a Foucault–Gramsci convergence gives rise to a theoretically worthwhile but specifically non-Marxist form of historical materialism.

Jane Kenway (1990) is among the researchers who have sought to utilize Foucault and Gramsci in a common frame of reference. She argues that considering Foucault in reference to Gramsci permits a more useful analysis than considering Foucault by himself. For this reason, Kenway contends that Foucault is usefully complemented by a "post-structuralist reading of Gramsci" (Kenway, 1990: 172). In fact, for Kenway, a Gramscian reading of Foucault helps free Foucault from the libertarian and right-wing implications that some have depicted in his work (Benton, 1984; Giddens, 1982, ch. 15). In addition, to see such compatabilities between Foucault and a neo-Marxist, while it may appear incongruous to those who have emphasized the incompatibility and difference between Foucault and Marxism, need not be considered an attempt to synthesize the two projects either in terms of "Foucault/Gramsci" or, more broadly, "modernism/postmodernism." Rather, for Kenway, the purpose is more limited and is aimed at demonstrating the more pragmatic advantages of "combining their different foci for the analysis of the incident under scrutiny" (Kenway, 1990: 202). Kenway's concern to treat both Gramsci and Foucault as complementary is paralleled by the similar efforts of Smart (1986), Mercer (1980), and Cocks (1989).

Another attempt to integrate Foucault and Gramsci has been made by the feminist philosopher Joan Cocks (1989). Like Kenway, Cocks argues that the ability to utilize both writers' insights in a common perspective has significant value in that both offer more by way of sociological insight when combined than each does individually. Her theoretical justification for such an enterprise is more elaborate than Kenway's, however. As she puts it,

There are [between Gramsci and Foucault] certain striking thematic repetitions, certain similar analytical obsessions—certain ways, too, in which their arguments and insights are reciprocally illuminating. What is flawed in each argument alone, moreover, is improved by the selective combination of the arguments together. For in some cases there is too great a faith in subjective agency, in others too great an emphasis on objective determination. Some defend an overly centrist strategy of resistance, others an overly localist one. In certain arguments we find a naive esteem for a final harmony in social relations, and in others, a hypertrophied sensitivity to the possibilities of repression in any collective way of life. (Cocks, 1989: 26)

In other words, the advantage of combining Foucault and Gramsci in a common frame of reference derives from the fact that each moderates the weaknesses of the other. Foucault's focus on the molecular and on the micro-physics of power supplements and enriches the Gramscian focus on structures in an analysis that enables a theorization of both the sources and structural basis of power in institutions as well as its consequences and capillary effects. Foucault's supplementation of Marxism thus enables him to correct and neutralize some of that perspective's well-documented deficiencies. According to Nancy Fraser,

Foucault rules out the crude marxist critiques of ideology and an overemphasis upon the state and economy, and instead rules in "the politics of everyday life". For if power circulates everywhere, even at the most mundane levels, then any effort to transform the regime must make an effort to address these everyday practices. Here we can see that while breaking with the totalising theory of marxism Foucault retains the link with a critical theory of society. Foucault unpacks the presupposition of grand theorising and addresses the plurality of forces, practices and regimes of power that exist within society. As such he subjects the micro politics of everyday life to scrutiny, often seeming to dissolve macro concerns into an analytic concentration of micro practices. (Fraser, 1989: 26)

The consequences of retaining Gramscian insights in relation to Foucault are also of value. Gramsci's theorization of power is much more materially grounded than Foucault's in that it maps the topography and articulates the structural sources of power. The significance of utilizing Gramscian insights is increased when one considers that Foucault's conception of power has been frequently criticized from a sociological point of view. As Derek Layder points out, for instance:

As Foucault does not define power, his analysis of domination lacks definition; it has no particular shape, no boundaries, no topography. As such it tends to flow or leak into everything else. Such a diffuse or amorphous notion of power makes it particularly difficult to understand its spheres of influence and the intensity of its effects. . . . Foucault's notion of power . . . pays little attention to the structural conditions under which power effects are produced in people. (Layder, 1994: 109)

For Nancy Fraser, "Foucault . . . adopts a concept of power that permits him no condemnation of any objectionable features of modern societies" (1989:33). In a related way, Charles Taylor criticizes Foucault's conception of power as a gross oversimplification: "Foucault's opposition between the old model of power based on sovereignty/obedience, and the new one based on domination/subjugation leaves out everything in Western history which has been animated by civic humanism or analogous movements. . . . Without this in one's conceptual armoury Western history and societies become incomprehensible" (Taylor, 1986: 83).[1]

In addition to the issue of power, Gramscian insights are also worthy of being retained in relation to the conceptualization of practices of the material or non-discursive level of reality. While Foucault acknowledges the existence of real-world necessities, they remain relatively undifferentiated within his general theory. As a consequence, the contexts of, and distinctions within, the material realm remain unspecified. Important in Gramsci is the distinction between power as *force* or *domination* (*dominio*) and power as *consent* (*consenso*), and between the *state* and *civil society*. In addition, Gramsci theorizes the relations between *structure* and *agency*, between individual agents and their contributions and historical collective movements in a way that Foucault fails to do. To be able to understand the way in which social contexts (structures, institutions) mold social activity linking individuals to group processes and to other forms of collective expression explains why notions such as resistance and the processes of oppositional politics are more theoretically intelligible in Gramsci than in Foucault. In short, Gramsci enables us to understand how the social circumstances in which action takes place make certain things possible, and how creativity, agency, and constraint are related through social activity.

Gramsci also enables a moderation of Foucault's radical historical nominalism. The doctrine of nominalism asserts a thesis about the unreality of abstractions and collective representations, and involves a prioritizing of individuality and uniqueness of historical events over the universality of historical laws. While Foucault is a holist, there is a sense in which the sociological form of nominalism that he adopts results in an atomistic view of society and a consistent sociological singularism. Foucault's project, as Thomas Flynn (1989, 1994) has observed, can be seen as expressing the strong nominalist tendency of the later Middle Ages, which regards individual elements as the only real existences and there being no reality at all in universal essences. Thus, although it needs careful qualification, there is some point to Flynn's view that "what Foucault calls his 'nominalism' is a form of methodological individualism. It treats such abstractions as 'man' and 'power' as reducible for the purposes of explanation to the individuals that comprise them. This is the context of his claim, for example, that 'power does not exist', that there are only individual instances of domination, manipulation, edification, control and the like" (Flynn, 1994: 39).

Flynn also notes that Foucault's nominalist claims are highly challengeable and that Foucault fails to defend such a perspective (Flynn, 1994: 44). Supplementing Foucault with Gramsci effectively moderates the nature of this nominalism from the radical version of the doctrine where only individual things exist and there are no universal regularities or entities to a milder version of the doctrine in which universality is considered to be at least as important as individuality in the makeup of the universe and its description (Gracia, 1988: 7–8). For many sociologists, on this issue alone, mixing Gramsci and Foucault has major beneficial sociological effects.

POST-STRUCTURALISM AND MARXISM

One of the major obstacles to such a convergence, and at the same time one of the major potential contributions of Foucault to Gramscianism, relates to the concept of social structure as embodied in the concepts of *totality* and *difference*.

Since Foucault's post-structuralist conception of difference ensures the openness of the social structure, in a sociological sense it overlays a pluralist model onto the structure of classical Marxist theory, and elevates difference as an ontological principle that replaces or at least balances unity as the central principle of social explanation.

Some commentators believe that Gramsci, under the influence of Croce and Hegel, overemphasizes the degree of consensus necessary for social reproduction. Adamson, for instance, refers to Gramsci's "unitarism" in the following manner:

As in the German Idealist tradition, Gramsci tended philosophically toward a unitarist rather than a pluralist position; he seemed to believe in a kind of anthropological impetus immanent in history which supports political movements and forms of political organization tending toward uniformity and against diversity. While Kant's politics led him in the same direction, he shied away in *Perpetual Peace* from the idea of a world state because he feared its tyrannical tendencies. Though Gramsci did not speak explicitly of a world state. . . . Given the influence of Hegel on him, one suspects that the culturally integrated totality that he foresaw would have been complexly mediated. Yet his failure to be fully explicit about the character of these mediations, coupled with other indications such as his treatment of language (e.g., the need to educate people away from regional dialects), casts doubt on this suspicion, especially when it is brought into conjunction with the politics of the "modern prince." (1980: 240–241)

Adamson goes on to argue that Gramsci's "ontological suppositions show a clear awareness of the importance of 'individuality' for human freedom . . . at odds with any static image of totalitarian control from above" (1980: 241). Because interpretations of Gramsci such as those given by Hughes (1961: 101), Lichtheim (1961: 369), or Bates (1976: 116, 124–129) depict the strategy of hegemony as inevitably producing a culturally integrated totality tending toward totalitarianism, however, Foucault's post-structuralist conception of difference can be seen as providing an important form of insurance against the possibility of such interpretations, thus ensuring the "openness" of the social system.

Notwithstanding the value of Foucault's correction as an insurance against those who would interpret Gramsci as a Hegelian, it should also be acknowledged that many writers would seek to defend Gramsci on this matter. A plausible case can be made to defend the claim that although Gramsci was interested in explaining unification, it was for him an empirical issue and not an a priori metaphysical premise. In that he was interested in unification, it was the *unification of Italy*. In that he seeks hegemonic relations as forms of common agreement, he considers both the *origin* of such agreements and *who benefits* from them. His concept of hegemony refers to a set of ideas which, rather than advance a metaphysical representation of the dominant ideological matrix, are dominant as a consequence of a particular structure of power. Such a view is supported by Adamson, who notes:

By stressing the integration of all the economic, political, or cultural expressions of a particular society, the concepts of hegemony and historic bloc suggested not how some of these spheres are reflected in others but rather how they are partial totalities of potentially equal significance which are knit together or drift apart in accordance with the political actions that people carry out in concrete historical circumstances. . . . The possibility of an alternative hegemony seems to presuppose a social order in which the existing hegemonic apparatus is not so powerful and pervasive as to disrupt all organized, collective challenges and yet which is sufficiently dependstent on that hegemonic apparatus for its stability so that an alternative hegemony would pose a serious threat. (Adamson, 1980: 179)

Hence, Adamson argues:

Certainly it was not [Gramsci's] intention to argue that a society's culture is very often, if ever, the perfect, totalized expression of its hegemonic apparatus. His assertion was that states seek to diffuse a hegemonic outlook as best they can, and that major works of art and literature are therefore likely to reflect and perhaps also to influence and shape this hegemony. (Adamson, 1980: 244)

Gramsci realized that hegemonic situations differ in intensity and degree of variation depending on the dynamics of historical development. On this view the potential for social disintegration is ever present, and conflict lurks just below the surface. This possibility would seem to be supported by Gramsci's rejection of Lukács's conception of "the point of view of the totality," through which history progressively realizes the point of view of the proletariat in a process of "unfolding," as a form of idealism (Gramsci, 1961: 448). Such a view is supported by Adamson who notes that "while Lukács's anthropological dialectic implied a sense of historical closure. . . . Gramsci's pragmatalogical dialectic seemed to deny the necessity of an historical movement toward totality." At the same time, Adamson seems to reluctantly concede that Gramsci at times "drifted toward a teleology of the proletariat as history's culmination," thus reinstating closure, making operationalizing the concept of hegemony, as an analytic guide to grasping the politics of cultural life, difficult. (Adamson, 1980: 138). If indeed reductionism is a tendency by which slippage occurs unwittingly, then Foucault's correction, through the application of difference, marks an important contribution.

While Marxism has always refused to make the theme of difference its organizing principle, it has always found a place for difference in relation to unity. What the post-structuralist correction involves, then, is altering the ontological weightings of "unity" and "difference" within the context of the theory as a whole. As Milton Fisk observes, "the materialist interpretation of history is certainly in the tradition of the theme of difference-in-unity, for it attempts to organise the different aspects of a society around its economy considered as a unity. . . . Post Marxists of the poststructuralist sort claim that privileging gets us into difficulty since it is inherently reductionist of differences" (Fisk, 1993: 326).

SIMILARITIES AND DIFFERENCES

The attempt at convergence does not founder in relation to epistemology, for Gramsci, like Foucault, was critical of materialists who assume a direct correspondence with reality unmediated by culture or language. In this respect, Gramsci shares Lukács's anathematization of any distinction between "thought and being" as a "false and rigid duality" (Lukács, 1971: 204), and he refers to the positing of material realities as entities that could be apprehended independently of discourse, or seen simply as a reflection of material processes without remainder, as "religious residues" (cited from Bhaskar, 1991: 165).

The originality of Gramsci's form of materialism, and its compatibility with Foucault's approach, stems in large part from the break it produced with mechanistic models of base and superstructure. For Gramsci, forms of Marxism that overemphasize the economic base of society neglect the diversity of the constitution of civil society and its autonomy from the economic. In attacking Bukharin's (1969) view of historical materialism, typically seen as the successor to Second International Marxism, Gramsci was stating his opposition to classical versions of historical materialism. "The claim, presented as an essential postulate of historical materialism, that every fluctuation of politics and ideology can be presented and expounded as an immediate expression of the structure, must be contested in theory as primitive infantilism" (Gramsci, 1971: 407).

Whereas political and cultural hegemony was always "based on the decisive function of the leading group in the decisive nucleus of economic activity" (Gramsci, 1971: 161), it was also distinct from it. Again, as Gramsci explains:

Politics becomes permanent action and gives birth to permanent organisations precisely in so far as it identifies itself with economics. But it is also distinct from it, which is why one may speak separately of economics and politics, and speak of "political passion" as of an immediate impulse to action which is born on the "permanent and organic" terrain of economic life but which transcends it, bringing into play emotions and aspirations in whose incandescent atmosphere even calculations involving individual human life itself obey different laws from those of individual profit, etc. (Gramsci, 1971: 139–140)

In his criticisms of Bukharin, Gramsci maintained that it is impossible to predict any determinate outcomes because outcomes depend on human conditions that are not themselves determined by their antecedent conditions. In opposition to Bukharin, history is governed by laws only in a highly restricted sense. Hence, Gramsci (1971: 412) says, "it is not a question of discovering a metaphysical law of 'determinism', or even of establishing a 'general law' of causality." History in this model is represented as infinite variety and multiplicity with continuous creation of unique patterns. "It is a question," says Gramsci, "of bringing out how in historical evolution relatively permanent forces are constituted which operate with a certain regularity and automatism" (412). Whereas Bukharin's search for uniformity and objective laws constituted a form of vulgar evolutionism, for Gramsci historical materialism was a set of concepts comprising tools for analysis, a guide to examining social situations rather than a predetermined ontology or methodology of the social order.

Gramsci's opposition to economism was central to his concentration on the autonomy of the cultural sphere, and on elements of culture such as the nation and ethnic identity which he saw as independent from economics. In addition, the stress on the role of education, on the constitution of identities in civil society, as well as on the role of intellectuals, was part of a constructionist dimension taken as much from Croce and Machiavelli as from Marx by which Gramsci emphasized the constitutive nature of human consciousness. The autonomy of the discursive is recognized also in relation to the universality of the philosophical dimension of reasoning. As Gramsci maintains:

It must first be shown that all men are "philosophers." . . . This philosophy is contained in: 1: language itself, which is a totality of determined notions of concepts and not just of words grammatically devoid of content; 2: "common sense" and "good sense"; 3: popular religion and, therefore, also in the entire system of beliefs, superstitions, opinions, ways of seeing things and of acting, which are collectively bundled together under the name of "folklore." (Gramsci, 1971: 323)

Because Gramsci saw ordinary language as containing philosophical notions that affected perceptions and actions, he regarded the limitations of using so-called ordinary language as a solution to philosophical problems in the manner of modern linguistic philosophy. Like Foucault, the importance Gramsci placed on language was on its role as a carrier of political and philosophical presuppositions. He was sensitive to the way language could be "at the same time a living thing and a museum of fossils of life and civilization" (Gramsci, 1971: 450). Languages are hegemonic instruments that can reinforce the values of common sense and potentially transmit new ones.

In that Gramsci believed that the intellectual poverty of orthodox Marxism could be resolved through "infusions of idealism" (Femia, 1987: 95), within the Communist Party, especially during the pre-prison years, Gramsci was frequently berated for "idealism" (see Davidson, 1977: 89). After 1919, as Femia notes, Gramsci's "wrestling match with Croce" resulted in a more critical and materialist approach, taking a serious interest in the material conditions that prevented men from directing their lives in accordance with their ideals. (Femia, 1987: 95). While Gramsci remained committed to certain Crocean ideas and themes, his central reaction was that, just as Bukharin had ignored culture, Croce ignored structure (Femia, 1987: 98—see Gramsci, 1971: 216–217). In his criticisms of Croce, Gramsci insists that ideas must be studied in relation to the social patterns in which they are embedded. Hence political activity, he says, must be "grounded in factual reality" (40). Similarly, in his analysis of "objective" and "subjective" factors in change, Gramsci depicts the former as independent of human will (180). In addition, he believed that producing change through a purely educational movement without regard to objective circumstances was an "anarchist fallacy" (149). History must not be seen as Croce did, as the history of concepts, but rather as a history of acting and thinking men. It is the notion that activity and thought are always related to a context that ultimately enables Gramsci to avoid idealism. He cautions against attributing too much causal weight to the material as against the ideational or discursive, however. He was never impressed by the radicalizing potential of economic crises. At best they could only "create a terrain more favourable to the dissemination of certain modes of thought" (184). Gramsci advances similar arguments against idealist interpretations of his work in *The Prison Notebooks* in the sections "Science and the Instruments of Science" (457–458) and in "The So-Called Question of the External World" (440–448). According to Femia (1987: 106), while Gramsci's terminology is influenced by idealism, a close inspection indicates that he is not denying the existence of nature prior to the human spirit, but only the relevance of intelligibility of such a natural order. Hence, although Gramsci frequently makes constructionist statements such as "we know reality only in relation to man" (Gramsci, 1971: 143), this is quite different, says Femia (1987: 116), from Croce's view that nature is a *creation* of human activity or that values and beliefs are the primary determinants of social life. "If Gramsci is an idealist," says Femia (113), "it is only in the attenuated sense that since Kant, we are all idealists."

Gramsci and Foucault also share similar views on the role of intellectuals. Gramsci's writings on intellectuals and on political education signal his profound distance from all forms of voluntarism or idealism. To be politically effective, leadership must be *organic* to the group whose interests it articulates. As Gramsci says:

A human mass does not "distinguish" itself, does not become independent in its own right without, in the widest sense, organising itself; and there is no organisation without intellectuals, that is, without organisers and leaders, in other words, without the theoretical aspect of the theory–practice nexus being distinguished concretely by the existence of a group of people "specialized" in conceptual and philosophical elaboration of ideas. (Gramsci, 1971: 334)

Although Gramsci sees "organic" intellectuals as articulating the goals and aspirations of subaltern groups against the "crystallising" function of "traditional" intellectuals, so Foucault champions the "specific" intellectual as someone who represents the claims of "local, marginalised, and disqualified knowledges" against the global theories of systematizing thought of

the "universal intellectuals" who seek to "uphold reason." For Foucault, a
"specific intellectual" is someone

working, not in the modality of the "universal," the "exemplary," the "just-and-
true-for-all," but within specific sectors, at the precise points where their own conditions of life or work situation them (housing, the hospital, the asylum, the
laboratory, the university, family and sexual relations). (Foucault, 1980b: 126)

For Foucault, like Gramsci, intellectuals have an important role as organ-
izers of culture and disseminators of truth. Every society has its dominant
and effective "regime of truth," as well as its "general politics of truth"
around which the nature and form of truth is contested. The disqualification
of local and regional forms of knowledge is achieved in Foucault's thought
through "the existence of a particular politico-economic regime of the production of truth" (Smart, 1985: 68). In this sense, his task is not to purify
science or truth by critiquing its ideological element but, as Smart says, "of
detaching the power of truth from its forms of hegemony, social, economic,
and cultural, within which it operates" (Smart, 1985: 68).
   In linking intellectuals and masses, Gramsci is also linking individuals to
collective processes of change in society. The processes by which groups,
organizations, and alliances form is *synthetic* rather than determined by the
mode of production or by metaphysical criteria, or by the historical level of
development in general. On several occasions in *The Prison Notebooks* Gramsci discusses the processes by which individuals link together and by which
relations between individual and collective are formed (Gramsci, 1971: 186–
191). When the distance between individuals and group aspirations or between intellectuals and masses narrows, groups coalesce into what Gramsci
calls an "intellectual/moral bloc" or an "historic bloc." A political party is
one example of an "historic bloc." It is (or may be) a hegemonic force in
the making. This sociological analysis as to how groups form and disperse,
which is at the basis of the theory of hegemony, is broadly compatible with
the view of social relations in the work of Foucault.
   One other important similarity between Gramsci and Foucault relates to
their view of history. They are both "absolute historicists," which is to say
that "the rationality of theoretical or philosophical systems is manifested
solely in relation to the historical processes of which they are a part" (Femia,
1987: 245). While this means that truth values are not determined by correspondence to some fixed standard, to an "objective" reality beyond the
reach of human volition, it does not mean that the truth of ideas or propositions contained in any theory or philosophy cannot be tested against
practice, or corroborated in relation to their coherence to other "mature"
discursive systems. For Gramsci, rational conceptions are those theoretical
formulations that come to prevail historically, partly as a consequence of
arrangements of power, partly through a handing down of custom and tra-

dition, partly because they meet human needs and aspirations, and, hence, as a consequence of all of these, form the "common sense" of an epoch.

Similarly, Foucault's approach attempts to describe history while denying the existence of historical laws, of a constant human nature, of subject-centered reason, or of any absolute or transhistorical values. Building on the epistemological work of Bachelard and Canguilhem, Foucault is interested in explaining the discontinuities, breaks, and ruptures that signal fundamental changes in discursive systems. He is also interested in the interrelations and entanglements between discursive formations and the various political, economic, social, and ideological practices that form the social structure. Foucault approaches ideas and values not in terms of absolute norms of truth and good but as the expressions of a specific age, culture, or people. If such values, ideas or knowledge systems are functions of historical conditions, then they may change with changes in those conditions, and no possible evaluation of their value or truth in general is possible.

Gramsci has similar problems in relation to the issue of relativism in that, like Foucault, he identifies history with philosophy. Similar to Foucault, too, Gramsci sees the subject as socially and historically constructed. Human nature is but "the totality of historically determined social relations" (Gramsci, 1971: 133). In addition, as Gramsci states: "One cannot . . . have a critical and coherent conception of the world, without having a consciousness of its historicity . . . [without] . . . 'knowing thyself' as a product of the historical process to date which has deposited in you an infinity of traces, without leaving an inventory" (Gramsci, 1971: 324).

Both thinkers also emphasize the independent and creative role of the human will within the historical process. Both are in this sense "optimists of the will." For Foucault, like Gramsci, one of the central tasks of the intellectual is educational in that it is orientated toward the possibilities for change. In this regard, Foucault clearly saw himself as an educator. As he explains in an interview:

My role . . . is to show people that they are much freer than they feel, that people accept as truth, as evidence, some themes which have been built up at a certain moment during history, and that this so-called evidence can be criticised and destroyed. To change something in the minds of people—that is the role of the intellectual. (Martin, Gutman, & Hutton, 1988: 10)

Foucault's ethic of freedom lies not in "self discovery," or "authenticity" in the Sartrean sense but, as Rajchman (1985: 38) describes it, "in a constant attempt at self disengagement and self invention." This was indeed Foucault's own ethic as writer and intellectual. It was the theoretical idea of testing limits (Simon, 1995: 13) which Foucault pursued both in intellectual work and at a practical level.

Gramsci also places a strong emphasis on the possibility of freedom. In this sense, for both thinkers, men are not determined, although they may be entrapped. Individuals operate within structurally determined limits, but they perform a creative and potentially autonomous role. However, such a role must be understood in relation to collective political action and in terms of the structural and institutional scope for self-creation. Hence, what Femia says for Gramsci applies equally to Foucault: "Men in history . . . are striving to realize their full potentialities, and this effort is a struggle to escape from being the plaything of forces that seem at once mysterious and irresistible; that is, to attain mastery over these forces, to subjugate them" (Femia, 1987: 119).

Gramsci also sees change as an essential function of intellectuals. For Gramsci, however, "counter-hegemony" links individuals to the cultural-historical process in a way Foucault doesn't do. For Gramsci, the result of counter-hegemony is a "higher" life achieved through collective political action. To this end, his concepts of "war of movement" (total revolution), "war of position" (limited strategic advance), "passive revolution" (gradualist incursion/advance), or "caesarism" (unexpected political intervention) mark Gramsci as a major strategist of change in a way in which Foucault is only left wanting.

Duccio Trombadori, in his interviews with Foucault in 1978, asked Foucault about the inability to conceptualize change in a way that transcends localistic issues and links the individual to groups and collective politics:

One of the observations that could be made of the way in which you confront the theme of power is this: the extreme fragmentation or "localization" of the questions ends up impeding the transition from a dimension that we might even call "corporate" to a vision of the totality within which the particular problem is inserted. (Foucault, 1991b: 150)

Foucault gives a long answer in which he says:

Yes, the problems that I pose are always concerned with local and particular issues . . . how could one do otherwise? (150–151)

To this response Trombadori raises an objection:

Perhaps I didn't explain myself. I do not dispute the need to raise local problems, even in a radical way, if it is necessary. Moreover, I am sensitive to what you say about intellectual work. Nevertheless, it seems to me that that way of confronting problems by particularizing them ends up inhibiting the possibility of their coordination in relation to other problems in the general understanding (*vision*) of a determinate historical and political situation. (152)

Foucault responds:

Localizing problems is indispensable for theoretical and political reasons. But that doesn't mean that they are not, however, general problems. After all, what is more general in a society than the way in which it defines the relation to madness. (152)

But Trombadori is still not satisfied.

When I spoke of a general understanding (*vision*), I was referring essentially to the political immersion of a problem and to the necessity of its articulation in a wider action or program that at the same time is linked to certain historico-political conditions. (153)

To this Foucault responds:

The generality that I try to make apparent is not of the same type as others. And when I am blamed for localizing problems, confusion is created between the local character of my analyses and an idea of generality similar to the one usually discussed by historians, sociologists, economists etc. I don't advance problems that are less general than those usually proposed by political parties or by certain great theoretical systems.

Somewhat frustrated, Trombadori endeavors to restate the problem:

What you say is perfectly acceptable. But you seem to confirm a certain closure, or unwillingness to open your discourse clearly onto the level of the "political." (154)

He continues to elaborate in an effort to clarify:

For every local problem one always faces the need to find solutions—even if provisional and temporary ones—in political terms. From this arises the need to shift one's way of seeing things from a particular analysis to the examination of real possibilities, within which a process of change and transformation can advance. It is in this balance between the local situation and the general picture that the "political" function is at stake. (156–157)

To which Foucault says:

I would respond in this way: for reasons that essentially pertain to my political choice, in the widest sense of the term, I absolutely will not play the part of one who prescribes solutions. I hold that the role of the intellectual today is not that of establishing laws or proposing solutions or prophesying, since by doing that one can only contribute to the functioning of a determinate situation of power that to my mind must be criticized. (157)

Trombadori remains unsatisfied, however, and asks Foucault whether "in the long run," by evading in some way the "political dimension," his proposal "risks representing a kind of 'distraction,' considering the contingent and complex stakes in question that are placed in society but have their immediate reflection on the level of institutions and parties" (164).

Foucault developed the concept of *governmentality* in the late 1970s and early 1980s in response to criticisms that his conception of power was too localistic and regional and didn't take the formation of national and international hegemonies into account. He developed the concept of the *strategic reversibility of power relations* at the same time, in an effort to explain how individuals exert *agency*, drawing on the very discursive systems through which they have been constructed, his ability to explain the subtle and complex relations between individuals, groups, and objective historical processes and movements, as well as the dynamics as to how change in social structures is effected. Yet Foucault is not as "tightly" theorized as is Gramsci. Foucault may also well have had less interest in doing so. To some extent, while Gramsci focused on political change, Foucault became more interested, especially toward the end of his life, in the development and care of the self. Yet although this signals a difference, Gramsci's theories of change are not incompatible with Foucault's conception of the discursive construction of individuals and of the relationship between individuals and social structures. This is to say, in effect, that Gramsci's theoretical insights can still be utilized within a more pluralist approach. Such a shift can also accommodate changes in the use of language as they reflect the different social ontologies between the thinkers. Hence Gramsci's use of language in the singular, reflecting as it does his more unitarist approach, resulting in the use of singular terms like "cultural and moral leadership," "cultural hegemony," and so on, can easily be adjusted to echo Foucault's mode of expression, where he speaks in the plural of "hegemonies," "knowledges," "regimes of truth" and so on. In short, while there are differences, they are not incompatibilities. They are in fact complementarities, and to "correct" Gramsci with Foucault by altering the ontological weight between "difference" and "unity" is both to "denationalize" Gramsci (i.e., to make his theoretical concepts and themes less concerned with or tied to the underlying dimension of unification at a national level), and therefore, also, to reconceptualize his theoretical project within a new pluralist framework, a framework much more relevant to the dispersal of power from national to international contexts in late twentieth-century capitalist contexts.

POWER, HEGEMONY, AND THE STATE

Although the dimensions discussed above can be seen as compatibilities between the two thinkers, the precondition for, consequence of, and ultimate cost of making the convergence thesis work is effected only on the basis that Gramsci "vacate[s] the theoretical problematic of Marxism" (Smart, 1983: 41). Hence only on the basis of a *transformed theoretical content* does Foucault use the concept of hegemony as he does, for example, in *The History of Sexuality*. As Balibar notes,

> Foucault . . . uses the notion of *hegemony* . . . in a way which makes it possible to get away from the "great binary division" (*VS*, p. 127) in which the necessity for a final crisis and collision is always ideally contained. The "social hegemonies" (*VS*, p. 122), or the "hegemonic effects" which make up the "great dominations" (*VS*, p. 124) and constitute the "focal points of resistance" on the basis of which a network of institutions and disciplinary practices spreads throughout the whole of society (*VS*, p. 169) have to be conceived of not as given in advance but as results or as resultants; "terminal forms," which are at the same time differential or relational forms. In the same way, revolutions have to be conceived of as "strategic codings of points of resistance" (*VS*, p. 127)—in other words, as the effects of contingent integration, not predetermined. (Balibar, 1992: 51)[2]

In that a Foucauldian reading of Gramsci signals a shift away from classical Marxism, readings of Gramsci that do not portray him as primarily or solely within the Marxist tradition, such as those provided by Maurice Finocchiaro (1988), Benedetto Fontana (1993), or Walter Adamson (1980), also help make such an approach possible. These writers, while acknowledging Gramsci's interest and attachment to Marxism, emphasize the eclecticism of his work, drawing as it does on writers such as Croce and Machiavelli. As Adamson notes, "most of the assumptions in Gramsci's 'autonomous science' of politics were rooted in Machiavelli's outlook" (1980: 204). Of particular note are the distinctions between *fortuna* and *virtù* (attesting to the distinction between "objective materiality" and the creative aspect of "will"), and between "leaders" and "led." In addition, as Adamson points out:

> Machiavelli had been among the first political theorists to base his political calculations on the "effective reality" of the social and economic world. He had conceived that world not statically but dynamically, as a "relation of forces in continuous motion" which could be shaped into a "new equilibrium" by a creative political will. And he had the great virtue of having written about politics "neither in the form of a cold utopia nor as learned theorizing, but rather as a creation of concrete fantasy which acts on a dispersed and shattered people to arouse and organize its collective will." For all of these reasons Machiavelli was an inspiration to Gramsci. (Adamson, 1980: 204)

Another effect of mixing Gramsci with Foucault is that we are forced to alter our idea of the structure of social conflict. Foucault doesn't see power as structured or binary between dominators/dominated or as exclusively repressive. Rather, as noted above, politics and power constitute a dimension present in all fields of human activity. As well as being repressive, power is also productive, and, far from being contained in the state or repressive apparatuses, power is exercised at all levels of society. Because he does not insist on the dominance of economic considerations, Foucault is able to consider power in relation to diverse domains, for example, the structures of enlightenment, knowledge, sexuality, rationality, medicine, discipline, and punishment.

According to Barry Smart (1986), it is in relation to the concepts of power and hegemony that the essential complementarity and utility of the two approaches is justified. Although Foucault's work has revealed the complex multiple processes from which the strategic constitution of the forms of hegemony may emerge, Gramsci's formulations contribute to and constitute a theory of the formation and of the *attempted* social cohesion of groups and classes in the wider social structure in response to external environmental conditions. In terms of this new combined perspective, then, attempts to constitute hegemony work not simply through practices of coercion, or simply through practices of consent, but *also* by way of other practices, techniques, and methods that infiltrate minds and bodies as well as cultural values and behaviors as apparently naturally occurring properties. Both Gramsci and Foucault share a dual analytic focus on forms of knowledge and relations of power through which the human subject has been objectified and constituted and on the techniques of the self and related discourses in terms of which human beings are made into subjects. Both focus on a concern with forms of government to which human beings are subjected, disciplined, modified, and reconstructed. Through such a common perspective, the dangers of interpreting hegemony as a form of socialization (from above) are averted. Rather, now it is represented as constituted through practices in concrete historical settings (from below). What Foucault adds to Gramsci, apart from a more open conception of social structure, then, is an understanding of how various complex social techniques and methods central to the construction of identities, values, and political settlements are constituted and how they operate. Foucault offers a more developed set of concepts through which the micro-physics of the constitution of hegemony is understood in terms of the exercise of multiple processes (techniques, strategies) of power and its effects. This is precisely what Gramsci on his own account was unable to do. In addition, Foucault manages to shift the focus away from the problematic of ideology, and in doing so he provides additional strength to arguments against economic determinism in Marxist theory. Rather, now with Foucault's contribution the issue becomes a consideration of the general relations between power and knowledge.

As well as considering the dynamics of the complex processes through which hegemonic forms are constituted, the overall achievements of the new synthesis are significant. Foucault's focus on power as both repressive and productive parallels Gramsci's distinction between power as exercised by the repressive state apparatuses on the one hand and power exercised through the mobilization of consent on the other. In addition, Foucault's description of the complex processes of governmentalization, which involve the emergence and development of new technologies of power on individuals and populations, accounts for the construction of different forms of social beliefs and values, and hence furthers our understanding of hegemony. It is also possible to utilize the concepts of both thinkers in a combined perspective. Thus an explanation of how new forms of power shape and govern the individual involves supplementing, in Barry Smart's words:

the "State"/"civil society" dichotomy . . . by an analytic focus upon the 'governmentalization' of power relations, that is the development of individualizing techniques and practices which are reducible neither to force nor to consent, techniques and practices which have transformed political conflict and struggle through the constitution of new forms of social cohesion. (Smart, 1986: 162)

In other words, Gramsci's distinctions between the *State* and *civil society*, and between *force* and *consent*, are now augmented by the concept of *governmentality*, which describes State power over populations and has the effect of more adequately theorizing power relations at both the micro and macro levels of social structure. While the State is not all-encompassing, in the sense of eradicating the sphere of civil society altogether (as it did for Althusser with his conception of Repressive State Apparatuses and Ideological State Apparatuses), it is still permitted a very real presence. This would appear to be in accord with Foucault's statement of his own intention, as expressed in an interview in the late 1970s:

I don't want to say that the State isn't important; what I want to say is that relations of power, and hence the analysis that must be made of them, necessarily extend beyond the limits of the State. . . . The State is superstructural in relation to a whole series of power networks that invest the body, sexuality, the family, kinship, knowledge, technology and so forth. (Foucault, 1980b: 122)

Smart expresses a similar idea:

Analytically Foucault's work pries open the problem of hegemony in so far as it decentres the question of the state, introduces a non-reductionist conception of power, and displaces the concept of ideology, through which Gramsci sought to theorise questions of "intellectual and moral leadership" central to the achievement of hegemony, with analyses of the relations of "truth" and "power" through which "men govern (themselves and others)." (Smart, 1986: 162)

Both authors believe that power functions as domination only insofar as those who are dominated consent to it. Without consent there can be no domination, and in this sense, as Holub (1992) points out, both see power as ubiquitous, and both also share a view of the production of consent as occurring within the systems and subsystems of everyday social relations and practices.

CONTEMPORARY FORMS OF POST-STRUCTURALIST MARXISM

In the twentieth century, various forms of post-Marxist scholarship have sought to integrate Gramsci with various forms of post-structuralism. Laclau and Mouffe's attempt to make the convergence thesis work is premised on their rejection of mechanistic versions of materialism and hence is the key to understanding their post-structuralist version of Marxism. The notion of "historic bloc," which "cross-cuts" traditional conceptions of base and superstructure, enables Gramsci to transcend economistic versions of Marxism and of the centrality of class, they argue. Because they fail to distinguish between the materialism of Foucault and the textualism of the later post-structuralists, however, their attempt ends linking Gramsci to the post-structuralists rather than the materialists, with consequent enormous costs in terms of analysis and explanation. As Laclau and Mouffe explain in their book *Hegemony and Socialist Strategy,*

Our analysis rejects the distinction between discursive and non-discursive practices. It affirms . . . that every object is constituted as an object of discourse, insofar as no object is given outside every discursive condition of emergence. . . . The fact that every object is constituted as an object of discourse has *nothing to do* with whether there is a world external to thought, or with the realism/idealism opposition. An earthquake or the falling of a brick is an event that certainly exists, in the sense that it occurs here and now, independently of my will. But whether their specificity as objects is constructed in terms of "natural phenomena" or "expressions of the wrath of God," depends upon the structuring of a discursive field. What is denied is not that such objects exist externally to thought, but *the rather different assertion that they could constitute themselves as objects outside any discursive condition of emergence.* (Laclau & Mouffe, 1985: 107–108)

The conception of society also changes in Laclau and Mouffe's form of post-Marxism in their attempt to incorporate difference as opposed to the Hegelian conception of totality as the backbone to a renewed conception of social structure. The initial argument for such a case was put forward by Laclau and Mouffe in their article "The Impossibility of Society" (1983). Here they say, "The incomplete character of every totality necessarily leads us to abandon, as a terrain of analysis, the premise of 'society' as a sutured and self-defined totality. Society is not a valid object of discourse. There is no single underlying principle fixing—and hence constituting—the whole social field of differences" (Laclau & Mouffe, 1983: 111).

Laclau and Mouffe use the concept of *suture* to make such a post-structuralist conception of social structure possible and to escape the notion of a social structure characterized by an underlying principle that fixes and hence constitutes the whole field of differences. Meaning in English, literally, "to stitch" (Barrett, 1988: 66), the concept for Laclau and Mouffe represents the *tension* between "totalization" and "difference." As Michèle Barrett explains, in seeking to clarify Laclau and Mouffe's position,

A "suture" marks the absence of former identity, as when a cut flesh heals but leaves a scar marking difference. Laclau and Mouffe present us with a body politic whose skin is permanently split open, necessitating ceaseless duty in the emergency room for the surgeons of hegemony whose fate it is to try and close, temporarily and with difficulty, the gaps. (This patient never makes it to the recovery ward.) (Barrett, 1988: 66)

Hence, for Laclau and Mouffe, "Hegemonic practices are suturing in so far as their field of operation is determined by the openness of the social, by the ultimately unfixed character of every signifier. This original lack is precisely what the hegemonic practices try to fill in" (Laclau & Mouffe, 1985, n.1).

In their attempts to forge a "convergence," Laclau and Mouffe see hegemony as discursively constituted in the same way that all social relations derive their social character from their discursive constitution. In this sense, connections among individuals and groups have to be constructed, articulated, and maintained. Within the textualist parameters of their resolution of the problem, however, the discursive is rendered as co-extensive with the social, and all social relations as being constituted in and through discourse. As subjects are social, so they too are constituted in and through discourse. Man is a discursively constructed "subject-position." The benefits of this, they claim, is that dimensions like "class" and "the mode of production" are not privileged. Rather than the nature of social life existing as "always already classed," class is now "constituted" rather than "pre-given" in the same way as race and gender are constituted from the elements already present in the "national-popular" culture. Rather than class subjectivities being determined by the subject's position in the relations of production, with equivalent political and ideological dispositions, class identities are formed as the outcome of political contestation as groups compete to create class alignments from the raw material in the discursive field. In this model, then, the convergence is forged by opposing the unity of the social order, opposing the idea of the class belongingness of subjects and practices, opposing the idea of a correspondence between the various levels or regions of the social system, opposing the idea of a single principle of explanation or causal model for all events, asserting the heterogeneity of social relations, affirming the synthetic nature of the constitution of groups, and recognizing the twin levels of discursive and extra-discursive as well as the variability of causal relations and principles of explanation. What they actually do, however, in

achieving all this, is privilege the discursive over the extra-discursive, thus
lapsing into a form of linguistic idealism that is more in keeping with the
textualism of Derrida rather than the more subtle materialist reading of *dis-
course/practice* to be found in Foucault. In the end, the practices of the real
material world drop out of their analysis altogether. Thus, as Ian Craib
states:

In the work of Laclau and Mouffe (1985) . . . we are presented with a permanently
open notion of articulation, of subjectivity sliding from meaning to meaning. The
problem then becomes that of suggesting how there can be sufficient "fixity" to be
able to say anything coherent at all. If any such point is suggested, it can be decon-
structed immediately, leaving us on a constant and eventually meaningless slide of
meaning. (Craib, 1977: 10)

CONCLUSION

Even if we can accept the positive implications that the post-structuralist
concept of difference has for an understanding of the openness of social
systems, it is still the case, as Fisk (1993) has observed, that difference and
totality have to be kept in balance, or that the ontological principle of difference cannot plausibly explain social relations on its own (Fisk, 1993:
324). This is why in classical philosophy the theme of otherness, which
underpins difference, was always paired with that of unity or identity. To
try to make one's philosophical orientation work solely on the grounds of
difference neglects equally strong arguments for unity. For to try to define
objects solely in terms of differences neglects equally compelling reasons for
considering them as objects of certain *kinds*. Similarly, if, as the post-
structuralist insists, it is not possible to achieve a final synthesis, this doesn't
mean, nor should it entail, that all unities or identities simply collapse into
differences or that social life is simply a process of endless, vicious regress.
In short, as Fisk (325) argues, unless the theory of difference is to result in
incoherence, there must be a minimal kind of unity. This is perhaps the
major reason for adding Gramsci to Foucault.

There will of course be those who are not satisfied. The Marxist writer
Norman Geras (1990) objects to any possible marriage between Foucault
and Gramsci on the grounds that Foucault's use of concepts such as hegemony or capitalism generates fundamental incompatibilities between divergent
world views, something along the lines of a paradigm conflict. Geras does
not believe that the concepts can be transformed in the process of convergence but sees any possible "meeting" as a "head-on collision." The central
axis of the conflict is "totality" and "difference," or between "necessity"
and "indeterminism." To use concepts such as capitalism or hegemony creates inconsistencies, in Geras's view, because the concepts come from (and

thereby imply) a theoretic that runs counter to the idea of difference as popularly theorized. Rather than invoke the open and non-structured nature of the social, it is apparent that, in Geras's view, these concepts stand in for a banished reality that postmodernists incorporate on each page as needed (Geras, 1990: 109). In addition, by their (essential) nature, they imply closure determined by and intelligible to one foundation or origin. In other words, says Geras, these concepts can only make sense in relation to a structured society where it is possible to fix the meaning of any event. In hegemony theory, for example, any discourse is constituted, he claims, by definition, as an attempt "to dominate the field of discursivity," "to arrest the flow of difference," that is, "to construct a centre" (Geras, 1990: 67).

In spite of the surface plausibility of Geras's arguments, they only constitute a handicap to a convergence if one expects the outcome to be some form of classical Marxism. This is clearly not the case for Foucault; nor is it for Laclau and Mouffe, who go to considerable lengths to separate themselves from the Marxist camp—hence the use of the term *post-Marxism*. What is altered beyond recognition is the *form* and *structure* of these concepts as utilized by Foucault within his post-structuralist perspective. In Foucault's usage, hegemony now simply becomes another structural concept that expresses the relations of power within a discursive field. The shift from unitarist to pluralist ontology also enables a parallel shift at the level of language, from singular to plural forms of expression. While one doesn't want to strike too discordant a note, the outcome is perhaps closer to Weber than to Marx. What it facilitates at a pragmatic level is the availability of two well-worked concepts—hegemony and discourse—which can now be utilized as analytic and explanatory tools in conventional sociological work.

Rather than conceptualize social relations as totalities, they are now constituted as relations of aggregates, of institutions, forms of organizations, series, practices, and agents in a new pluralist mix. While Foucault recognizes no pre-given center or structure, he searches in each age, following Nietzsche's example, with adherence to almost positivist principles of historical analysis, for the regulating mechanisms by which closure is directed. Hegemony is an attempt to produce such a closure. In the final analysis, however, such attempts are never successful, which is to say that hegemonies are always incomplete, always contested, breaking down, needing to be remade and rewon. The consequence of reading Gramsci after Foucault is that this incompleteness becomes of central importance and receives greater emphasis. The consequence of retaining Gramscian insights, however, is that Foucault's nominalist individualism is moderated by a conception that allows for the theorization of structures, for an understanding of how groups, organizations, and alliances form and cohere, and for an understanding of how part and whole cohere as organized collective expression. Gramsci's nonreductionist problematic of hegemony and conception of power allows that, far from being localized in the repressive state apparatuses, power is exercised at all levels of society. As such, power is therefore consistent with the strategic conception of power in the work of Foucault.

In the final analysis, Gramsci and Foucault present a more powerful perspective on social structure taken together than each does on his own. It produces what can be seen as a new form of historical materialism. Although it is not specifically a Marxist conception in that it is not a theory of the economic base of society, or a critique of political economy or of the traditional Marxist dialectical method, it still provides for a general theory of domination which, consistent with historical materialism, takes all social, economic, and political practices as transitory and all intellectual and discursive formations as inseparably connected to power and social relations. Given fundamental shifts in the structure of capitalism—in terms of a general post-Fordist diversification of economic structures, in terms of increased globalization, or in terms of a shift from a "mode of production" to a "mode of information" (Poster, 1984)—such a conception of historical materialism must be viewed as having considerable analytic and theoretical importance.

NOTES

1. Other writers who similarly criticize Foucault's concept of power along similar lines for subverting the possibility of a social and political criticism include Benhabib (1989: 369–370), Walzer (1986: 64), White (1991: 18), and Wolin (1988: 186, 193–194).

2. VS represents "La Volonté de Savoir," the subtitle of *The History of Sexuality* in the French edition.

Part III

Foucault and the
Tasks of Education

Chapter 8

Foucault and Critical Theory

A critique is not a matter of saying that things are not right as they are. It is a matter of pointing out on what kinds of assumptions, what kinds of familiar, unchallenged, unconsidered modes of thought, the practices that we accept rest. . . . Criticism is a matter of flushing out that thought and trying to change it: to show that things are not as self-evident as one believed, to see that what is accepted as self-evident will no longer be accepted as such. Practising criticism is a matter of making facile gestures difficult. (Foucault, 1988i: 154–155)

Critique, for Foucault, aims at identifying and exposing the unrecognized forms of power in people's lives, to expose and move beyond the forms in which we are entrapped in relation to the diverse ways that we act and think. In this sense, critique aims to free us from the historically transitory constraints of contemporary consciousness as realized in and through discursive practices. Such constraints impose limitations that have become so intimately a part of the way people experience their lives that they no longer experience these systems as limitations but embrace them as the very structure of normal and natural human behavior. Within these limits, seen as both the limits of reason and the limits of nature, freedom is subordinated to reason which is subordinated to nature, and it is against such a reduction of reason to nature that Foucault struggles. His commitment is to a form of "permanent criticism" which must be seen as linked to his broader program of freedom of thought. It is the freedom to think differently from what we already know. Thought and life achieve realization through an attitude of "permanent criticism" whose aim is not an objective of absolute emancipation or absolute enlightenment, but rather limited and partial operations on the world as well as acts of aesthetic self-creation framed within a critical ontology of ourselves and supported by an ethics and aesthetics of existence.

FOUCAULT, KANT, AND THE ENLIGHTENMENT

Foucault sees in Kant's essay "What Is Enlightenment?" (1784) the origin of a critical ontology of the present. In Foucault's view, Kant founded the two great critical traditions between which modern philosophy has been divided. On the one hand, Kant laid down and founded that critical tradition of philosophy that defines the conditions under which a true knowledge is possible, of which a whole area of modern philosophy since the nineteenth century has been presented and developed on that basis as an analytic of truth. On the other hand, he initiated a mode of critical interrogation that is immanent in the movement of the Enlightenment and that directs our attention to the present and asks, "What is the contemporary field of possible experience?" It is in this latter emphasis, starting with Hegel and leading through Nietzsche, Weber, and the Frankfurt School, that Foucault locates his own work.

Foucault summarizes Kant's definition of the concept of Enlightenment as a measure of man's "release from his self-incurred tutelage" (Kant, 1992: 90). Kant defines Enlightenment, says Foucault, "in an entirely negative way, as an *Ausgang*, an 'exit' or 'way out' . . . he is looking for a difference: what difference does today introduce with respect to yesterday?" (1984a: 34). In this, Foucault discovers Kant as "an archer," as Habermas (1986: 105) has put it, "who aims his arrow at the heart of the most actual features of the present and so opens the discourse of modernity." As Foucault puts it:

The question that seems to me to appear for the first time in this text by Kant is the question of the present, the question of what is happening now. . . . And what is this "now" within which all of us find ourselves . . . it seems to me that with this text on the *Aufklärung* we see philosophy . . . problematizing its own discursive contemporaneity: a contemporaneity that it questions as an event. (Foucault, 1988q: 87–88)

In considering the Enlightenment, what also must be taken into account, says Foucault (1988q: 89), is that "the *Aufklärung* calls itself *Aufklärung*. It is certainly a very singular cultural process that became aware of itself by naming itself. By situating itself in relation to its past and its future, and by designating the operations that it must carry out within its own present." Thus, as Foucault (1984a: 34) summarizes it, Kant indicates in his essay that the "way out" that characterizes the Enlightenment is a process that releases us from the status of our own immaturity, an immaturity in which we accept someone else's authority to lead us in areas where the use of reason is called for.

Kant links the process of release from immaturity to man himself. He notes that "man himself is responsible for his immature status . . . that he is able to escape from it only by a change that he himself will bring about in himself." Hence Kant's motto for the Enlightenment: *aude sapere* (dare to know) (1984a: 35).

The Enlightenment for Kant, says Foucault, is therefore both a *collective process* and an *act of personal courage* (35). As integral to the conditions for escape from immaturity, Kant seeks to distinguish the realm of obedience and reason. Hence one must obey as a condition of being able to reason freely. (Kant gives the example of paying one's taxes while being free to reason about the system of taxation in operation.) Thus central to the Enlightenment in Kant's view is the public use of reason which "must be free . . . [for] it alone can bring about enlightenment among men" (Kant, 1992: 92). To resolve the issue as to how the public use of free reason can coexist with obedience to the law, Kant proposes his famous contract with Frederick II. This, as Foucault puts it, "might be called the contract of rational despotism with free reason: the public and free use of autonomous reason will be the best guarantee of obedience, on condition, however, that the political principle that must be obeyed itself be in conformity with universal reason" (Foucault, 1984a: 37).

There is a connection, in Foucault's view, between the brief article "What Is Enlightenment?" and Kant's three Critiques,[1] for Kant describes the Enlightenment as the moment when humanity is going to put its own reason to use, without subjecting itself to any authority. It is precisely at this moment, however, that the critique is necessary since, as Foucault (1984a: 37–38) states, "its role is that of defining the conditions under which the use of reason is legitimate. . . . The critique is, in a sense, the handbook of reason that has grown up in Enlightenment; and, conversely, the Enlightenment is the age of the critique." Thus, Kant's short essay on the Enlightenment constitutes "a reflection . . . on the contemporary status of his own enterprise." It is in this sense, as Foucault maintains, that "this little text is located . . . at the crossroads of critical reflection and reflection on history" (38).

Foucault takes Kant's text as the point of emergence of the question of modernity. As he puts it,

the question of modernity had been posed in classical culture according to an axis with two poles, antiquity and modernity; it had been formulated either in terms of an authority to be accepted or rejected . . . or else in the form . . . of a comparative evaluation: are the Ancients superior to the Moderns? are we living in a period of decadence? and so forth. There now appears a new way of posing the question of modernity, no longer within a longitudinal relationship to the Ancients, but rather in what one might call a "sagital" relation to one's own present-ness. Discourse has to take account of its own present-ness, in order to find its own place, to pronounce its meaning, and to specify the mode of action which it is capable of exercising within this present. What is my present? What is the meaning of this present? And what am I doing when I speak of this present? Such is, it seems to me, the substance of this new interrogation on modernity. (Foucault, 1986c: 90)

Hence, for Foucault, Kant's essay introduces a new type of question into the field of philosophical reflection, one that sees philosophy "problematizing its own discursive present-ness" within the context of history. (1986c: 89). It is this historical contextualization that was Kant's reason for undertaking his work at the particular time, in the first place. In fact, the question he was addressing was one put to him and other *Aufklärer* by the *Berlinische Monatsschrift*. Fifteen years later, Kant posed a similar question in response to the French Revolution. In his article "The Conflict of the Faculties,"[2] Kant considers the question as to the nature of the French Revolution. What he was searching for was a "sign" of progress of the human race. In order to judge progress, reasoned Kant, rather than seek to follow the threads of a "teleological fabric which would make progress possible" Kant thought it necessary "to isolate and identify in history an event that will serve as a sign for progress" (92).

[T]he event that will be able to allow us to decide whether there is progress will be a sign: *rememorativum, demonstrativum, prognosticum*. It must be a sign that shows that it has already been like that (the rememorative sign), a sign that shows that things are also taking place now (the demonstrative), and a sign that shows that it will always happen like that (the prognostic sign). In this way we can be sure that the cause that makes progress possible has not just acted at a particular moment, but that it guarantees a general tendency of mankind as a whole to move in a direction of progress. (Foucault, 1988q: 91)

Is there such a sign? Kant answered that the French Revolution has such signifying value, although it is not the revolution as an event that constitutes the sign but rather "the way the Revolution operates as spectacle, the way it is generally received by spectators who did not take part in it but watch it, witness it and, for better or worse, allow themselves to be swept along by it" (1988: 92). It doesn't even matter whether the Revolution succeeds or fails. What constitutes the *sign of progress* is the fact, as Kant expresses it, that the Revolution is surrounded by "a wishful participation that borders closely on enthusiasm" (cited in Foucault, 1986c: 93).

Hence, for Kant, the enthusiasm for the Revolution "is the sign of a moral disposition of humanity" (Foucault, 1986c: 93); it completes and continues the process of the Enlightenment, that event that denotes the long journey from humanity's immaturity to maturity. In Foucault's view, Kant's two questions—"What Is Enlightenment?" and "What Is Revolution?"—are the two forms in which he poses the question of his own present. They are also the two questions "which have continued to haunt if not all modern philosophy since the nineteenth century, at least a great part of it." For Kant, says Foucault, the Enlightenment constitutes both a "singular event inaugurating European modernity and as a permanent process manifesting itself in the history of reason" (95).

Foucault is less convinced than Kant that the Enlightenment is a long, slow, uphill pilgrimage based on the directing capacities of reason or that the Revolution constitutes a sign of progress. For Foucault, rather than being a period or event based on conviction and certainty in man's newfound, mature dependence on reason, the Enlightenment signifies uncertainty and the need for caution. Similarly, the Revolution is not an event marked by the passage of enthusiasm which serves as a sure sign of progress, but an event that is an ambiguous occurrence and always potentially dangerous: "liable to succeed or miscarry, or to succeed at unacceptable cost" (1986c: 92). Hence, while Foucault respects Kant's argument, he finds it flawed on several grounds: "many things in our experience convince us that the historical event of the Enlightenment did not make us mature adults, and we have not reached that stage yet" (1984a: 49–50). The Revolution that Kant took to be a sign of progress, although "born of rationalism . . . one is entitled to ask what part is played in the effects of despotism in which that hope lost itself" (Foucault, 1980l: 54).

Foucault also rejects the notion that reason has a universal form, and he sees Kant as trying to safeguard reason's role in response to the collapse of metaphysics. Foucault's approach to history and reason will not be taken seriously by anyone who agrees with Kant that "maturity" involves a recognition of the "limits" beyond which reason cannot go. Yet, as Ian Hacking (1986b: 238) points out, "Foucault was a remarkably able Kantian." In *The Order of Things*, he describes Kant's work as characterized by an "analytic of finitude" (1970: 313–318). This involves the claim that man, for Kant, exists at the center of the universe as a finite being who can reason within limits that he cannot go beyond. Such a notion generates insoluble contradictions for the human sciences because it is based on incompatible conceptions of what man, his history, and mind are (312–313). Foucault traces the play of these contradictions as they have emerged alongside the empirical human sciences. Hence on the one hand our knowledge must be limited, as man knows himself as a finite being, as an objective of nature; on the other hand that finitude which establishes the limits of human understanding is claimed to be the condition that makes knowledge of this finitude possible (314–315). Thus the possibility of knowledge is established on limits to reason that deny it (317–318).

Kant's philosophical thesis concerning the limits of reason was initially presented as an answer to Hume's skepticism in which certainty in knowledge is undermined. While Hume thought that there was no integrating principle underpinning human identity, Kant held that there was: that there is a "condition of possibility" which constitutes the unity of the individual subject; that conscious experience is not just a matter of "associative linkage" and cannot be reduced to transient states, impressions, desires, and so on. In Kant's view, knowledge is limited by a priori categories that human beings use to make sense of the world. These categories and concepts by which human beings structure experience, and which concern such dimensions as space and time, make the world intelligible, but only in a limited sense. They permit knowledge of the "phenomenal world," that is, the world "for us"; but they do not give us knowledge of "things in themselves." Hence, there are definite limits beyond which knowledge of the world cannot be obtained and of which it is pointless to ask if we are to avoid speculative errors. Because our minds impose or construct a structure, it is useless to ask what the world is like in itself unmediated by human perception.

Kant gives a much more complex account of the limits imposed on reason which prevent it from going beyond what is given in experience. Through his division of knowledge into three spheres—science, morality, and aesthetics—Kant imposes additional limits on the human faculties, for each sphere of knowledge is associated and restricted to its own type of reasoning. Hence it is illegitimate to use forms of reasoning appropriate for one particular sphere (e.g., science) when arbitrating claims in one of the others (e.g., in terms of morality or of aesthetics).

Kant's argument is transcendental in the sense that the existence of a priori categories are deduced to constitute the consciousness of the human subject as that which organizes perception and are seen as timeless and self-evident universal structures. For Foucault, the unresolved tension of Kant's philosophical project is that he fails to appreciate the contingent and historically contextualized character of all truth-claims, that is, to advocate a notion of critique which claims to transcend specific historical conditions through the exercise of cognitive faculties (of understanding, reason, and judgment) deduced a priori as timeless structures. In this sense, Foucault rejects Kant's claims to have established the universal grounds for the conditions of possibility of human knowledge, and Kant's claims for transcendental reason are replaced for Foucault by a principle of permanent contingency. By extension, Foucault disputes Kant's claim to have established a secure foundation by which to differentiate various types of knowledge claims, relating to science, practical reason, or aesthetics. The objective is to switch from a conception of critique which is transcendentally grounded to a conception of critique which conceives it as practical and as historically specific. Hence, as to Kant's famous questions "What can I know," "What ought I to do?" and "What may I hope for?," Foucault would, as James Bernauer expresses it, "de-nature" and "historicize" them:

Not "What can I know?," but rather, "How have my questions been produced? How has the path of my knowing been determined?" Not "What ought I to do?," but rather, "How have I been situated to experience the real? How have exclusions operated in delineating the realm of obligation for me?" Not "What may I hope for?," but rather, "What are the struggles in which I am engaged? How have the parameters for my aspirations been defined?" (1991b: 46)

Underpinning Kant's transcendentalism is an anthropological conception of the subject. Foucault opposes Kantian humanism in the same way he opposed Hegelianism and Phenomenology and their philosophy of the subject. Although influenced by Nietzsche's anti-humanism in the sense that Foucault sees no "doer" behind the deed and no subject as such, there is a certain obvious sense, as Norris (1993: 80) points out, that Foucault's conception of the subject marks a retreat from Kant back to Hume in that Foucault recognizes no "unity," "essence," or integral identity to the subject.[3] Foucault's critique of humanism is consistent throughout his work but receives its earliest systematic treatment in *The Order of Things*. As he expressed it later, anthropological humanism takes various forms and can be seen in Christianity, Marxism, Existentialism, Phenomenology, even Nazism and Stalinism, says Foucault. In addition:

Humanism is . . . a theme, or rather, a set of themes that have reappeared on several occasions over time, in European societies; these themes, always tied to value judgements, have obviously varied greatly in their content, as well as in the values they have preserved. . . . From this we must not conclude that everything that has ever been linked with humanism is to be rejected, but that the humanistic thematic is in itself too supple, too diverse, too inconsistent to serve as an axis for reflection. And it is a fact that, at least since the seventeenth century, what is called humanism has always been obliged to lean on certain conceptions of man borrowed from religion, science, or politics. Humanism serves to color and to justify the conceptions of man to which it is, after all, obliged to take recourse. (1984a: 44)

Humanism, in fact, constitutes a condition of possibility of the Enlightenment episteme. It focuses on the study of man and places the subject at the center of life. Hence Kantianism sees man as a transcendental arbiter of reason and as both the subject and object of knowledge, leading in Foucault's view to the fundamental incompatibilities in the conception of what man is and in the nature of modernist knowledge that he analyzed in *The Order of Things* (1970: 316–322). For Foucault, man cannot be seen as a foundation or origin or condition of possibility of discourse. Kant's attempt to do so was part of his search for an original foundation "that would make rationality the telos of mankind, and link the whole history of thought to the preservation of this rationality" (Foucault, 1972: 13).

For Foucault, then, because the Enlightenment has not evacuated the problems and dangers of earlier periods in history, the basis of critique must be as a form of permanent interrogative thinking: "The thread that may connect us with the Enlightenment is not faithfulness to doctrinal elements, but rather the permanent reactivation of an attitude—that is, of a philosophical ethos that could be described as a permanent critique of our historical era" (Foucault, 1984a: 42).

In that the Enlightenment emphasizes a "permanent critique," it emphasizes a form of philosophical interrogation that "simultaneously problematizes man's relation to the present, man's historical mode of being, and the constitution of the self as an autonomous subject," says Foucault (1984a: 42). Critique, then, is defined as "ethos" which has both a negative and a positive heuristic. In terms of its negative heuristic, Foucault identifies the need to refuse what he calls "the 'blackmail' of the Enlightenment" (42). This refers to the pressure to be either "for or against the Enlightenment," to "accept the Enlightenment and remain with the tradition of its rationalism . . . or [to] criticise the Enlightenment and then try to escape from its principles of rationality" (43). Rather:

We must try to proceed with the analysis of ourselves as beings who are historically determined, to a certain extent, by the Enlightenment. Such an analysis implies a series of historical inquiries that are as precise as possible; and these inquiries will not be orientated retrospectively toward the "essential kernel of rationality" that can be found in the Enlightenment and that would have to be preserved in any event; they will be orientated toward the "contemporary limits of the necessary," that is, toward what is not or is no longer indispensable for the constitution of ourselves as autonomous subjects. (43)

For Foucault, the Enlightenment comprises a set of events and complex historical processes located at a certain point in the development of European societies, and the philosophical ethos of critique may be characterized as a *limit-attitude*, but in a different sense from that suggested by Kant:

Criticism indeed consists of analyzing and reflecting upon limits. But if the Kantian question was that of knowing what limits knowledge has to renounce transgressing, it seems to me that the critical question today has to be turned back into a positive one: in what is given to us as universal, necessary, obligatory, what place is occupied by whatever is singular, contingent, and the product of arbitrary constraints? The point, in brief, is to transform the critique conducted in the form of necessary limitation into a practical critique that takes the form of a possible transgression. (Foucault, 1984a: 45)

Foucault thus transforms Kant's dissertation on Enlightenment into a form of "historico-philosophical critique." Rather than accepting preestablished limits to reason based on Kant's transcendental analysis, the theoretical task becomes that of testing the limits which establish to what extent we can move beyond them. In addition, says Foucault, this historico-critical attitude must be an experimental one. It must reject "radical and global" forms of analysis, as "we know from experience," he says, "that the claim to escape from the system of contemporary reality so as to produce the overall programs of another society, of another way of thinking, another culture, another vision of the world, has led only to the return of the most dangerous traditions." Thus Foucault analyzes "specific transformations," which are experimental, practical, and local (1984a: 46). But this does not mean that nothing can be done "except in disorder and contingency" (48). Neither is it to say that its qualities are those of an "obtuse, naive, or primitive empiricism" (Foucault, 1980f: 81). We will return to the specific practical injunctions of Foucault's conception after briefly considering his location in relation to other major forms of intellectual thought.

FOUCAULT, HABERMAS, AND THE QUESTION OF MODERNITY

Foucault's conception of critique does not appeal to standards in the past, in the future, or in reason, yet it seeks to expose unrecognized operation of power in social practices. In this respect, Foucault's conception of critique differs from that of Marxism, the Frankfurt School, or Habermas. Foucault's aim is not the realization of a rational society, but more pragmatically, to reveal "the contemporary limits of the necessary." His critique, in that it is not Kantian, also does not share the faith of a future utopia of the sort advocated by Marxists or by the leading writers of the Frankfurt School such as Adorno, Horkheimer, or Habermas. As Rajchman says, citing Geuss (1981), Foucault sees the model of an "inverted Enlightenment" as definitive of the very idea of the model of critical theory that has been developed within Marxism, and most especially by the Frankfurt School (1985: 80). Such models presuppose, in Foucault's view, the revelation of some concealed emancipatory truth about our "real" natures, just as much as they do about the real nature and limits to reason. It is the absence of some implicit or explicit ultimate measure or standard by which truth is assessed that explains why Foucault terms his own form of critical interrogation as "practical." In this sense, its most immediate and central concern is to sound a warning on the dangers of power, and this becomes the main function of philosophy. As Foucault states, "on the critical side . . . philosophy is precisely the challenging of all phenomena of domination at whatever level or whatever form they present themselves—political, economic, sexual, institutional, and so on" (1991a: 20).

For Habermas, critical theory has both Hegelian and Kantian moments in that it attempts to realize an ideal historical state as well as to maintain universal claims for truth and moral reasoning. In addition, Habermas's critical theory shares the Kantian theme of the unity of knowledge underpinned by a conception of anthropological interests. In Habermas's conception there are three "interests" of humanity which correspond to the different relevant interests of inquiry. The first "interest" corresponds to the natural sciences, yields instrumental "means-ends" knowledge, and is based on an interest in explaining; the second corresponds to the human sciences, yields interpretive knowledge, and is based on an interest in understanding; and the third corresponds to critical knowledge and is based on an interest in emancipation or in becoming mature. For Habermas, knowledge acquired through these interests is rational to the extent that it is not corrupted by domination or oppression, which is to say that communication is rational to the extent that it is unconstrained by force. Hence Habermas promotes a transhistorical and cross-cultural conception of rationality which locates it neither in the subject nor the world, but rather in the nature of *unconstrained communication*, as resolved through *argumentation* or *deliberation*. Presupposed in every speech act, says Habermas, is the possibility of separating the "strategic" from the "communicative" uses of language, a circumstance that makes it possible to assess the validity of perspectives based on the *force of the better argument alone* (see Habermas, 1971, 1984).

Foucault sees Habermas's conception of critique as an idealist conception that traces the process of the Enlightenment as the story of its movement toward its ideal realization or end-state. This is the Hegelian theme that links Habermas's idea of critique to the realization of history's ultimate goal and that sees history as the self-realization of humanity. He also rejects Habermas's assumptions concerning the nature of knowledge based in the different interests of the human race, which grounds for Habermas, following Kant and Fichte, the major divisions in the sciences of inquiry. This, in Foucault's view, is to ground one's form of critique in an analytic framework of anthropological interests that underpin both the Hegelian and Kantian moments. Hence, Foucault attempts to purge both the humanist and the idealist aims of critique as they occur in Habermas's project, replacing them, following Nietzsche, with a model of history as a continuous and never-ending process of changing practices.

Foucault thus opposes Habermas in terms of his Hegelianism and his Kantianism: he rejects his conception of history, his conception of anthropological interests, his conception of reason, as well as his "utopianism" which together give rise to Habermas's notion of a rationality premised, according to Jameson, on the idea of a "noisefree, transparent, fully communicational society" (1984: vii) where "so-called validity claims immanent in ordinary conversation can be discursively redeemed at the level of discourse" (Peters, 1996: 40). With regard to this issue, Foucault states,

[In Habermas's work] there is always something which causes me a problem. It is when he assigns a very important place to relations of communication and also a function that I would call "utopian." The thought that there could be a state of communication which would be such that the games of truth could circulate freely, without obstacles, without constraint, and without coercive effects, seems to me to be Utopia. It is being blind to the fact that relations of power are not something bad in themselves, from which one must free oneself. I don't believe there can be a society without relations of power. . . . The problem is not of trying to dissolve them in the utopia of a perfectly transparent communication, but to give one's self the rules of law, the techniques of management, and also the ethics, the *ēthos*, the practice of self, which would allow these games of power to be played with a minimum of domination. (Foucault, 1991a: 18)

For Foucault, "strategic" action, conceived broadly as politically or ideologically distorted dialogue, necessarily supervenes on "communicative" action. It is always the question of maintaining the correct balance of power relations in the present rather than seeking to exclude all forms of power from the world in the search for a different order of society. Hence Foucault rejects the idea, which he sees in Habermas, Marxism, and the Frankfurt School, of conceiving history as a single rational trajectory along which humanity fulfills its essential nature. For Foucault, power is more ubiquitous, diffuse, and corporeal; it infiltrates the fine textures of social existence as well as self-identity, and hence it is impossible to know one's true humanity apart from power's distorting effects (Foucault, 1980f: 96, 101).

For his part, Habermas labels Foucault as a "young conservative," similar to the 'young conservatives' of the Weimar Republic. This accusation goes to the heart of the difference between himself and Foucault: their relations to the issue of "modernity." Habermas designates himself as a defender of the "project of modernity" which aims to preserve the emancipatory impulse of the Enlightenment, against the anti-modern sentiments of a line of French post-structuralist thinkers "running from Bataille to Derrida by way of Foucault" (cited in Foucault, 1988a: 34). Hence, for Habermas, Foucault is a "post-modernist" who manifests an opposition to modernity which he defines, as did Weber, as a movement that privileges the tradition of reason. "Post-modernity," then, as Raulet summarizes it in his interview with Foucault (1988a: 35), is "the crumbling away or the break-up of reason."

When confronted with this "accusation" by interviewer Raulet in 1983, Foucault professes "not to be up-to-date on the issue of post-modernity" and "not to understand what kind of problem is common to the people we call post-modern or post-structuralist" (Foucault, 1988a: 33–34). Once Raulet links it to the "break up of reason," Foucault dissents completely.

That is not my problem . . . I am not prepared to identify reason entirely with the totality of rational forms which have come to dominate—at any given moment, in our own era and even very recently—in types of knowledge, forms of technique and modalities of government or domination. . . . For me, no given form of rationality is actually reason. So I do not see how we can say that the forms of rationality which have been dominant . . . are in the process of collapsing and disappearing. . . . I can see multiple transformations, but I cannot see why we should call this transformation a collapse of reason . . . there is no sense at all in the proposition that reason is a long narrative which is now finished, and that another narrative is under way. (Foucault, 1988a: 35)

Foucault goes on to caution against seeing the present as a "present of rupture, or a high point, or of completion, or of a returning down" and maintains that while there are "forms of rationality," there is no "unique line of reason." Again he complains of "blackmail" against the possibility of a critical enquiry into the history of rationality ("either you accept rationality or you fall prey to the irrational"), and dissents even when told of Habermas's praise for his recognition of the "moment when reason bifurcated" (into instrumental and moral reason) when Kant asked the question "What Is Enlightenment?" (27). Foucault admits this was an "important event" but denies it was a "unique phenomenon": rather than a single division, there has been an "abundance of branchings, ramifications, breaks, and ruptures" (28). Each time a type of rationality asserts itself, it does so, as Raulet expresses the point, by "a kind of cut-out—by exclusion, or by self-demarcation, drawing a boundary between self and other" (29). Hence, if modernity means anything for Foucault, it is probably best represented in the form of an answer as given by Dreyfus and Rabinow: "modernity is not a specific historical event, but a historical conjuncture which has happened several times in our history, albeit with different form and content: for example, the breakdown of the traditional virtues in Athens at the time of Socrates and Aristophanes, the decline of the Hellenistic world, the end of metaphysics at the time of Kant" (1986: 117).

NIETZSCHE, FREUD, MARX, AND HEIDEGGER

In his article "Nietzsche, Freud, Marx" (1986b), Foucault speaks of the historicity of techniques of cultural interpretation based in the works of Nietzsche, Freud, and Marx that introduced a new critical frame of reference which provided the possibility of moving beyond the Renaissance search for "resemblances" toward a new hermeneutic. In this grid of intelligibility a new mode of interpretation, one that "always reflects back on itself," where "we are perpetually sent back in a perpetual play of mirrors" was initiated (1986b: 2). Here Foucault questions whether Nietzsche, Freud, and Marx have not in some way multiplied the signs in the Western world. Rather than giving new meaning to things that had no meaning, "they have in reality changed the nature of the sign and modified the fashion in which the sign can in general be interpreted," modifying the "space of distribution in which signs can be signs" (2). With these three thinkers, says Foucault, "interpretation has become an infinite task" (3). While in the sixteenth century the epistemic principle of "resemblance" underpinned and limited the interpretive function, Foucault points out that with Nietzsche, Freud, and Marx what was introduced was a conceptual framework built on "irreducible gaping and openness." This is not because, for Foucault, interpretation is "without borders" (3) but because interpretation with Nietzsche, Freud, and Marx is preoccupied solely with "already present interpretation, which it must overthrow, upset, shatter, with the blow of a hammer":

One sees this already in Marx, who interprets not the history of relations of production, but a relation already offering itself as an interpretation, since it appears as nature. Likewise, Freud interprets not signs but interpretations. . . . In the same manner, Nietzsche seizes interpretations that have already seized each other. For Nietzsche there is no original signified. Words themselves are nothing but interpretations . . . and ultimately they signify only because they are essentially nothing but interpretations. (1986b: 4)

Here Foucault is explaining historical shifts in discursive systems of interpretation which proceed according to different principles. Nietzsche, Freud, and Marx introduced a "suspicious" form of interpretation that questioned already accepted interpretations trading under the title of "truth," such as those embodied in the conception of an Enlightenment. In all three thinkers, signs are revealed as "masks." "Thus money functions in the way that one sees it defined in *The Critique of Political Economy* and above all in the first volume of *Capital*. Thus symptoms function in Freud. And in Nietzsche, words, justice, binary classifications of Good and Evil, and consequently signs, are masks" (4). Foucault explains that one effect of these "suspicious" forms of interpretation is to be "thrown back on the interpretor, on 'psychology' in Nietzsche's sense." Another is that the interpretation cannot fail to be turned back on itself.

In his own form of materialism, which rejects the "suspicious stance," Foucault eclectically utilizes Nietzsche. Although he admits he took Nietzsche "seriously," especially the works that Nietzsche wrote around 1880, just as he claims for Deleuze, there is no "deafening reference to Nietzsche . . . nor any attempt to wave the Nietzschean flag for rhetorical or political ends" (1986b: 4). What Foucault takes from Nietzsche is his antihumanism, his conception of history as constituted through complexity and chance, and a conception of difference which represents life as a haphazard, endless struggle, where the essence of things lies in their relation to each other, based on a truncated dialectic (without synthesis) of opposing forces of power. Foucault shares Nietzsche's conception whereby the nature of things varies depending on the position they occupy within the changing hierarchy of domination and subordination. In this view the will to power is not that of an individual or subject but is universally applicable to human society and the relations of force of which it is constituted. Hence Foucault, like Nietzsche, abandons the Platonic quest for unity and puts in its place a pluralism of the essence of things, a critique of existing values, a commitment to nomadic structure, and a representation of life as aesthetic self-creation. Nietzsche's approach to truth also recognizes its constructionist dimension, in the sense that knowledge is seen as "invented" in a sense that at times goes well beyond Foucault's appropriations. In *Beyond Good and Evil* (1966: 17–19), Nietzsche turns Kant's questions around and asks why knowledge is necessary. Only, he decides, for the preservation of life. What matters is not the truth but what we believe to be true. Humans have a "will to truth" (and are as happy with true as with false judgments) which also is a "will to power," that is, a will to affirm life (11–12). The idea that knowledge is discovered is replaced by the view that it is invented. Nietzsche sees scientific and moral knowledge as possibly wrong yet life-affirming; hence he affirms a philosophy "beyond good and evil" (12). Although Foucault was influenced by Nietzsche's writings regarding truth, power, and the subject, as Foucault admitted to Gérard Raulet (1988a: 31), it is a mistake to overstate his dependence on Nietzsche. Foucault certainly did not share Nietzsche's disdain of collective political resistance on behalf of the marginalized and the downtrodden; nor did he share Nietzsche's ethical elitism as entailed in the celebration in the interests and struggles of the *Übermensch*; nor did he share the irrationalist view that one finds in Nietzsche an unconstrained constructionism, that the constraints of the world do not matter, that one can invent whatever one likes, and so on. Yet Nietzsche was also useful to Foucault, for as already noted (Chapter 6) it was through thinkers like Nietzsche that Foucault was able to distance himself from Phenomenology and Marxism. By distancing himself from Phenomenology it meant he could avoid the philosophy of the subject, while in relation to Marxism it meant he could avoid the theoretical and methodological entrapments of Marxist forms of critique, as well as of the general Marxist vision of history and society.

In this regard, Foucault's version of critical theory rejects both Marxist concepts like ideology and Freudo-Marxist concepts like repression. His objections to the concept of ideology are succinctly stated in his essay *Truth and Power*:

The notion of ideology appears to me to be difficult to make use of, for three reasons. The first is that, like it or not, it always stands in virtual opposition to something else which is supposed to count as truth. Now I believe that the problem does not consist in drawing the line between that in a discourse which falls under the category of scientificity or truth, and that which comes under some other category, but in seeing historically how effects of truth are produced within discourses which in themselves are neither true nor false. The second drawback is that the concept of ideology refers, I think necessarily, to something in the order of a subject. Third, ideology stands in a secondary position relative to something which functions as its infrastructure, as its material economic determinant, etc. For these three reasons, I think that this is a notion that cannot be used without circumspection. (1980b: 118)

Hence, to expose an ideology is to expose our "true" interests and at the same time to liberate the alienated subject. One of Foucault's central objections to such a concept is that power operates on bodies in much more subtle and concrete ways than merely through the socialization into irrational beliefs. To see power as simply accompanied by ideological production is to overgeneralize. For Foucault, it must be seen, as he puts it, as "both much more and much less than ideology" (1980f: 102). It relates to the production of specific effective instruments for the formation and accumulation of knowledge: specific methods of observation; specific techniques of registration; specific procedures for investigation and research; and apparatuses of control (102).

On similar grounds to his rejection of ideology within Marxism, Foucault rejects the use of the concept by Habermas based on a Kantian model that counterpoises the "irrational" to an ideal of rational agreement among autonomous rational agents. In place of such a view which distinguishes ideology from science or truth, Foucault substitutes his theoretical notion of "discursive practice" based on a minute and detailed analysis of practices that make particular forms of historical practice possible. The concept of discursive practice does not dissolve truth but rejects the distinction between ideology and truth or ideology and science. As our identities and our bodies are constructed through such discursive practices, the partitioning of truth from falsehood is problematic—much more difficult in Foucault's view than has hitherto been previously thought, and something that is never finally assured. In addition, discursive practices are always complex articulations of the true, but in a particular historical juncture and dependent on that juncture. Hence Foucault analyzes how discursive practices constitute norms that provide a perspective within a particular normative context of possible thought and action which become legitimized as "true" expressions.

A discursive practice is not in this sense ideological but the complex articulation of elements within an historically generated complex structure. Such a structure is always changing, is relatively autonomous, is not directed by a single person or group, and has unforeseen and unintended consequences. What Foucault analyzes is the emergence of norms that guide action and conduct as a consequence of a multitude of practices. Rather than seek to reveal some deep truth in the melange of historical practices, which could give sense to a concept of ideology, he seeks to account through a microscopic materialism for the emergence of our present truths.

Although Foucault therefore has major reservations about use of the concept of ideology, these reservations apply largely to its specific use within Marxist theory, for employment of the concept suffers from the general problems of the theory. Outside of Marxist theory Foucault sometimes uses the concept himself, and in *The Archaeology of Knowledge*, in the section titled "Knowledge (*savoir*) and Ideology" (1972: 184–186), he articulates a legitimate theoretical use of the concept, arguing that (a) ideological practice must be seen as one practice among others; (b) ideology is not exclusive of scientificity, that is, because something is ideological does not mean that the totality of its statements are undermined by error, contradiction, lacunae, or defect; and (c) by correcting itself, by rectifying its errors, a discourse does not necessarily undo its relations with ideology (186). "To tackle the ideological function of a science", he says, "must take into account the analysis of the discursive formation that gave rise to it and the group of objects, concepts, and theoretical choices that it had to develop and systematize" (186). By so doing, one must show "how the discursive practice that gave rise to such a positivity functioned amongst other practices that might have been of a discursive, but also of a political or economic, order" (86). In this sense, some discursive systems are "entirely penetrated with ideology" (178), "political economy" being a case in point. In Foucault's words, "broadly speaking, and setting aside all mediation and specificity, it can be said that political economy has a role in capitalist society, that it serves the interests of the bourgeois class, that it was made by and for that class, and that it bears the mark of its origins even in its concepts and logical architecture" (185).

Foucault also opposes the concept of repression as used by Freud and by Freudo-Marxists, and he views the concept as even more insidious than that of ideology (Foucault, 1980b: 117). As he states in his interview with Stephen Riggins, however, "it is not a question of denying the existence of repression. It's one of showing that repression is always a part of a much more complex political strategy regarding sexuality" (Foucault, 1988j: 9). As he expressed elsewhere (Foucault, 1980b: 117), just as behind the concept of ideology there is a nostalgia for a quasi-transparent form of knowledge, free from all error and illusion, so behind the concept of repression lies a longing for a form of power innocent of all coercion, discipline, and normalization. Not only does it deny the productive dimensions of power, but also it presupposes an essentialist conception of the subject as having a vital being "held down," prevented from self-realization.

In *The History of Sexuality*, Volume 1, Foucault specifically objects to the following theses as developed by Freudo-Marxism and Wilhelm Reich in particular:

- That sexuality in the nineteenth century was repressed as part of a broader strategy of the exploitation and oppression of the workforce. Here repression meant that sexuality was "rejected," "refused," "blocked," "concealed," "masked," "confined," "placed within a binary system of licit and illicit," and "prohibited" except in certain restricted contexts.

- That sexual liberation is tied to and consequent upon political, social, and economic liberation.

- That the body has a natural vital energy that is thwarted by bourgeois social institutions such as the family, the state, and the economy.

• That sexuality was censored or talk of sexuality was prevented by the policing functions of social, education, economic, or political institutions (1978a: 83–85).

In Foucault's view, "things are not merely repressed. There is about sexuality a lot of defective regulations in which the negative effects of inhibition are counterbalanced by the positive effects of stimulation. The way in which sexuality in the nineteenth century was both repressed but also put in light, underlined, analyzed through techniques like psychology and psychiatry, shows very well that it was not simply a question of repression" (1988j: 9). What Foucault seeks to do by challenging the concept of repression, like that of ideology, is question the clarity and effectiveness of a certain form of left-wing thinking. He specifically directs a number of arguments against the Freudo-Marxists. First, he opposes their biologism/essentialism regarding their conception of the subject; second, he challenges the historical accuracy of the repression thesis, claiming that to the extent that sexuality was censored from the late eighteenth century, it also received constant attention; third, it depends on a purely negative, juridical notion of power common to both Marxism and psychoanalysis based on the idea of "subjugation-obedience" (Foucault, 1978a: 85) and correlative with the notion of "alienation"; and fourth, he claims that such a notion presupposes the principle of an expressive totality whereby the parts simply "express" or "reflect" the whole.

Foucault's opposition to the concept of repression as employed by the Freudo-Marxists is based on an opposition to *both* Marxism *and* Freudianism. It is accurate to say that Foucault had much less respect for Freud and psychoanalysis than he did for Marxism. His general view of psychoanalysis, as Miller notes, is tainted with "sarcasm" (1992: 58). He regards it, archaeologically, as "something dead, or about to die" (59). He initially criticized it in his 1954 book *Maladie Mentale et Personalité* (see Foucault, 1987b), and it receives further extended treatment in *The Order of Things*.

Foucault sees its origins as belonging to a structure whose historical emergence is contemporary with the human sciences. The concept of man that it depends on emerges only at the end of the eighteenth century and in the first years of the nineteenth. It is essentially Cartesian man, the man of the human sciences, a "man" unthinkable during the Classical period. From the perspective of psychoanalysis, this model of the mind, as "ideas" or "images" that represent the outside world, may correspond with varying degrees of adequacy to what is actually out in the world (see Foucault, 1987b: 31).

In addition to its philosophical conception of the subject, Foucault opposes psychoanalysis for its approach to science, by which it seeks to explain the forces underlying the human personality, in terms of the causal models of the *Naturwissenschaften*. In this model, sexual desire is explained in terms of natural laws.

In *The Order of Things* psychoanalysis also experiences the paradox of the "empirical-transcendental doublet" of which Kant is identified as the prime mover. Kant accepted the finitude of human reason as the basis for man's positive powers. As Foucault asserts, "to make the limits of knowledge provide a foundation for the possibility of knowing" (1970: 317) creates a paradox. Hence man functions as both the source of meaning and a meaningless object, a paradox that posits a finite system of representations as the basis of all knowledge about man. Psychoanalysis is doubly mistaken, for it seeks to understand the unconscious through the conscious. Any science of psychology must deal with this paradox that man's self and mental life are opaque and foreign to him, while at the same time they constitute the source of all meaning: man is both the subject and object of knowledge. As Foucault says, "psychoanalysis stands as close as possible, in fact, to that critical function which as we have seen, exists within all human sciences. In setting itself the task of making the discourse of the unconscious speak through consciousness, psychoanalysis is advancing in the direction of that fundamental region in which the relations of representation and finitude come into play" (1970: 374). Hence, as Dreyfus maintains, "Freud's view of therapy as the interminable task of searching out and bringing to light the self's concealed motivations is the culmination of that structure of the sciences of man that demands that one think the unthought . . . the unthought must be . . . accessible to thought" (1987: xvii).

Rather than explain sexuality as a function of natural laws, as a natural urge located deep within the organism, Foucault sees it as an apparatus (*dispotif*) explainable through power mechanisms and comprising institutions, forms of behavior, discursive and nondiscursive practices. Hence the concept of sexuality that Freud depends on is historically bourgeois, arising from the middle of the eighteenth century. Yet an "archaeology" of psychoanalysis shows that the history of the apparatus of sexuality cannot represent sexual desire as an organic function operating in terms of natural laws, for it presupposes a false unity. Foucault proposes that "the notion of 'sex' made it possible to group together, in an artificial unity, anatomical elements, biological functions, conducts, sensations, and pleasures, and it enabled one to make use of this fictitious unity as a causal principle, an omnipresent meaning, a secret to be discovered everywhere" (1978a: 154).

As well as criticizing Freud and Marx, and appropriating from Nietzsche, Foucault adopts aspects from the writings of Heidegger, an influence that until the work of Machery (1986) and Dreyfus (1987, 1992) has been understated, despite the obvious difference that Foucault was an historian in the sense that Heidegger certainly was not.

Dreyfus (1987: xv) points out that when Foucault wrote *Maladie Mentale et Personalité* in the early 1950s (first published 1954), Foucault's approach represented an eclectic mix of existential phenomenology of the early Heidegger and writers like Binswanger, as well as the classical version of Marxist materialism which he adopted in order to combat Cartesian Representation-ism and psychological viewpoints that sought to develop scientific accounts of the human mind based on the methods of the natural sciences.

Central to the existential phenomenology of the early Heidegger was a representation of mental life in terms of "intentionality" which presupposed a "context" in terms of which objects in the world made sense and through which Foucault could provide a descriptive rather than a scientific account of human pathology. This context in turn presupposed an "ontology," a background understanding of *Being*, including presuppositions, things, tools, language, institutions, shared understandings, and other people, which determines what is deemed possible or impossible, what counts as important or unimportant, or what events are meaningful or unmeaningful.

A culture's understanding of *Being* creates what Heidegger calls a "clear-ing" (*Lichtung*) in which objects take meaning for individuals and through which possibilities and options are opened up, made possible, or closed off, or blocked. The "clearing" determines what it is possible to think and achieve, say or do.

As Dreyfus observes, Foucault's approach to explaining mental illness in his early publication was also based on a classical materialist account of psy-chological pathology as located in objective material life contradictions. In this, he "simply reverses the classical story. . . . In Foucault's account, social contradictions cause alienation, alienation causes defenses, defenses cause brain malfunction, and brain malfunction causes abnormal behaviour" (Dreyfus, 1987: xxvi). In Foucault's words, he sought to show "how each morbid individuality must be understood through the practices of the en-vironment" (1987b: 12).

One can see why Foucault (1984e: 334) claimed to be "unsatisfied" with this early work and why he opposed its republication in 1962,[4] for he came to reject the anthropological assumptions of existential phenomenology as well as the specific form of the materialist view of history. These committed him, as Dreyfus claims, citing Paul Ricoeur, to a "hermeneutics of suspi-cion" by which the present is understood to be a "cover-up of truth" (class struggle, libido, anxiety) which, when unmasked, will result in liberation (Dreyfus, 1987: xxviii).

Influenced by the late Heidegger, who came to reject the view of a con-stant, ahistorical, universal truth, Foucault ultimately modified the exact na-ture of his materialism. He rejected the "hermeneutics of suspicion" which led him to progressively distance himself from the themes of the early Hei-degger and Marx and reject the understanding of the experience of madness as an unchanging, ahistorical construct, or as a constant underlying state waiting to be revealed. What he came to reject, in more general terms, was the idea that there existed some general ahistorical structure of experience which could be liberated by simply changing social circumstances. What he replaced it with was a more nuanced materialism that saw the structures of experiences, and human beings as well, as *constituted* through historical practices.

On this model, then, there is no universal truth of the human condition to be discovered. Following Nietzsche and the later Heidegger, Foucault forges a nominalist reduction of the ontological dimensions of personality, illness, and all forms of experience, which means that they have no essential core apart from the practices that give them meaning. Thus historical constitution becomes the key to the understanding of experience, society, and self. Although it is possible to adduce various "costs" and "benefits" by considering experiences within the configuration of life experience as a whole, there is no fundamental truth to be revealed, and no ideal state needs be achieved. The best for people is *immanent* in their present life conditions. Human beings must work with what they have.

Foucault believed that the critical task becomes to understand discursive historical practices that *constitute* and therefore define forms of historical experience such as madness, or sexuality, or discipline, or punishment, and to understand how cultures impose limits, exclusions, and restrictions on the scope of human possibility.

Madness and Civilization, which Foucault wrote in the early 1960s, contains resonances of the early Heidegger, which can be evidenced in the continued appeal to concepts such as strangeness, fear, anxiety, or silence. By the time of *The Birth of the Clinic* and *The Order of Things*, however, Foucault had rejected hermeneutics as an approach that would reveal the deep truth underpinning ordinary experience, including the claim that madness has been silenced and must be liberated. As Dreyfus says, Foucault has changed from "digging out the ahistorical structure of *Dasein* to interpreting the historical constitution of western man" (1987: xxxiv).

Foucault shared with the later Heidegger the themes that experience is constituted in history, that history is a strategy without a consciously directing subject, and that the driving forces of history have to do with power and control. In relation to this later theme, Foucault's conception of normalization can be regarded as similar to Heidegger's view in seeing the expansion of the processes of rational control over human subjects through the "total mobilization" of technology to all aspects of life. For Foucault, the expansion of normalizing power through science and technology progressively incorporates each and every anomaly, and through the human sciences, such as psychiatry, psychology, and statistics, enables knowledge of individuals to be assumed under a type and to be classified by locating individuals and the population in relation to the same epistemic and conceptual space. Hence normalization eradicates the possibility or desirability of *difference*. It functions in terms of educational technologies such as the normal curve, which was first used in the educational and psychological sciences by Francis Galton in the second half of the nineteenth century to classify intelligence, to situate the individual within an epistemic field or framework, without reducing the individual to the typical. Hence, as Foucault states, normalizing judgment produced "a whole range of degrees of normality indicating membership of a homogeneous social body but also playing a part in classification, hierarchization, and the distribution of rank. In this sense, the power of normalization imposes homogeneity, but it individualizes by making it possible to measure gaps, to determine levels, to fix specialities, and to render the differences useful by fitting them one to another" (1977a: 184).

Foucault, like Heidegger, sees the modern age as being marked by a tendency toward the total ordering of all beings through disciplinary bio-power, which distorts the social order and our relations to other beings. Hence, for Foucault, like Heidegger, the continued trend toward total mobilization of Western society poses our greatest danger, for while previous "clearings" have been incomplete, leaving spaces of ungovernability, in the present epoch human beings are being subjected to greater and greater surveillance and control.

THE PRACTICE OF CRITICISM

What criticism represents for Foucault, in a concrete and practical sense, is an autonomous, non-centralized kind of theoretical production, whose validity is not dependent on the approval of the established regimes of thought. In this sense, criticism involves the role of the "specific intellectual" and is linked to the insurrection of subjugated knowledges. By subjugated knowledges, Foucault means the historical contents of knowledges that have been disqualified as inadequate to their task or insufficiently elaborated—naive knowledges that are defined as operating low down on the hierarchy of formal knowledge below an acceptable level of cognition or scientificity. It is through the reemergence of these low-ranking subordinate knowledges that criticism performs its task (see Foucault, 1980f).

In that the task of criticism is not linked to the objective of absolute emancipation, the commitment is part of a broader program of freedom of the thinker which involves an ascetical moment of the transgression of self. In this sense, critique for Foucault has two components—work on oneself and response to one's time. On this point Norris misrepresents Foucault when he claims that Foucault "turns to aesthetics as an analogue, or a substitute for the misguided labors of epistemological or ethico-political critique" (1993: 80). Foucault sees critique as both "on the world" (cognitively, ethically, politically) and "on oneself." As we will see in the next chapter, Foucault developed new forms of relating to the self, most clearly expressed in the context of revolt and the possibility which Bernauer claims "witnesses the capacity for an ecstatic transcendence of any history which asserts its necessity" (1991: 70). As a modern example of work on oneself, Foucault points to Baudelaire whose "consciousness of modernity is widely recognised as one of the most acute in the nineteenth century" (Foucault, 1984a: 39). Baudelaire defines modernity as "the will to 'heroize' the present." Modern man is the man who tries to invent himself through an ascetic elaboration of self which can only be produced, says Baudelaire, in art. The Enlightenment, says Foucault, emphasizes "a type of philosophical interrogation . . . that simultaneously problematizes man's relation to the present, man's historical mode of being, and the constitution of the self as an autonomous subject" (Foucault, 1984a: 42).

Central to the task of critique is its relationship to the *transformation of real-world structures*. "Criticism," Foucault observes, "is absolutely indispensable for any transformation" (Foucault, 1988i: 155), "a transformation that remains within the same mode of thought, a transformation that is only a way of adjusting the same thought more closely to the reality of things can merely be a superficial transformation . . . as soon as one can no longer think things as one formerly thought them, transformation becomes both very urgent, very difficult, and quite possible" (155). So criticism is integrally related to transformation and change, which, Foucault states, can only be carried out in a free atmosphere. This gives a programmatic role for the "specific intellectual" and for "thought." Since he works specifically in the realm of thought, his role is to see how far the liberation of thought can make these transformations urgent enough for people to want to carry them out:

Out of these conflicts, these confrontations, a new power relation must emerge, whose first, temporary expression will be a reform. If at the base there has not been the work of thought upon itself and if, in fact, modes of thought, that is to say modes of action, have not been altered, whatever the project for reform, we know that it will be swamped, digested by modes of behaviour and institutions that will always be the same. (156)

Thought, then, is a crucial factor in the process of criticism. Thought exists independently of systems and structures of discourse. It is something that is often hidden but that always animates everyday behavior (Foucault, 1988i: 154–155). A critique is not a question of criticizing things as not being right as they are. Rather, says Foucault, "it is a matter of pointing out on what kinds of assumptions, what kinds of familiar, unchallenged, unconsidered modes of thought the practices that we accept rest . . . Criticism is a matter of flushing out that thought and trying to change it: to show that things are not as self-evident as one believed, to see that what is accepted as self-evident will no longer be accepted as such (154–155).

Thought is also the context for the realization of freedom. Foucault's antihumanist conception of freedom echoes Heidegger's rather than Sartre's in that rather than seeing freedom as a natural right, or fundamental choice relating to a conception of our fundamental being, Foucault sees it as relating to the possibilities generated through "clearing away" the illusions of the age and becoming conscious of the historical and social mainsprings of our actions. Rajchman calls it "the freeing or 'clearing' of the possibilities of an age" (1985: 44–45).

Freedom is also permitted a space in relation to Foucault's conception of change, says Rajchman. In the archaeological scheme of things, change while non-deliberate is not caused or necessitated by internal contradictions or by external forces on their own. Thus a space is provided for a new type of freedom in which "new systems of possibility opened-up, or 'cleared' " (45).

For a long period, says Foucault, the "left" intellectual spoke and was acknowledged in the capacity of truth and justice, as the "spokesman of the universal . . . the consciousness/conscience of us all" (1980b: 126). This role is that of a "faded Marxism," and it is diminishing. Intellectuals have increasingly become used to working in "specific" sites since the Second World War (127). Rather than being a generalist, a writer, a "universal consciousness," his or her specific activity increasingly serves as the basis for politicization, and she or he develops "lateral connections across different forms of knowledge and from one focus of politicization to another. Magistrates and psychiatrists, doctors and social workers, laboratory technicians and sociologists have become able to participate, both within their own fields and through mutual exchange and support, in a global process of politicization of intellectuals" (126). Foucault identifies Robert Oppenheimer as marking the point of transition between the universal and specific intellectual. "It's because he had a direct and localised relation to scientific knowledge and institutions that the atomic scientist could make his intervention. . . . And for the first time . . . the intellectual was hounded by political powers, no longer on account of the general discourse which he conducted, but because of the knowledge at his disposal: it was at this level that he constituted a political threat" (128).

If Oppenheimer symbolically typifies this new emergent figure at one level, Foucault indicates that his precursors can be seen in the debates between Darwin and the post-Darwinian evolutionists and their stormy debates with the socialists on the topics related to evolution (crime, psychiatry, eugenics) and in the politicization of events around biology and physics. Today the specific intellectual is a product of newly emerging "technic-scientific structures" and faces "the danger of remaining at the level of conjunctural struggles, pressing demands restricted to particular sectors." Hence, says Foucault, there exists "the risk of being unable to develop these struggles for lack of a global strategy or outside support; the risk, too, of not being followed, or only by very limited groups" (1980b: 130).

It would be a dangerous error to discount the specific intellectual politically in relation to his local form of power, either on the grounds that he is simply a specialist or that his interests do not concern the masses, or to see him or her as merely a servant of capital or the State. For it is the intellectual as the occupier of a "specific position," rather than as the "bearer of universal values," that most directly links to the apparatus of truth and enables the intellectual to engage in struggle, not simply in relation to professional or sectoral interests, but at the "general level of the regime of truth" (132).

There is a battle "for truth," or at least "around truth"—it being understood . . . that by truth I do not mean "the ensemble of truths which are to be discovered and accepted," but rather "the ensemble of rules according to which the true and the false are separated and specific effects of the power attached to the true," it being understood also that it's not a matter of a battle "on behalf" of the truth, but of a battle about the status of truth and the economic and political role it plays. (132)

For Foucault, then, historico-critical investigations constitute an historical ontology that aims to study specific interconnections in terms of *knowledge, power,* and *ethics,* and that bears on the issue of truth. Such an historical ontology of ourselves has to answer an open series of questions and make an indefinite number of enquiries. They are practical in the sense that they derive their starting point in terms of problematizations in relation to actual, concrete, human existence. Although such investigations are "specific" in the sense that they always bear upon "a material, an epoch, a body of determined practices, and discourses" (1984a: 49), they are also "general" in the sense that such problems are relevant to Western societies and include such issues as the relations between sanity and insanity, sickness and health. Finally, says Foucault, "what is at stake is this: how can the growth of capabilities be disconnected from the intensification of power relations?" (148). This may ultimately be seen as the intended purpose or goal of critique.

Like Marx, through the arm of critique, Foucault wants to change our world, not simply our idea of it. As an intellectual, he was opposed to the Enlightenment emphasis on unity and normality, and the lack of toleration for diversity as evidenced in the technocratic ways our cultures deal with sickness, insanity, crime, and sexuality. The homogenizing and totalizing forms of culture work in and through the apparatuses of education in conjunction with the Enlightenment project based on the sciences of Man. Yet the modern ethos, the lucid and heroic ability to face up to the crises of the present, is not what Foucault calls maturity. Maturity consists not only of the heroic attitude but what Foucault calls an ironic stance toward one's present situation. Maturity as ironic, says Dreyfus and Rabinow, entails "an abandonment of traditional seriousness while preserving active engagement in the concerns of the present. It seeks to avoid preserving some special status for truth which grounds serious involvement, and also to avoid the frivolity which arises when one abandons all seriousness to chance on the grave of god, or logos, or phallocentrism, etc." (1986: 117). Hence the ironic stance involves utilizing those practices that offer the possibility of a new way of acting. This concern with ascetic self-creation became a central theme of Foucault's later writings, and it is to this subject that we shall now turn.

NOTES

1. The Critique of Pure Reason, The Critique of Practical Reason, The Critique of Judgement.

2. *The Conflict of the Faculties* is a collection of three dissertations on the relations between the different faculties that make up the university. The second dissertation concerns the conflict between Law and Philosophy and asks the question "Is there such a thing as constant progress for mankind?" In seeking an answer to this question, Kant raised the issue of the French Revolution.

3. This "retreat," while suggestive of a similarity, cannot be pushed too far, for it could not involve a return to Cartesianism, as Foucault and the post-structuralists would reject such a position.

4. Foucault's dissatisfaction remained in spite of the fact that the 1962 edition was revised to represent the changes taking place in his thought.

Chapter 9

Educating the Self

So it is not enough to say that the subject is constituted in a symbolic system. It is not just in the play of symbols that the subject is constituted. It is constituted in real practices—historically analyzable practices. There is a technology of the constitution of the self which cuts across symbolic systems while using them. (Foucault, 1997d: 277)

Such is the basis of Foucault's materialism of the self. Although the self is constituted by practices, it is always possible to make something out of what it has been made into, once it learns how to pull the strings. This is the basis of ethical work. Ethical work, says Foucault, is the work one performs in the attempt to transform oneself into an ethical subject of one's own behavior, the means by which we change ourselves in order to become ethical subjects. Such a history of ethics is a history of ascetics. In his interview "On the Genealogy of Ethics," Foucault explains that there is "another side to these moral prescriptions which most of the time is not isolated as such but is, I think, very important: the kind of relationship you ought to have with yourself, *rapport à soi*, which I call ethics, and which determines how the individual is supposed to constitute himself as a moral subject of his own actions" (1983d: 237–238). The question of how to conceptualize ethics and how to write its history led Foucault to a study of ancient cultures in the tradition of historians of ancient thought such as Paul Veyne, Georges Dumézil, Pierre Hadot, and Jean-Pierre Vernant (Davidson, 1994: 64). Foucault's concern with ethics in the last two volumes of *The History of Sexuality*, constituted a reconceptualization and reorientation of his original project on sex in *The History of Sexuality*, Volume 1 (Davidson, 1994: 64).

Now, sex would be conceptualized in relation to ethics, and ethics was to become, in his latter works, specifically the framework for interpreting Greek and Roman problematizations of sex. Ethics, as such, was a part of morality, but, rather than focus exclusively on codes of moral behavior, it concentrated on the self's relationship to the self, for the way we relate to ourselves contributes to the way that we construct ourselves and form our identities as well as the ways we lead our lives and govern our conduct.

In this newfound concern with ethical action, there is on the surface a shift in relation to Foucault's interest away from knowledge as a coercive practice of subjection to being a practice of the self-formation of the subject. Yet this positing of a more active, volitional subject does not involve a radical break with his earlier work, nor is it inconsistent with it (Foucault, 1991a: 11; 1989q: 296). In *Madness and Civilization*, Foucault states that it was a matter of knowing how one "governed" "the mad" (1989q: 296); in his last two works, it was a matter of how one "governs" oneself. In addition, he says:

if now I am interested . . . in the way in which the subject constitutes himself in an active fashion, by the practices of the self, these practices are nevertheless not something that the individual invents by himself. They are patterns that he finds in his culture and which are proposed, suggested and imposed on him by his culture, his society and his social group. (Foucault, 1991a: 11)

ETHICS, SELF-CREATION, AND THE CARE OF THE SELF

In Volumes 2 and 3 of *The History of Sexuality*, Foucault became concerned with a set of practices that were very important in classical and late antiquity. These practices, he explains, had to do with what the Greeks called *epimeleia heautou* and in Latin *cura sui*—the principle that one needs to attend to one's self or take care of one's self, which referred to forms of practice of the self. This phenomenon had been important since Greek and Roman times, even though it had hardly been studied. In the civilizations of Greece and Rome, these practices of self played a much greater importance than they did later on when such practices of the self were taken over by institutions of religion, psychiatry, and a pedagogical kind (see Foucault, 1986a: 45).

In providing historical examples of the "care for the self," Foucault presents the example of Socrates. In the *Apology*, Socrates presents himself to his judges as the teacher of self-concern. Socrates accosts strangers and berates them for being concerned with wealth, reputation, and honors, but not with their souls. Socrates challenges them to "care for themselves." Christian asceticism, like ancient philosophy, also takes the care of the self seriously and "makes the obligation to know one's self one of the elements of this essential care" (Foucault, 1997b: 94). Foucault gives the example of Gregory of Nyssa, who applies the notion of *epimeleia heautou* to the impulses to "renounce marriage, detach one's self from the flesh, and through the virginity of one's heart and body regain the immortality from which one had fallen" (94).

In both of these later volumes of *The History of Sexuality* Foucault was inspired by the work of Pierre Hadot (1987, 1997). As Davidson puts it, "In order fully to understand Foucault's motivations and his object of study one must take into account the way in which Hadot's work on ancient spiritual exercises helped to form the entire project. . . . If as is now widely recognised the work of Georges Canguilhem is indispensable to understanding the early Foucault, the work of Pierre Hadot is crucial to understanding his last writings" (1997: 200–201).

What Hadot did was to open up dimensions of ancient philosophy typically overlooked and forgotten. Foucault, being a keen reader of Hadot's work, sought to reinstate philosophy as "a mode of life, as an act of living, as a way of being" (Davidson, 1997: 195) by seeking to isolate philosophical and spiritual exercises that lead to the philosophical way of life. Hadot had argued that such exercises were eclipsed by the reduction of philosophy from a way of life to an abstract theoretical activity locked within a discipline. Similarly, Foucault argues that "codes of behaviour became emphasised at the expense of forms of subjectivation" (201). In both *The Use of Pleasure* and *The Care of the Self*, Foucault borrows Hadot's notion of spiritual exercises, directing his attention to the history of ethics as a history of *askēsis* or practices of self, focusing attention on classical Greece as well as Hellenistic and Roman philosophy as places where these elements of *askēsis* were most emphasized, strongest, and most dynamic (201).

Hadot acknowledges in turn a debt to Pierre Courcelle's work on Hellenistic literature,[1] which explored themes such as "self knowledge, historically following them "across the years . . . as they evolved in the western tradition" (Hadot, 1997: 206). An important concept was that of *philosophia*, which as a form of life required spiritual exercises aimed at realizing a transformation of one's vision of the world. Such exercises, involved learning how to live the philosophical life (Hadot, 1987: 196). The lesson of ancient philosophy, Hadot says, consisted in "an invitation for a man to transform himself. Philosophy is conversion, transformation of the way of being and the way of living, the quest for wisdom" (Hadot, 1987: 227). Starting with Ancient Greece and traversing the Hellenistic and Roman cultures, Hadot considers the philosophical orientations of the different schools—the Platonists, the Aristoteleans, the Epicureans, the Stoics, the Academicians— and notes how each school has its fundamental approach to life and regimen of exercises.

According to Arnold Davidson, "the idea of philosophy as a way of life . . . is one of the most forceful and provocative directions of Foucault's later thought" (1994: 70–1). To emphasize philosophy as a "way of life" must be seen as distinct from everyday life, for, as Hadot has written with respect to the ancients, the idea of a "way of life" "implies a rupture with what the skeptics called *bios,* that is daily life" (cited in Davidson, 1994: 70). "It was this experience of philosophy as a way of life, and not simply as a theoretical doctrine, that brought Socrates into deadly conflict with the authorities" (71). For Foucault, "philosophy was a spiritual exercise, an exercise of one-self in which one submitted to modifications and tests, underwent changes, in order to learn to think differently" (71).

In considering various sorts of ethical action in ancient cultures, Foucault surveys different senses of the care of the self related to the work one does on oneself: as a philosophical style of life; as a form of spiritual "conversion to self" (*epistrophē eis heautou*); as a preparation for death (*meleté thanatou*); as directed towards self-sufficiency (*autarkeia*); and as a practice of truth telling (*parrhésia*). Ethical action was always undertaken in the context of real-life existence, however, and pertains to practical activity exercised on the world. In this sense, ethics concerns the power we exercise in relation to what power does to us and to the forms of subjection we experience, in order to constitute ourselves as the subjects of knowledge. Foucault refers to these self-formative practices as "ascetical" practices; he interprets ascet-ical in a broader sense than that used by Weber, not as "abnegation," but as an "exercise of self upon self by which one tries to work out, to transform one's self and to attain a certain mode of being" (Foucault, 1991a: 2). In this sense, ethics is about "techniques of self-improvement," to use Ian Hacking's (1986) phrase. Foucault lists among the various aspects of ethical practice: *ethical substance,* the aspect of our behavior relevant for ethical judgment; *the mode of subjectivation,* or what is used in order to internalize these concerns; *various self-forming techniques,* used to get ethics to work (self-denial, asceticism, etc.); and *teleology,* referring to the kind of being which we aspire to be as moral beings (1985a: 26–27; 1997d: 262–265).

By ethics, Foucault refers not to morality in the narrow sense of the term, but rather to *customs* and *practices*—what Kant meant by *Sitten* (Hacking, 1986: 239). Hence, ethics is not intended in the Kantian sense, as pertaining to something "utterly internal, the private duty of reason" (Hacking: 239) but more in the sense of Ancient Greece where ethics was concerned with the good life.

The Greeks . . . considered this freedom as a problem and the freedom of the indi-vidual as an ethical problem. But ethical in the sense that Greeks could understand. *Ethos* was the deportment and the way to behave. It was the subject's mode of being and a certain manner of acting visible to others. One's ethos was seen by his dress, by his bearing, by his gait, by the poise with which he reacts to events, etc. For them that is the complete expression of liberty. (Foucault, 1991a: 6)

In this regard, Hacking says that Foucault reverses Kant. Kant had held that we construct our ethical position by recourse to reason. As Hacking observes, "but the innovation is not reason but construction" (1986: 239). In other words, Kant taught us that we make the moral law, and that is what makes us moral. Foucault incorporates this "constructionist" dimension into his historicism, meaning that "morality leads away from the letter of the law of Kant, but curiously preserves Kant's spirit" (1986: 239). As Hacking concludes, "those who criticise Foucault for not giving us a place to stand might start their critique with Kant" (1986: 239).

Closely related to the Greek view of ethics, ethical action demands *stylization* which is an aesthetics of existence. In this sense, ethical self-creation of one's life as a work of art extends Nietzsche's concept that life has value as an aesthetic achievement and that one must give style to one's life by integrating the diffuse nature of oneself into a coherent whole. The question of style was crucial in ancient experience: stylization of one's relationship to oneself, style of conduct, and stylization of one's relationship to others. In the Greco-Roman empire of the second and third centuries, style was regarded as a moral code (Foucault, 1989s: 319). According to Davidson, this theme of aesthetics as involving a *style of existence* is another of Foucault's central ideas in his later writings[2] (1994: 70–71). "Styles of existence" refers to how one lives a life philosophically. The problem of ethics is in choosing a *style* of life. As Paul Veyne notes, "*style* does not mean distinction here; the word is to be taken in the sense of the Greeks, for whom artist was first of all an artisan and a work of art was first of all a work" (Davidson, 1994: 67). One of Foucault's concerns was in the style of life of the homosexual community by which he sought to "advance . . . a homosexual *askēsis* that would make us work on ourselves and invent, I do not say discover, a manner of being that is still improbable" (Foucault, 1989b: 206, cited in Davidson, 1994: 72). Hence, as Davidson points out, the homosexual style of life involves new forms of friendship and yields "a culture and an ethics aimed at the creation of a homo-sexual mode of life" (1994: 72).

Ethical action presupposes a certain political and social structure with respect to liberty. According to Foucault, "liberty is the ontological condition of ethics. But ethics is the deliberate form assumed by liberty" (1991a: 4). For liberty or civic freedom to exist, there must be a certain level of liberation conceived as the absence of domination. In this, Foucault disputes the view "more or less derived from Hegel" in terms of which "the liberty of the individual would have no importance when faced with the noble totality of the city" (5). The concern for liberty as expressed in ancient societies— in not being a slave, for instance—was a basic, constant issue during eight centuries of ancient culture. We have there an entire ethics that turned about the care of the self, premised on liberty, and that gave ancient ethics its distinctive form (5). Thus the subject's activity is intrinsically mediated through power which coexists with freedom in that relationships of power are changeable relations that can modify themselves. But where states of domination result in relations of power being fixed "in such a way that they are perpetually asymmetrical [then the] margin of liberty is extremely limited" (12). Foucault gives the example of the traditional conjugal relation in the eighteenth and nineteenth centuries: "we cannot say that there was only male power; the woman herself could do a lot of things: be unfaithful to him, extract money from him, refuse him sexually. She was, however, subject to a state of domination, in the measure where all that was finally no more than a certain number of tricks which never brought about a reversal of the situation" (12). Such states of domination entail relations of power which "instead of being variable and allowing different partners a strategy which alters them, find themselves firmly set and congealed. When an individual or social group manages to block the field of relations of power . . . to prevent all reversibility of movement . . . we are facing what can be called a state of domination" (3). In such a situation, liberty is "extremely confined or limited," and in this sense a certain degree of liberation is a precondition for liberty, which in turn is a precondition for the ethical practices of the self. Such ethical practices of self on self involve choices that are essentially moral choices, says Foucault (3).

Just as ethical work presupposes liberty, it also is intrinsically political. As Foucault explains, "it is political in the measure that non-slavery with respect to others is a condition: a slave has no ethics. Liberty is itself political. And then it has a political model, in the measure where being free means not being a slave to one's self and to one's appetites, which supposes that one establishes over one's self a certain relation of domination, of mastery, which was called *arche*—power, authority" (1991a: 6).

Practices of the self are political also in that they constitute relations of power, they are ways of controlling and limiting. As such they raise the problem of the abuse of power, when one imposes on others "one's whims, one's appetites, one's desires."

There we see the image of the tyrant or simply of the powerful and wealthy man who takes advantage of his power and his wealth to misuse others, to impose on them undue power. But one sees—at least that is what the Greek philosophers say— that this man is in reality a slave to his appetites. And the good ruler is precisely the one who exercises his power correctly, i.e., by exercising at the same time his power on himself. And it is the power over self which will regulate the power over others . . . if you care for yourself correctly, i.e., if you know ontologically what you are . . . then you cannot abuse your power over others. (Foucault, 1991a: 8)

The care of the self thus posits a politically active subject, involving practices of the self which include governance as well as the problems of practical politics. These in turn involve managerial imperatives, including decision making, the interpretation and application of rules, gambits, risks, knowing when to act and when to hold back, or being able if necessary to attack or defend. These skills required *autarkeia* (self-sufficiency) which pertained in the ancient schools to a form of internal freedom "located in the faculty of judgement, not in some psychologically thick form of introspection" (Davidson, 1994: 76–77).

Hence the care of the self does not just refer to "attention to oneself" in the narrow sense; nor is it concerned solely with the avoidance of mistakes and dangers; nor does it designate primarily an attitude toward one's self or a form of awareness of self. Rather, it designates a "regulated occupation, a work with its methods and objectives" (Foucault, 1986a: 50; 1997b: 95). This work is by its very nature political, for it contains integral to it notions concerning the management of self and others. This is evident, says Foucault, in the meaning of the word *epimeleia* and its various uses. Xenophon employs the word to designate the work of a master of the household who supervises its farming, and it is a word also used to pay ritual homage to the dead and to the gods. In addition, Dio of Prusa uses it to refer to the activity of the sovereign who looks after his people and leads the city-state. Also, in the comparison of Plato's *Alcibiades* with texts from the first and second centuries, Foucault points out that the care of the self is related to politics, pedagogy, and self-knowledge (1986a: 50; 1997b: 95).

CARE OF THE SELF/KNOWLEDGE OF THE SELF

For Foucault, "care of the self" precedes "knowing the self." In the cultures of Antiquity, philosophy revolved about the self, and knowledge of the world came afterward and as support for the care of the self (Foucault, 1986a: 14). Thus the Ancients' concern for care of the self can be actualized against the modernist concern for truth. Philosophy reversed the priority of caring for self over the Delphic principle of knowing the self (*gnōthi seautou*). In Greek and Roman texts, the injunction of having to know oneself was always associated with the other principle of the care of the self, and it was that need to care for oneself that brought the Delphic maxim into operation (Foucault, 1997e: 226). Foucault maintains that it is implicit in all Greek and Roman cultures and has been explicit since Plato's *Alcibiades*. Thus concern with care of the self was present in the Socratic dialogues, in Xenophon, in Hippocrates, and in the Neoplatonist tradition from Albinus on. One had to occupy oneself with oneself before the Delphic principle could be brought into action. Hence, "there was a subordination of the second principle to the former" (Foucault, 1997e: 226).

Foucault gives several examples (228–230). The first philosophical elaboration of the concern with taking care of oneself Foucault finds in Plato's *Alcibiades 1*, where "taking care of oneself is its first principle" (229–230). In 127d of the *Alcibiades* we find the first appearance of the phrase *epi-*

meleisthai sautou, which expresses "something more serious than the simple fact of paying attention to oneself" (1997e: 230). Socrates shows the ambitious young man that it is quite presumptuous of him to want to take charge of the city, or even manage his affairs, unless he has first learned to take care of himself (1986a: 44). In the *Apology* it is as a master of the art of care of the self that Socrates presents himself to his judges (44). Care of the self thus involves various things: taking pains with one's holdings and one's health. It is always a real activity and not simply an attitude (1997e: 230). It is used in reference to a farmer tending his fields, his cattle, and his house, or to the occupation of the ruler in taking care of the city and citizens. In addition, it is also used as a medical term to signify the fact of caring (1986a: 50, 1997e: 230).

In *Alcibiades 1,* concern for the self, says Foucault, is related to defective pedagogy—one that concerns political ambition at a particular moment. In the remainder of the text, Plato explores two questions—first, what is the nature of the self of which one has to take care? and, second, what is the nature of that care? The answer to the first question is that the self is not a substance but a form of activity. The answer to the second is that to take care of oneself consists of knowing oneself. In this Plato gave priority to the Delphic maxim "know yourself," which eventually absorbed the principle of caring for the self (Foucault, 1997c: 231).

While the privileged position of "know yourself" is characteristic of all Platonists, later in the Hellenistic and Greco-Roman periods this is reversed: the accent was not on knowing yourself but on caring for yourself. Hence "in the Hellenistic and imperial periods, the Socratic notion of 'the care of the self' became a common universal philosophical theme" (231), accepted as a primary orientation by Epicurus and his followers, by the Cynics, and by Stoics such as Seneca, Rufus, and Galen (232).

Although with Descartes, "it is striking to find that in the *Méditations* there is exactly this same spiritual care to accede to a mode of being where doubt would not be allowed and where finally we would know," it is *in fact* with Descartes that this "mode of being is entirely determined by knowledge, and it is as access to a knowing subject . . . that philosophy would define itself" (1991a: 14).

Until the sixteenth century truth had a price: "no access to truth without ascesis." Furthermore "in western culture up to the sixteenth century, asceticism and access to truth are always more or less obscurely linked" (Foucault, 1997d: 279):

Even if it is true that Greek philosophy founded rationality, it always held that a subject could not have access to the truth if he did not first operate upon himself a certain work that would make him susceptible to knowing the truth—a work of purification, conversion of the soul by contemplation of the soul itself. . . . But the extraordinary thing in Descartes' texts is that he succeeded in substituting a subject as founder of practices of knowledge for a subject constituted through practices of the self. (278–279)

With Descartes, then, the link between care of the self and knowing the self is broken:

Evidence is substituted for ascesis at the point where the relationship to the self intersects the relationship to others and the world. The relationship to self no longer needs to be ascetic to get into relation to the truth. It suffices that the relationship to the self reveals to me the obvious truth of what I see for me to apprehend the truth definitively. Thus, I can be immoral and know the truth. . . . With Descartes direct evidence is enough. (279)

TRANSFORMATIONS

Compared to Greek life in Plato's time, in the Hellenistic and Greco-Roman periods, the specific form of caring for the self differed in the sense that it was no longer exclusively a preparation for political life. Rather, in the latter periods it became a way of life and a universal principle based on the idea that one must leave politics in order to take care of oneself. Such developments were related to broader material changes in politics and culture associated with the decline of the city-states as autonomous entities, a decline that started around the third century B.C. This in turn led to a change in the role of the citizenry which saw a movement of a "retreat into the self" and a growing individualism that accorded increasing importance to the private aspects of existence, to the values of personal conduct, and to the interest that people focused on themselves (1986a: 41–42). Individualism, in this sense, refers (1) to a particular attitude, characterized by the "absolute value attributed to the individual in his singularity and by the degree of independence conceded to him vis-à-vis the group to which he belongs and the institutions to which he is answerable" (42); (2) to the "positive valuation of private life, that refers to the importance granted to family relationships, to forms of domestic activity and to the domain of patriarchal interests" (42); as well as (3) to the intensity of the relations to self. Thus in Roman times:

Whereas formerly ethics implied a close connection between power over oneself and power over others, and therefore had to refer to an aesthetics of life that accorded with one's status, the new rules of the political game made it more difficult to define the relations between what one was, what one could do, and what one was expected to accomplish. The formation of oneself as the ethical subject of one's own actions became more problematic. (84)

The new rules of the political game were ushered in because of the rise of centralized imperialism under the Empire. One must approach the issue of explaining the changes that occurred in terms of the "organisation of a complex space": imperial society was "more flexible," "more differentiated," "less rigidly hierarchized" than was Athenian society (Foucault, 1986a: 82). As a consequence, new forms of the political game emerge which amount to forms of privatized retreat (85). There is a "return to oneself" in Hellenistic and Roman thought which is in part an alternative to the civic activity and political responsibilities of Athenian society, and which were marked by certain "withdrawal behaviors" and problematized political behavior in certain crucial ways (86). The importance of starting with the self as a basis for political rule becomes emphasized. Hence, Foucault cites Plutarch, who stresses that before they can be involved in public life it is necessary that the individual must "retreat within himself"; that before he can be involved in political rule he must "set his soul straight" and "properly establish his own *ēthos*" (91–92). Thus, in the Hellenistic period and at the beginning of the Empire, the three types of authority— over self, household, and others—became modified, and a growth of public constraints and prohibitions saw an individualistic withdrawal into private life (96). Hence, there is a crisis of the subject (96). Self-knowledge now becomes just one aspect of care of the self, and a medical model was substituted for Plato's pedagogical model, that is, the care of the self becomes permanent medical care. The goal of the care of the self becomes the goal of the complete achievement of life. The dominant form of pedagogical relation also shifted away from the importance placed on dialectic as dialogue to a master–student relationship based not on question and answer but on silent listening. Truth was no longer "within one" as it was for Plato, but in the *logoi*, the teachings of the masters. The dominant practices of the self became to subjectivate these teachings, to assimilate, acquire, and transform these teachings into "a permanent principle of action" (1997e: 232).

Techniques of the self can be found in all cultures in different forms (Foucault, 1997d: 277). Just as Hellenistic and Roman culture differed from Athenian society in certain respects, so too there were changes with the emergence of Christian experience. In Christian culture, strict obligations of truth, dogma, and canon imposed a set of rules of behavior for a certain transformation of the self. Christian experience implied an obligation to obey rules as each person had an obligation to know who he was, to know what was happening inside of him, to acknowledge faults, to recognize temptations, and so on. There was also an obligation to disclose the self as was made obvious through the development of different forms of discovering and deciphering the truth about themselves, such as *exomologēsis* which constituted an obligation to recognize oneself as a sinner and penitent, an obligation that "rubs out the sin and yet reveals the sinner" (1997e: 244); through *exagoreusis*, a form of "self-examination . . . reminiscent of the verbalizing exercises in relation to the teacher–master of the pagan philosophical schools" (245) and incorporating the Christian spiritual principles of obedience and spirituality; and later in terms of the sacrament of penance and the confession of sins (243). Christian obedience constituted a "new technology of the self" that was more concerned with "inner hidden thought" related to "inner impurity" than with action, and that represented a renunciation of self and a surrender of autonomy.

From the eighteenth century to the present, these techniques of Christian obedience have been "reinserted in a different context by the so-called human sciences in order to use them without renunciation of the self but to constitute, positively, a new self" (Foucault, 1997e: 249). This constitutes a decisive break (249). While Descartes symbolizes this break, there are complex material causes. At a particular time, the "care of the self" became suspect, says Foucault. Caring for the self gradually became transformed into self-love, a form of egoism or individual interest, rather than linked, as it was in antiquity, to the care for others, involving necessary sacrifice of the self. This was partly due to developments within Christian experience, which involved new individualizing forms of power.

With Christianity, there occurred a slow, gradual shift in relation to the moralities of Antiquity, which were essentially a practice, a style of liberty. Of course, there had also been certain norms of behaviour that governed each individual's behaviour. But the will to be a moral subject and the search for an ethics of existence were, in Antiquity, mainly an attempt to affirm one's liberty and to give to one's own life a certain form in which one could recognise oneself, be recognised by others, and which even posterity might take as an example. This elaboration of one's own life as a personal work of art, even if it obeyed certain collective canons, was at the centre, it seems to me, of moral experience, of the will to morality in Antiquity, whereas in Christianity, with the religion of the text, the idea of the will of God, the principle of obedience, morality took on increasingly the form of a code of rules. . . . From Antiquity to Christianity, we pass from a morality that was essentially the search for a personal ethics to a morality as obedience to a system of rules (Foucault, 1988n: 49)

Foucault was interested in antiquity, not because he admired the lives of the Ancients, but with the idea of morality as obedience to a code of rules disappearing, the idea of morality as the search for an aesthetics of existence becomes more urgent. Although Foucault did not judge it desirable to reinstate Greek ethics (1989s: 319), he considered the element of ethical action involved in the work of self on self to be capable of taking on some contemporary significance. In this sense, as an interviewer suggested to him, his return to the Greeks can be seen as "shaking up the ground on which we think and live" (1989s: 319).

SELF AND OTHERS

The onset of modernity also involved forms of power in relation not only to religion but to philosophy, economics, politics, and culture. If at the start of this period there was an uncoupling of the imperative to "care for the self" from its twin to "know the self," with the latter imperative gradually eclipsing the former, the social effects of this process in undermining community and in promoting individualizing forms of power were also important for Foucault.

From Descartes to Husserl, the imperative to "know thyself" increasingly predominated over that to "take care of thyself". As the "care of the self" had traditionally passed through or entailed relationships with others, this disproportionate weighting of knowledge has contributed to the "universal unbrotherliness" that caused Weber so much pain and which he lacked the tools to do more than decry. For Foucault the equation of philosophical *askēsis* with renunciation of family, solidarity, and care for one's self and for others—as the price for knowledge—was one of our biggest wrong turnings. (Rabinow, 1997: xxv)

Although Kant reintroduced ethics as an applied form of procedural rationality after Descartes had cut ethics and reason loose, Kant's solution did not reintegrate knowledge of the self with the care of the self. Rather, it demanded a universal subject that nonetheless necessitated an ethical attitude whereby we recognize ourselves as universal subjects by conforming to universal rules (Foucault, 1997d: 279–280).

In the premodern period, care of the self implied the care for others, and thus the care of the self was always ethical in itself. As Foucault states in relation to the Greeks, "For the Greeks it is not because it is care for others that it is ethical. Care for the self is ethical in itself, but it implies complex relations with others, in the measure where this ethics of freedom is also a way of caring for others" (1991a: 7).

The relation of self for others was evident among the Greeks in relation to the responsibilities of governance in the home, of the city, or in interindividual relationships whether formal or based on friendship, or in educational relationships based on the "teachings of a master . . . a guide, a counsellor, a friend—someone who will tell you the truth" (Foucault, 1991a: 7). Thus, "the problem of relationships with others is present all along in this development of care for self" (7). As Horrocks and Jevtic explain, "the commitment of self . . . needed a greater understanding of how to balance 'withdrawal' and 'commitment' in order to find the purpose of man's existence in and out of the home" (1997: 157).

In one of his interviews, Foucault states his central interest in *The History of Sexuality*, Volume 3 as being "how an experience is formed where the relationship to self and to others is linked" (1989g: 296). Care of the self, then, is always at the same time concerned with care for others. Ethical practice in this sense is communal, and "ethos implies a relation with others to the extent that care for self renders one competent to occupy a place in the city, in the community . . . whether it be to exercise a magistracy or to have friendly relationships" (Foucault, 1991a: 7). Foucault notes how this indeed was the ethical imperative of Socrates. In Greek society, "One who cared for himself correctly found himself by that very fact, in a measure to behave correctly in relationship to others and for others. A city in which everyone would be correctly concerned for self would be a city that would be doing well, and it would find therein the ethical principle of its stability." There is a temporal and logical order, however: "One must not have the care for others precede the care for self. The care for the self takes moral precedence in the measure that the relationship to self takes ontological precedence" (7).

PRACTICES OF THE SELF

Practices of the self (*askēsis*) refer to "a set of practices by which one can acquire, assimilate, and transform truths into a permanent principle of action" (1997e: 235). The practices of caring for oneself involve self-knowledge (the Socratic-Platonic aspect), knowledge of rules of conduct or of principles that are truths, and various self-forming activities. Together these form a total orientation to life (235). Hence *epimeleia heautou* is not just a principle but a constant practice: "We may say that in all of ancient philosophy the care of the self was considered as both a duty and a technique, a basic obligation and a set of carefully worked-out procedures" (Foucault, 1997b: 95). Among the various techniques highlighted by Foucault as reasonably constant across history are the following:

1. One must study philosophy. Socrates advises Alcibiades to take advantage of his youth to look after himself and embark on a study of philosophy.

2. The care of the self must be constant and exercised throughout one's whole life (1986a: 49; 1997b: 96).

3. Attending to one's self is a "form of living" (1997b: 96). Alcibiades realized that he must attend to himself if he hoped to attend to others.

4. The common goal of these practices of self can be characterized by the principle of "conversion to one's self." This goal involves a turning-in upon oneself (*epistrophē eis heautou*) (1986a: 64). For Alcibiades this is to occur through the impulse by which the soul turns to itself and by which one's gaze is drawn "aloft"—toward the divine element (1997b: 96). For Seneca, Plutarch, and Epictetus the conversion is accomplished by "setting into one-self" and by "taking up residence in oneself." In addition, in a conversion to oneself one establishes various relations to oneself—to control oneself, to enjoy oneself (96). The conversion of self is the final goal of all the practices of self. It implies a shift of attention whereby the self gains access to the self, resulting in pleasure (1986a: 66).

5. *Pedagogy.* In the *Alcibiades*, the deficiencies of education meant that one must take care of it oneself, to provide a *formation* (Foucault, 1997b:

96). This includes (a) a critical function, relating to un-learning, getting rid of bad habits, or moderating the lessons of teachers and parents; (b) struggle—practices of the self involve "permanent battle" and "the individual must be given the weapons and the courage that will enable him to fight all his life" (97). Foucault draws on metaphors of the athletic contest and of warfare, the latter of which suggests that "the mind must be deployed like an army that the enemy is always liable to attack" (97); (c) a curative and therapeutic function, which aims to cure the diseases of the soul, which conceives of philosophy and medicine as a "single domain" (*mia chōra*) (97), and which links medicine and education, in the model of Epictetus, as an *iatreion* or "dispensary for the soul."

6. *A teacher*: Universally, Greek writing and the writings of the first and second centuries emphasized the importance of a teacher or director. Thus, "it was a generally accepted principle that one could not attend to oneself without the help of another" (97). The role of teacher could, however, take various forms: strictly educational organizations (e.g., Epictetus's school); private counselors, especially in Rome but also in family relations (Seneca writes a consolation to his mother on the occasion of his exile); relations of protection (the same Seneca looks after the career and education of the young Serenus); relations of friendship (Seneca and Lucilius); and so on (98). In Hellenistic and Roman times, too, there was a right to appeal for guidance and counseling to another. Galen, for instance, advises anyone who wants to take proper care of himself to seek the aid of another (1986a: 53).

7. *Askēsis*: This term refers to a set of exercises that enable us to keep control in the face of events that may take place; that enable us not to be overwhelmed or "thrown" by events or by emotions within us. The Greeks characterize two poles of these exercises or practices as *maletē* and *gymnasia*. *Maletē* refers to meditation (*meditatio*) suggestive of a preparation by improvisation of thinking over arguments, by conducting exercises in imagination, for the Stoics, *praemeditatio malorum*, or an ethical imaginary exercise. *Gymnasia* is at the opposite pole and refers to "training" in a real-life situation rather than an imaginary experience in thought. It can involve sexual abstinence, physical privation, and other rituals of purification. Between *maletē* and *gymnasia* lie a whole series of intermediate possibilities (1997b: 98–99).

8. *Logoi*: In order to keep control of ourselves, we need access to certain "discourses" understood as true discourses (*logoi*), or what Lucretius calls *veridicta dicta*, which enable us to face reality and protect ourselves when an unforeseen event occurs (99). The "nature" of these *logoi* was disputed, a dispute that had to do with the need for theoretical knowledge (*theoria*). The Epicureans emphasized knowledge of the "principles that govern the world," whereas the Stoics emphasized *dogmata* (theoretical principles related to practical prescriptions), and others stressed *concrete rules of behavior* (99–100).[3] A further question, says Foucault (100), concerns how these

logoi exist within us, whether by memory (Plutarch), or what the Greeks mean by *prokheiron ekhein,* or what Seneca and Plutarch suggest is the absorption of a truth so thoroughly that it becomes part of oneself—"an abiding, always-active, inner principle of action" internalized "through a more and more thorough appropriation" (101).

Such internalized true discourses, says Foucault (100), are not merely a simple memory that can be recalled. Foucault draws on various metaphorical indications that characterize such true discourses. Plutarch compares them to a medical metaphor (*pharmakon*) which provides us with protection against all the vicissitudes of existence. Marcus Aurelius compares them to an instrument kit that a surgeon uses. Plutarch refers to the metaphor of "friendship" which is "always at hand" and "the surest and best of which are those whose useful presence in adversity lends assistance to us" (100).

9. *Medicine*: The care of the self has a close correlation with medical thought and practice all the way back to Ancient Greek culture. By Greco-Roman times, this correlation was so strong that Plutarch was able to say, at the beginning of *Advice about Keeping Well,* that philosophy and medicine are concerned with "a single field" (*mia chōra*) (Foucault, 1986a:54). Both drew on a shared set of notions whose central element is the concept of pathos.

It applies to the passions as well as to physical illness, to the distress of the body and to the involuntary movement of the soul; and in both cases alike, it refers to a state of passivity, which for the body takes the form of a disorder that upsets the balance of its humours or its qualities and which for the soul takes the form of a movement capable of carrying it away in spite of itself. (54)

Hence Foucault says that the improvement, the perfecting of the soul that one seeks in philosophy, the *paideia* that philosophy is supposed to ensure, increasingly assumes a medical coloration (55).

10. *Education*: There is also a strong relation between care of the self and education of the self from Ancient Greece through to Greco-Roman times. In this sense, educating oneself and caring for oneself are interconnected activities, especially those aspects of the care of the self for which one seeks a teacher, making them forms of adult education—of *Erwachsenerziehung* (50). Educating the self also assumes a certain involvement with the medical cultivation of the self (55). Thus Epictetus sees his school as a "dispensary to the soul" and the philosopher's school as a "physician's consulting room" (*iatreion*) (55). The "crossover point" where agitation and troubles concern both body and soul appears to have been expressed through a particular and intense form of attention to the body (56).

11. *Methods of appropriation*: Foucault states that a series of technical questions crop up, 1997b: 100) concerning the methods of appropriation. Here he stresses (a) progressive exercises of memorization, and the impor-

tance of (b) listening, (c) writing, and (d) habitual self-reflection. In *The History of Sexuality*, Volume 3, he also considers (e) testing procedures, comprising various practical tests, such as abstinence (1986a: 58), and (f) exercises in self-examination in order to scrutinize the self (1986a: 61–62).

With reference to the various exercises of self-examination, these include the evaluation of one's progress, self-scrutinization, as well as the "necessary labor of thought upon itself to form a steady screening of representations, examining them, monitoring them, sorting them out" (63). "More than an exercise done at regular intervals, it is a constant attitude that one must take toward oneself." Hence, in the *Apology*, Socrates says that "an unexamined life (*anexetastos bios*) is not worth living" (63), while Epictetus uses the metaphor of the "night watchman" and the "money changer" to speak of the control of thought, advancing the view that "we must not accept mental representations unsubjected to examination" (63).

With reference to "listening," Foucault compares Socrates, who questions people, trying to get them to say what they know, to the Stoics and Epicureans, who stress silence and listening by the disciple. Thus Plutarch or Philo of Alexandria develop a set of rules for proper listening covering such subjects as the physical posture to take, how to direct one's attention, as well as the way to retain what has been said (1997b: 101).

With reference to writing, Foucault includes the cultivation of personal writing, taking notes, conducting conversations, reflecting on what one hears or does, as well as keeping notebooks (what the Greeks call *hupomnēmata*). He notes the importance of written notation as an indispensable element in the ascetic life in the cultures of antiquity and later. Writing about oneself performs a number of functions:

It palliates the dangers of solitude; it offers what one has done or thought to a possible gaze; the fact of obliging oneself to write plays the role of a companion by giving rise to the fear of disapproval and to shame . . . what others are to the ascetic in a community, the notebook is to the recluse . . . the constraint that the presence of others exerts in the domain of conduct, writing will exert in the domain of inner impulses of the soul. (Foucault, 1997c: 207–208)

Drawing from characters such as Seneca, Plutarch, and Marcus Aurelius, sees Foucault self-writing as playing a role very close to that of confession to the priest. Self-writing played a role in the cultivation of the self prior to Christianity, serving to enforce "its close link with companionship, its application to the impulses of thought, its role as a truth test" (208). Self-writing requires exercise (*askēsis*). So the art of living (*tekhnē tou biou*) requires an *askēsis* that must be understood as a training of the self by the self.

Compared to practices such as abstinence, memorization, self-examination, meditation, silence, and listening to others, writing came rather late, but it came to play a considerable role. "By means of this nightly

description an important step is taken towards the description of the self"
(Foucault, 1997d: 275). Writing came into vogue in Plato's time for personal and administrative use (272) and permitted a politics of the self: "the
ancients carried on this politics of themselves with these notebooks just as
governments and those who manage enterprises administered by keeping
registers" (272). Foucault points out that the texts from the imperial epoch
of Greco-Roman culture also placed a good deal of emphasis on writing as
evidenced by Seneca and Epictetus. For Epictetus, though offering an exclusively oral teaching, writing was nonetheless emphasized as a "personal
exercise." For Epictetus, Foucault observes (1997c: 208–209), writing appears regularly associated with "meditation, with that exercise of thought
on itself that reactivates what it knows, calls to mind a principle, a rule, an
example, reflects on them, assimilates them, and in this manner prepares
itself to face reality" (209).

Foucault believed that writing is associated with *thought* in two different
ways:

One takes the form of a linear "series": it goes from meditation to the activity of
writing and from there to *gumnazein*, that is, to training and trial in a real situation—
a labor of thought, a labor through writing, a labor in reality. The other is circular:
the meditation precedes the notes which enable the rereading which in turn re-
initiates the meditation. In any case, whatever the cycle of exercise in which it takes
place, writing constitutes an essential stage in the process to which the whole *askēsis*
leads: namely, the fashioning of accepted discourses, recognised as true, into rational
principles of action. As an element of self-training, writing has, to use an expression
that one finds in Plutarch, an *ethopoietic* function: it is an agent of the transformation
of truth into *ēthos*.

Keeping notebooks (*hupomnēmata*) is also important as an aid to *memory*:

Their use as books of life, as guides for conduct, seems to have become a common
thing for a whole cultivated public. One wrote down quotes in them, extracts from
books, examples and actions that one had witnessed or read about, reflections or
meanings that one had heard or that had come to mind. They constituted a material
record of things read, heard, or thought, thus offering them up as a kind of accumulated treasure for subsequent rereading and meditation. They also formed a raw
material for the drafting of more systematic treatises, in which one presented arguments and means for struggling against some weakness (such as anger, envy, gossip,
flattery) or for overcoming some deficient circumstance (a grief, an exile, ruin, dis-
grace). (1997c:209–210)

These *hupomnēmata* should not be seen simply as a memory support or as
"private" but serve as supports to friendship, advice, public documents, and
for "truth production." Hence, the aim of *hupomnēmata* is "to make one's
recollection of the fragmentary logos, transmitted through teaching, listening, or reading, a means of establishing a relationship of oneself with one-

self" (211). Writing prevents *stultitia* which exclusive attention to reading produces (212). Stultitia is mental agitation or distraction involving constant and frequent change of opinion and weakness in the face of events because the mind is prevented from providing a fixed point for itself in the possession of an acquired truth. Hence writing was seen as necessary for the soul, and hence *hupomnēmata* must be a regular and deliberate practice.

12. *Parrhésia*: In his last lectures at the Collège de France, in his interpretations of various works by Plato,[4] Foucault argues that Socratic *parrhésia*, the practice of truth telling, is a specifically ethical practice. *Parrhésia* has the objective of inciting each person to be concerned with their own self; thus it was a moral virtue as opposed to a political virtue (Flynn, 1991: 102). In this sense, "truth telling involves the presence of an other. . . . What was expected in the case of telling the truth about oneself was that the other likewise be a truth teller, not a flatterer or coward (this was the condition of the parrhesiastic 'contract' established between the two parties)" (Flynn: 103). Foucault distinguishes different basic modalities of truth telling relating to the prophet, the sage, the teacher-technician, and the parrhesiast. Each is concerned with a different form of truth—as destiny, as being, as *technē*, and as *ēthos* (103–104). Socrates could play each of these roles, but he was depicted by Plato primarily as a parrhesiastic, says Flynn. Although each of the four modes of speaking the truth has maintained a different degree of dominance and importance in different societies at different historical times, in the Western philosophical tradition truth telling has primarily concerned being and *ēthos* (104).

CONCLUSION

Foucault wins Richard Rorty's (1991) approval when he speaks of aesthetic self-invention; yet Rorty misinterprets Foucault, downplaying the political and radical implications of his work and understating the Aristotelian sense of community that Foucault directs our attention to. Rorty presents a "private-aestheticist" reading of Foucault, which is a reading "in the tradition of liberal irony we have come to associate with Rorty" (Norris, (1993: 46).

Whether Foucault's scholarship in regard to the Ancients is at times inaccurate, as Pierre Hadot (1992) questions, is an issue that is not disputed here. According to Hadot, Foucault makes several errors in his interpretation and assessment of ancient culture. Hadot notes "some inexactitude" (226) in Foucault's presentation of the ethic of the Greco-Roman world as an "ethic of pleasure," specifically Foucault's failure to distinguish pleasure (*voluptus*) from joy (*gaudium*) in the works of Seneca; his lack of emphasis on the themes of divinization, the pursuit of wisdom, and "belonging to the Whole of the human community, to the cosmic Whole" (227); his lack of attention to the Epicureans; his interpretation of the function of *hupomnēmata* as inclining the soul toward meditation of the past, rather, as Hadot

(228) claims, to promote pleasure in the meditation of the present moment. As Hadot puts it:

> It is not, then, as Foucault thought . . . by writing and reading disparate thoughts that the individual forges his spiritual identity. First, as we have seen, these thoughts are not disparate, but chosen for their coherence. Secondly—and most importantly—the point was not to forge a spiritual identity by writing but to free oneself from one's individuality, to raise oneself to universality. It is therefore inaccurate to talk of "writing about the self"; not only is it not oneself that one is writing about, but also the writing does not constitute the self: as in other spiritual exercises, it changes the level of the self; it universalizes it. (Hadot, 1992: 229)

Hadot accuses Foucault of representing a "new form of dandyism" and of advancing a conception of the self that was "too purely aesthetic" (230). Yet, at the same time, Hadot (226) appreciates why Foucault may have glossed over some aspects. His return to an examination of ancient cultures was not simply an historical study but "was meant also to offer contemporary man a model of life" (226). Hadot concedes that because Foucault saw themes such as universalization as problematic and divinization as too individualistic, he may well have parenthesized them as lacking importance within the problematization of self related to the present conjuncture of forces within which he wrote. As Foucault states to Gilles Barbadette, "the search for styles of existence as different as possible from each other appears to me to be one of the points around which contemporary research could be initiated in particular groups in the past" (1989s: 330).

Foucault's treatment of ethics is, then, an "education of the self" based on a conception of *ēthos* which he derives from an examination of ancient cultures: a culturation of life stages through practices of aesthetic self-fashioning which allow the individual a measure of autonomy in the context of a broader community. In this Foucault reexamines the uses of pleasure in the Greek and Greco-Roman works in order to promote an "art of living" (*tekhnē tou biou*).[5]

Whether Foucault's vision is "too purely aesthetic," as Hadot claims, is disputable in that the aesthetic form of the Enlightenment must be seen as supplementing the critical form, as has been dealt with earlier, which was also essential in Foucault's conception. The aesthetic form is established on the basis of surpassing Enlightenment claims in order to create new forms of autonomy and new types of society. For Foucault aesthetic self-creation is an alternative to Kantian practical reason—in fact to all of modernist ethics—because it assists us in viewing ethical life as a form of self-creation rather than as a form of self-knowledge.

NOTES

1. *Les lettres greques en Occident de Macrobe à Cassiodore* (Paris: E. de Boccard, 1943).

2. Foucault acknowledges a debt in his use of *style* to Peter Brown, *The Making of Late Antiquity* (Boston: Harvard University Press, 1978). See Foucault (1989s: 320).

3. Foucault cites Seneca, *Lettres à Lucilius* (trans. H. Noblot), Paris: Belles Lettres, 1945–1964, vol. 4, pp. 27–50; *Ad Lucilium Epistulae Morales* (trans. R. M. Gunmere), Cambridge, Mass.: Harvard University Press, 1962, vol. 2, pp. 395–449.

4. *The Apology, Crito,* and *Phaedo.*

5. Foucault was attracted to both Classical Greek and especially Greco-Roman antiquity. One of the main Greek sources of influence on Foucault's ethics are the Stoics, although as Paul Veyne puts it,

clearly no one will accuse him of aspiring to renew the Stoic ethics of the Greeks . . . the solution to a contemporary problem will never be found in a problem raised in another era, which is not the same except through a false resemblance. . . . From one age to another problems are not similar, any more than is nature or reason; the eternal return is also an eternal departure (he had been fond of this expression of Char's); only successive valorizations exist. (cited in Davidson, 1997: 226)

In spite of Veyne's comment, there are parallels between Foucault's approach and that of the Stoics, especially with regard to the issue of freedom and the resolution of determinism and free will. There are, for instance, parallels between Foucault's treatment of the issue with the general approach of writers such as Chrysippus (see related comment in Chapter 11, note 2). The problem of determinism and free will only became acute in the post-Aristotelian period in Stoic philosophy as the earlier pre-Socratics, such as Leucippus and Democritus, showed no awareness of the problem. In addition, Epicurus's attempted resolution was so unsatisfactory that it provides few insights, but like liberalism in the modern era, comprises an assertion of free will while ignoring the sheer weight of the evidence of man's dependence on causal factors and of his constitution by them. Relatedly, the Stoic conceptions of the "continuum" and of the "interdependence of things" are much more in accord with Foucault's materialism than is the approach of the Epicureans. Aristotle too had a notion of "continuum," although it was a more passive conception than that of the Stoics, which represented the whole cosmos as constituted of parts in dynamic interplay. Attributing exclusive affinity between Foucault and specific schools of thought is problematic due to his general eclecticism, however, as he is also at times influenced by Aristotle, and there also appear affinities or parallels to various of the pre-Socratics such as Anaximander and Anaxagoras. While any attempts to be more specific on Foucault's relation to the Greeks would require further study, one important common thread which animates Foucault, like that which animated Canguilhem, is the postulation of an active, intelligent life force, residing not in an ontology of reason (Plato, Descartes) or in a transcendental subject (Kant) or in a psychological subject, but inherent in *matter*. The *a prioris* is not in other words on the aside of the subject, but on the side of the material world and immanent in it. Hence, life is meaning inscribed in matter. It is not formal, but material.

Chapter 10

Foucault's Influence in Educational Research

Foucault has had a major impact on the social sciences and a smaller, yet growing, impact on educational studies. In 1989 James Marshall could note that "educationalists had little to say on the subject" (1989: 98). In reviewing the works influenced directly by Foucault, Marshall refers to studies by Jones and Williamson (1979), Hoskin (1979), as well as the critical psychology of Henriques, Hollway, Urwin, Venn, and Walkerdine (1984). In the few years after Marshall made this observation, the situation began to alter. Publications by Cherryholmes (1988), Ellesworth (1989), McLaren and Hammer (1989), Walkerdine (1989), Davies (1989), Marshall (1989, 1990), Ball (1990), Miller (1990), Pagano (1990), Aronowitz and Giroux (1991), Britzman (1991), Lather (1991), McLaren (1991), Giroux (1991), and Olssen (1993), to name just some, established a veritable explosion of works influenced by Foucault or by post-structuralism generally. Indeed, since 1991 the influence of Foucault and post-structuralism on education has continued to grow, affecting almost every area of study, although Marshall's observation that "it is far from clear that the theoretical radicalness of the work has been grasped" (1989: 98) would still seem to be relevant. In addition, notwithstanding an increasing volume of literature, in many places Foucault's ideas are still marginalized within the mainstream discourses of educational scholarship.

Many of the works that appeared in the late 1980s and early 1990s relating Foucault to education simply sought to explain the relevance of Foucault's distinctive orientation to education, or of post-structuralism generally (e.g., Cherryholmes, 1988, or Marshall, 1989). Others sought some sort of integration or synthesis between post-structuralism and critical theory (Giroux, 1990; Aronowitz & Giroux, 1991; Lather, 1991; Ellesworth, 1989), proposing post-structuralism as a theory of emancipation toward a more equitable society. The appeal of Foucault, as of other post-structuralist writers, was that he problematized the meta-narratives of the Enlightenment and advocated the possibility of treating all knowledge and forms of pedagogy as *contingent, specific, local,* and *historical* (Aronowitz & Giroux, 1991: 81). It also permitted the realization of historically constituted forms of knowledge and pedagogy as "regimes of truth" (Gore, 1993: Ch. 6) without resorting to "top-heavy" critical meta-narratives such as Marxism.

Of relevance to educational psychology, the study by Henriques, Hollway, Urwin, Venn, and Walkerdine (1984) explored the way in which psychology is involved in particular constructions of the individual and society. After mapping the effects of nineteenth-century individualism on psychology, the authors seek to demonstrate, utilizing Foucault and other post-structuralist thinkers, the way educational psychologies such as those of Piaget contribute to the normalization and surveillance of children. Much of the problem, it is argued, stems from the ontological conception of the individual, which results from a certain model of individual and society relations that dominated the Victorian context out of which psychology developed. Such a model of the person warps both psychology's development and its operations. In order to correct the individualist bias of Western psychology, the authors seek to explore the applicability of various sociological theories in their attempt find a more appropriate model of "individual-society" relations as a basis for the discipline. Rejecting Marxist theories as being too "totalistic," focusing on structures of the economy as mechanically determining individuals responses and actions in a rigid way reflecting class interests, the authors utilize Foucault and other post-structuralists in order to represent individuals as constituted by dispotifs of discourse/practices with multiple sites of origin.

Also with respect to educational psychology, some of my own work (Olssen, 1993), utilizes Foucauldian theory in order to throw light on the origins of educational psychology by tracing it as a particular discourse to its emergence in the nineteenth century. My aim was to trace the way that educational psychology, like psychology in general, contained deep within the "hard core" of its scientific research program the political ideology of seventeenth to nineteenth-century individualism. This ideology of individualism derived from three sources: (1) from political and economic liberalisms, emerging in the seventeenth century; (2) from the epistemological emphasis on methodological individualism, emerging in the sixteenth and seventeenth centuries; and (3) from the sciences of biology and evolution as they developed in the late eighteenth and nineteenth centuries. In each of these three areas, specific proposals (political obligation, scientific method) confounded various senses or forms of individualism—descriptive, moral, political—asserting what in essence was a *metaphysic of individualism* against the more social and communitarian metaphysic of the *ancien regime.* The implication of this was to fashion a conception of the individual as "proprietor of his own person and capacities," a conception that privileges *nature* over *nurture*, and that Foucault contends is fallacious in terms of both ontology and psychology. Yet without this conception of the "possessive individual" (Macpherson, 1962: 263), sciences like mental testing and individual difference psychology would never have gotten off the ground or become institutionalized as powerful forms of technical control within Western education systems during the twentieth century.

Sciences like mental testing and educational psychology defined new ways of relating to the world, new means of administrative control, new ways of defining and talking about people—in short, new means of normalization and surveillance by which order and discipline in modern Western nations is made effective. Through these new sciences, individual human subjects were represented in biologically essentialist terms, and societies were depicted as "reflecting" or "adapting to" the real natures of their citizens. The doctrine of ontological individualism in which the human subject was represented as "pre-social," because of its dominance in European culture at the end of the nineteenth century, made possible the emergence of a discipline such as educational psychology. Such an individualism has in turn had major consequences for its development as an empirical science. Put another way, the emergence of educational psychologies in the second half of the nineteenth century reflected the cultural and political postulates of Benthamite individualism and was something of a contradiction to the tide of collectivist thinking which became ascendant in the final decades of the nineteenth century. The cultural individualism that gave rise to policies of social amelioration based on self-help and individual enterprise was a central consequence of the Enlightenment prioritizing of the individual as the foundation stone of political and civic obligation. Rather than see individuals as perfectible only in the context of a society, as had been maintained by leading thinkers from the time of ancient Greece to the seventeenth century, with the Enlightenment faith in subject-centered reason came the view that we can understand individuals only by perfecting individuals. Similarly, the view that we can understand individuals only by understanding the form of society in which they live was replaced by the contention that we can understand society only through an understanding of its individual members.

As I also pointed out (Olssen, 1993), although a Foucauldian approach to psychology might well support a "limited program," as Wundt originally proposed, confining psychology to neuroscience, the study of "higher mental faculties" would be left to history and sociology. As I stated:

Consistent with developing lines of thought in Germany, Wundt viewed the scope of human experimental psychology as distinctly limited. Believing that mind was a social phenomenon, he agreed with his contemporary, the sociologist Durkheim, that the social was not reducible to the individual and that the best way to study the concepts of consciousness was through the study of what Durkheim called "social facts"—myths, traditions and customs. (Olssen, 1993: 157)

In the nineteenth century both Marx and Durkheim took the view that society is independent to individuals and that the individual mind is socially and historically constructed. Against those theorists who argued that the individual is "pre-social" or biologically constituted, Marx argued that the individual is *always already social*: that is, the individual is a social being from the first. As he summed it up in the preface to *A Contribution to the Critique of Political Economy*, "it is not the consciousness of men that determines their existence, but their social existence that determines their consciousness" (Marx, 1968: 21). The dual position with respect to the ontological privileging of individual or society is clearly expressed in this quotation.

Durkheim also claimed the importance of society over the individual, arguing that no study of the individual can give us an understanding of society. In his *Rules of Sociological Method* (1933), he argued that, although society is made up of individuals, it is different and distinct from the component parts. If we think of language, or marriage, or of the various legal or moral codes in the world, then it becomes clear, argued Durkheim, that by studying the individual person we could never come to an understanding of such institutions. Yet without studying these structural features of society, we cannot understand the individual either. By the term "social," Durkheim meant those "general" or "collective" dimensions of reality as they are expressed in patterns or structures. Certain ideas or value systems, such as Christian thought, can be found throughout society and persist for a long period of time. In many cases they are more enduring than the individual members of the society. They were there before the individual was born and will be there after he or she is dead. When the individual comes into the world, reality in the form of language, belief systems, schooling, and so on is already constituted. It is not an immutable natural state of affairs but is historically constructed and is different in different societies. Durkeim maintained, that even an act as intimately personal as suicide was a social rather than a psychological phenomenon. In his study on suicide, Durkheim argues and presents evidence for the hypothesis that the cause of suicide is the degree of social and moral integration of the society: it was not something that could be explained by looking at individuals.

The ontological priority of the individual was reinforced by a broad spectrum of social and political theory and is closely tied to social, economic, and political changes from the sixteenth century onward. The Reformation and the attendant Protestant religion gave rise to a new spirit of individualism whereby each individual could communicate directly with God and was solely responsible for his (or even her) salvation. With the expansion of empire, the growth of science, and the Enlightenment belief in progress, the idea that the individual was master of his fate was further encouraged. This was partly inspired by the successful methods of the physical sciences which employed mathematical laws and measurement quantification, and based itself on a metaphysic of atomism, reducing complex physical phenomena to their smallest component particles. Believing that the social world could be studied in the same way was to generally endorse the search for the truth of life in the individual.

Classical liberal individualism encompassed all aspects of life. In *The Wealth of Nations*, published in 1776, Adam Smith sought to explain laissez-faire capitalism as a consequence of the natural competition of the individual in much the same way, with respect to basic postulates, that Darwin later sought to explain the processes of natural selection at work in the origins and evolution of species. In political philosophy, John Stuart Mill was to frame a political conception of liberty to safeguard political freedom within a laissez-faire approach to capitalism. Others, such as Jeremy Bentham and Herbert Spencer, were to legitimize "non-intervention," "individual liberty," and "unregulated competition" as being part of the *natural order of things*, reinforcing what was an ascendant view of society as a consequence of solely individual initiatives.

C. B. Macpherson has described the strain of thought in his book *The Political Theory of Possessive Individualism* (1962) and shows how, through a variety of thinkers from Thomas Hobbes to John Locke English political and social thought in the seventeenth century is characterized by the idea of possessive individualism. This idea, says Macpherson, became axiomatic to liberal democratic thought and to scientific movements. During the eighteenth and nineteenth centuries it became an underlying and unifying assumption. Its "possessive" quality is found in the condition of the individual as essentially the proprietor of his (or presumably her) own person or capacities, owing nothing to society for them. Thus for theorists such as Thomas Hobbes, John Locke, Adam Smith, Herbert Spencer, Jeremy Bentham, John Stuart Mill, and Francis Galton, the individual "pre-figures" society, and society will be happy and secure to the extent that individuals are happy and secure. Not only does the individual own his or her own capacities, but, more crucially, each is morally and legally responsible for himself or herself. Freedom from dependence on others means freedom from relations with others except those relations entered into voluntarily out of self-interest. Human society is simply a series of market relations between self-interested subjects. For Adam Smith it is guided by an "invisible hand." For John Locke society is a "joint stock company" of which individuals are shareholders.

Paradoxically, while the impact of individualism was dominant in relation to the social, political, educational, and scientific ideas of the late nineteenth, early twentieth century, this period actually marked a major extension of the State's authority over every aspect of the individual's life and to every corner of society. The problems of urbanization, population increases, immigration, war, and a major concern with eugenics (MacKenzie, 1979) gave rise to more regulation and control, leading to the State's encouragement of various forms of social research (see Abrams, 1968).

Notwithstanding this paradox, the impact of classical liberal individualism on psychology was secure. It can be summed up with reference to several features. Psychology took the individual as a unitary rational actor and as the primary object of investigation. *It was a science of the single case abstracted from culture.* In that social factors were important at all, they were simply seen as contaminating influences.

Biologism was one form of individualism and was central to the psychologies of individual differences and Freudianism. In individual difference psychology, almost no social influences were acknowledged at all, the genetic structure of the individual being seen as determining behavior and capacity in all important respects.

In Freud's theories, although environmental factors could act to affect development, the derivation and nature of development was determined by biologically shaped drives. The role of society was to serve to repress and constrain, and ultimately channel, these drives into socially useful activities. Freud's implicit theory of social structure was premised on the idea of conflict and aggression between individuals. In this sense he had a view of society similar to that held by Thomas Hobbes: a zero-sum model of competition and mutually excluding trade-offs between individuals motivated by chaotic psychic energies (Ingleby, 1987).

Cognitive developmental psychologies accorded biology a less direct role but still conceptualized the individual as a unitary rational actor, seeing behaviors, attitudes, emotions, language, and dispositions and so on as things *in* the individual and part of the individual's cognitive makeup. Development was seen as a consequence of *inner mechanisms* and capacities were viewed as individual and as logically distinct from social processes. Without a social perspective, cognitive psychology distorted the notion of development, reducing it to a series of cognitive rules.

Behaviorism was another form of individualism. Although the behaviorists rejected biology, stressing the environmental determination of behavior, the approach was still in accord with the dictates of methodological and liberal individualism. It was, in fact, the psychology of the single case *par excellence.* The focus was still on the individual as logically distinct from culture (Ingleby, 1987). Although individual dispositions could be modified by the environment, the nature of dispositions remains located firmly inside the child's immediate environment and this, as Ingleby puts it, "occludes social structure as effectively as the hereditarians" (Ingleby, 1987: 299). There was no recognition of structural or collective aspects of culture or society as impacting on individuals' lives at all.

In this sense, from a Foucauldian perspective, psychology is inadequate for the task of explaining the social nature of development, for it is premised on a fallacy in ontology constituted in modernism in terms of an episteme that excluded the possibility that an individual subject could be understood in terms of the externality of the structures of the social world. For Foucault, psychological science can be seen as a discursive formation that produced new categories and classificatory systems which became inscribed in the practices and organizational structures of daily life. In addition, it invented new concepts—intelligence, behavioral problem, reinforcement schedule, hyperactivity, ego control, the unconscious, stages of development, child-centered pedagogy, means analysis, scaling, normal development, slow development, and so on—which became in Foucauldian terms deeply implicated in producing the very reality that they claimed to discover. Hence the discourse of psychology formulates a way of organizing the world, and in doing so it positions people in relation to the categories and classifications it constructs.

In recent years there have been a number of more substantial analyses utilizing Foucauldian approaches to educational issues. In a number of papers and books spanning several years, James Marshall (1989, 1990, 1995, 1996a, 1996b) has presented a Foucauldian analysis of liberal education principles focusing on (1) personal autonomy, (2) notions of identity, (3) the adequacy of the liberal concept of authority, and (4) the idea of the improvement or progress of human beings through education or in society.

Maintaining the Foucauldian thesis that the autos or self has been constructed politically by power-knowledge, Marshall critiques the view that education is involved in the pursuit of personal autonomy or that rational autonomy is the aim of education. For Foucault, says Marshall, the pursuit of personal autonomy in such Enlightenment terms is a social construction and is destined to fail because it masks the fact that any such persons have been constituted by political acts. As Marshall puts it, "the notion of a self able to deliberate upon and accept laws so as to act autonomously as opposed to following laws heteronomously is a fiction, furnished upon the western world post-Kant as the basis for moral action but, for Foucault in the cause of governmentality" (1996a: 113). Rather, for Foucault, says Marshall, our conception of ourselves as "free agents" is an illusion, and he argues that liberal educators like P. H. Hirst, R. F. Dearden, and R. S. Peters, who advocate personal autonomy as a fundamental aim of education, do not understand how modern power, through the technologies of domination and of the self, has produced individuals who are governable. For Marshall, the very concepts that we use to construct our identities are such as to make independence and autonomy illusory. Hence education via governmentality affects the production of a new form of subject—those who believe they are free. Such an education simply introduces a new form of social control and socialization and new and more insidious forms of indoctrination where a belief in our own authorship binds us to the conditions of our own production and constitutes an identity that makes us governable. In that "selves" do emerge, it is as "pathologised" into certain types of human beings who are discursively constructed.

The human sciences have been pivotal here as technologies of the self in the construction of human subjects as autonomous. The human sciences have produced knowledge about man during the period of the Enlightenment. This, says Marshall, entails a "messy involvement":

> Man enters the scene as both speaking subject and as an object that is spoken about. As speaking subject, Man represents the very conditions of possibility of content knowledge about the object man. Foucault argues that Man as subject in the human sciences has a continuous messy involvement in knowledge about the object Man. Or, to put it another way, whereas the very conditions for the possibilities of knowledge should be separate from the contents of knowledge, or that there should be a dividing line between the transcendental and the empirical, Foucault believes that in the human sciences they are not and *cannot* be so divided. (1996a: 120)

In a related sense, utilizing Foucault's concept of governmentality, Marshall (1995, 1996a, 1996b) and Peters and Marshall (1996) examine the neo-liberal notion of the autonomous chooser as embodying a particular conception of human nature, as a model of the security of the state, and as a particular model of surveillance and control. Focusing on the massive changes in political policies regarding education, as well as other social services, which have taken place in New Zealand since 1987, Marshall develops a Foucauldian analysis of the reforms in terms of notions such as choice, quality, freedom, and autonomy. In a way similar to his analysis of autonomy as a liberal educational goal, what is presupposed in the notion of the autonomous chooser, says Marshall, is that the notion of autonomy needed to make choices, and the notion of needs and interests entailed as a result, have not been manipulated or imposed in some way upon the chooser but are the subject's own. A Foucauldian critique rejects such a possibility.

Further work on Foucault and education has been carried out in Australia by Ian Hunter (1994, 1996), who stresses the distinctiveness of Foucault's approach to the school as an apparatus for the social determination of subjectivity. For Foucault, says Hunter, historical phenomena are seen to emerge not as realizations of underlying principles or developmental laws but as contingent assemblages put together under "blind" historical circumstances. Foucault would not be concerned with education in reproducing labor power or ideology, says Hunter (1996: 47), but rather with the effects of the school through a variety of technologies of domination concerned with the disciplinary organization of the school: special architectures; devices for organizing space and time; body techniques; practices of surveillance and supervision; pedagogical relationships; procedures of administration and examination. Foucault thus forces us to consider that it is not educational principles but school premises and modes of organization that are important for understanding the constitution of subjectivity. And rather than representing the school as an agency of the economy or of the Repressive State Apparatuses, for Foucault it is a form of disciplinary and bureaucratic governance. It initially arose, says Hunter (149), from the pastoral disciplines whereby the production of a self-monitoring and self-regulating subject was made into a central disciplinary objective.

In the eighteenth century, says Hunter, the happiness of citizens and the highest good of the State were inseparable, premised on freedom within limits, assured property, and flourishing industry. (see Hunter, 1996: 155–156). With Kant the highest good became moral enlightenment, considered as a break from the "self-incurred tutelage" of medieval European society and a commitment to "self-realization," relying on the individual's own faculties of conscience and consciousness characteristic of the Enlightenment. For Kant the State should embody this rational and self-determining moral law. This begs the question of exactly how the State could fulfill the conditions of individual reason. As Hunter points out, Kant was happy to acknowledge Frederick the Great as the democratic embodiment of the people, thus defending in the final analysis an "army backed enlightenment" (156).

Notwithstanding such a paradox, Kant remained the champion of an ethical individualism and universalism which asserted the supremacy of the individual conscience as expressed in the categorical imperative. This meant in the final analysis that civic or governmental interests do not have a moral authority equivalent to the inner moral sense. This "make[s] it impossible for him to reach a positive historical understanding of the separation of governmental and intellectual-spiritual (*geistlich*) spheres" (Hunter, 1996: 157), resulting in a split between the "civic" and the "moral" person. Hence, while for Kant the State must encourage the creation of rational capacities in its citizens, Kantian philosophy also contains "two incompatible views: a *de facto* acknowledgement that rational conduct is an effect of the State's pacification and training of the population; and an unblinking faith of an intellectual elite that such conduct arises from intellectual self-reflection alone" (157). Herein lies the paradox between liberal and Marxist viewpoints: "For the liberal paradox of a community of rational individuals that uses schooling to form itself, and the Marxian dialectic of 'learning (human development) and choosing (human freedom)', are latter-day variants of the Kantian circle. Like Kant's, these views are incapable of reflecting on the school system as one of the arational, disciplinary means through which states began to form populations capable of civic conduct" (157).

Foucault's project, like those of Schiller, Hegel, and Marx before him, has been to challenge Kant's presumption of the "morally ultimate character of self-reflective personhood" (Hunter: 157), seeking instead to historicize

Kant by tying the development of the person to that of society. In this Foucault rejects both the Kantian and the Hegelian-Marxist view of the formation of the subject. The subject is neither "self-reflective" nor "incorporable" to history or class. Rather, says Hunter, Foucault focuses on the specific spiritual practices and disciplines through which individuals become "ethically self-concerned" and seek to compose themselves as subjects of their own conduct (158). Thus for Foucault the "reflective subject" is understood as a particular practice of the person deriving from the spiritual disciplines of the Greco-Roman and Christian cultures of the West—stoic self-testing; Christian interrogation of the flesh; the Catholic confessional; Protestant self-examination; sexual austerity; fasting—these are all inventions for taking an interest in ourselves as subjects of our own conduct.

Hunter says that from Foucault's viewpoint it is necessary to give up the idea that the subject might freely choose its own form "through a rational inspection of moral principles or competing versions of the good life." Freedom is possible with regard to individual action only after conduct has undergone moral problematization, but individuals cannot freely choose the form in which they will undergo problematization. Rather, individuals will be subject to dominant modes of the culture. Hunter draws on Weber's (1930) account of the rise of the Protestant ethic in the sixteenth and seventeenth centuries in order to provide a Foucauldian description of the exercise of spiritual training of the population. Fundamental to this development was the transfer of power of ethical determination from the priesthood to the population. Such a transfer involved the systematic use of devices for mass spiritual problematization. Hunter notes in particular the doctrine of predestination which he claims destroyed the certitude of salvation and encouraged the transmission of particular forms of ethical labor— practices of self-watchfulness, self control, special forms of devotional reading and writing—through which the faithful reassured themselves of their own ethical standing: "The result was a profound dissemination and individualization of Christian spirituality as ordinary members of flock were inducted into a practice of ethical life that made them 'personally' responsible for their own salvation" (159).

It is against this background that Hunter seeks to explain the rise of the first popular school systems in Europe by the churches as instruments for the intensification and dissemination of Christian spiritual discipline and pastoral guidance beginning in the continental States of Europe in the sixteenth and seventeenth centuries and reaching its height under eighteenth-century pietism and puritanism. Schooling then was a specifically religious effort by the Reformed Churches to Christianize the European peasantries, as a method of "injecting religion into daily life" (159). The object of pastoral pedagogy was not to produce "docile workers" or social automatons, and it cannot be understood as religious brainwashing, as Marxist historians are wont to do. Rather, it was to form the capacities required for individuals to comport themselves as self-reflective and self-governing persons. What critical historians fail to understand, and what Foucault corrects, says Hunter (160), is that the capacities of the self-reflective person emerge only *after* individuals have been initiated into the arts of self-concern and self-regulation. Foucault enables us to understand then the construction of "self-reflective personhood," not in Kantian terms, but as "the construction of that special pedagogical milieu in which such personhood is formed as a disciplined comportment" (161). The school's function was to transmit the disciplines of ethical self-concern and ethical labor into the daily life of the laity.

It was, says Hunter, Christian pedagogy's existence as a discipline, rather than as an ideology, that allowed it to slip its theological moorings and to reappear in the form of secular moral education. It effectively could become "humanist" pedagogy which utilizes the practices of ethical labor adopted and adapted from its Christian prototype. But for all that the self-reflective, self-regulating students that it forms are no less the product of an unconditional initiation into the discursive disciplines of conscience.

Based on such an analysis, Hunter suggests that a Foucauldian approach reinstates Weber against Marx. State schooling, rather than being represented as an expression of the interests and capacities of class politics, must be seen instead as the outcome of technical faculties of administration and as a vehicle for transmitting of pastoral pedagogy. It was through Christian pastoralism that the school disseminated the comportment of the self-reflective person, via a pedagogy of moral subjectification. Through a piece-meal series of exchanges between the State and the Christian pastorate, the school—through its architecture, pedagogy, and administration—became employed as an instrument of social governance of citizens and the spiritual disciplining of souls.

Foucauldian approaches to education provide a distinctive view of history and historical method which marks a radical departure and rejection from both Liberal and Marxist accounts of the emergence and functions of mass schooling in the Western world. Against Marxist and traditional critical accounts Foucault opposes all forms of materialist reductionism or explanation in terms of economic factors. Rather, his own approach stresses the multiplicity of material causes. Against Liberals he displaces the ontological priority placed on the individual as the authors of their own selves and the moral individualism that such an approach entails. Criticisms of Foucault's approach focus on the moral and epistemological relativism of his approach; on his approach to power, and by extension, on the consequences of the philosophical nominalism that underpins his analysis.

Chapter 11

Postscript:
Autonomy, History, Materialism

Christopher Norris takes issue with Foucault. While recognizing that Foucault is giving the subject a degree of autonomy, Norris finds it "hard to comprehend how the subject (in Foucault) could achieve any degree of autonomy, given the extent to which, on Foucault's own submission, this freedom is necessarily shaped or constrained by existing structures of regulative control" (1993: 32). Norris thus fails to see how Foucault can envisage "a realm of ethical values-of-choice, responsibility, and self determination," noting that "there still seems little room within this spartan regime for any notion of the 'subject' beyond what is produced by a clash of opposing values systems or an arena of endlessly contending discourses devoid of effective moral agency and choice" (33). For Norris, Foucault's subject is nothing much more than "a place-filler . . . a recipient of moral directives . . . a localized point of intersection . . . and a product of various contending forces" (34). Because in his later works Foucault speaks of ethical self-creation and autonomy, Norris accuses him of being inconsistent.

What emerges [in the final decades] is not so much a radical re-thinking of these issues as a shift in rhetorical strategy, one that allows [Foucault] to place more emphasis on the active, self-shaping, volitional aspects of human conduct and thought, but which signally fails to explain how such impulses could ever take rise, given the self's inescapable subjection to a range of pre-existing disciplinary codes and imperatives that between them determine the very shape and limits of its "freedom." (34–35)

Norris sees Foucault's post-structuralism as premised on the argument that subjectivity is a mere effect of various signifying systems or orders of discursive representation. And the doubt extends, he says, to Foucault's later writings in that Foucault continued to respect structuralist concepts even as he "insisted" that we "rethink" the question of the subject. Norris thus sees the pressure exerted by the structuralist paradigm as fatal in that it "generates strictly insoluble antimonies in the realm of ethical thought" (35).

Such criticisms, though commonly directed at Foucault, miss their mark, in Norris's case, by a fairly wide margin. Foucault doesn't see subjectivity entirely in terms of discursive formations and, as I have argued in earlier chapters, one of Foucault's central themes is against such a reductionism. Although he sees history and discourses as prior to and constitutive of the individual subject, the subject cannot be reduced to such discursive factors. As he says in *The Archaeology of Knowledge*:

If I suspended all reference to the speaking subject, it was not to discover laws of construction or forms that could be applied in the same way by all speaking subjects, nor was it to give voice to the great universal discourse that is common to all men at a particular period. On the contrary, my aim was to show what the differences consisted of, how it was possible for men, within the same discursive practice, to speak of different objects, to have contrary opinions . . . in short, I want not to exclude the problem of the subject, but to define positions and functions that the subject could occupy in the diversity of discourse. (1972: 200)

It must also be reasserted that Foucault never changed his orientation, as he himself insisted to be the case: "I have said nothing different from what I was already saying" (Racevskis, 1991: 28–29). He had in fact always been concerned about explaining the autonomy of the subject in the context of its embeddedness in social structures. With relation to *thought*, for instance, Foucault explains it as an original creative response in relation to social determinants:

For a domain of action, a behaviour, to enter the field of thought, it is necessary to have made it lose its familiarity, or to have provoked a certain number of difficulties around it. These elements result from social, economic, or political processes. But here their only role is that of castigation. They can exist and perform their action for a very long time, before there is effective problematization by thought. And when thought intervenes, it doesn't assume a unique form that is the direct result or the necessary expression of these difficulties; *it is an original or specific response*—often taking many forms, sometimes even contradictory in its different aspects—to these difficulties, which are defined for it by a situation or a context and which hold true as a possible question. (1984g: 388–389) (emphasis added)

Thought, then, arises as a unique event from a context of rules. Hence, it is always the case that "to a single set of difficulties, several responses can be made. . . . But what has to be understood is what makes them simultaneously possible: it is the point in which their simultaneity is rooted; it is the soil that can flourish them all in their diversity and sometimes in spite of their contradictions" (Foucault 1984g: 389).

Thomas Flynn claims that a "lingering uneasiness remains. . . . As Sartre reminded the Marxist 'economists', Flaubert may be a *petit bourgeois*, but not all *petit bourgeois* are Flauberts" (1991b: 114). Yet Flynn finally gives Foucault the benefit of the doubt:

Foucault was facing an issue that many have regarded the Achilles' heel of Marxism and Structuralism alike: the moral implications of their theories of history and society. Do they lead to a sterile amoralism, rendering inconsistent any viable moral theory? Foucault's Nietzschean sympathies made him hostile to moral norms as commonly conceived. But the increasing importance given the moral subject in his later work as well as the interrelation of power and truth in its self-constitution suggests Foucault's account might leave room for moral creativity in a way that eluded both Marx and the structuralists. (114)

Foucault can be defended more emphatically in terms of preserving the autonomy and creativity of the subject, both individually and as a group. What Foucault essentially advances is a theory of holism-particularism in terms of which, because novelty and complexity in history are essential characteristics, there will only ever be *one* Flaubert, although Flaubert will also share certain characteristics with other petit bourgeois individuals, as well as with the individuals of other social classes.[1]

Foucault makes his position clear in his interview with Noam Chomsky (Foucault & Chomsky, 1997) where he indicates that he does not dispute the existence of "extrinsic mental schematism" and that he didn't dispute the Chomskian-type answers to the "so-called what questions: why we possess language—not just how language functions, but what's the *reason* for our having language" (114). Apart from "one or two little historical points" which he wants to dispute, Foucault claims to be in essential accord with Chomsky. This accord especially applies, he says, to the recognition of "free creation within a system of rules."

One can only, in terms of language or of knowledge, produce something new by putting into play a certain number of rules. . . . Thus we can roughly say that linguists before Mr Chomsky mainly insisted on the rules of construction of statements and less on the innovation represented by every new statement. . . . And in the history of science or in the history of thought, we place more emphasis on individual creation, and we had kept aside and left in the shadows these communal general rules, which obscurely manifest themselves through every scientific discovery, every scientific invention, and even every philosophical innovation. (Foucault & Chomsky 1997: 119–120)

In this sense, Foucault explains the autonomy and originality of the subject in the same way, using the same arguments as he explains the autonomy of statements (*énoncés*). In the interview with Chomsky, Foucault agrees that "rules and freedom are not opposed to each other." In fact, the point he is at pains to stress in the interview with Chomsky is that within any system of rules, in the long run "what is striking is the proliferation of possibilities by divergencies" (121–122). As he says:

[C]reativity is possible in putting into play a system of rules; it is not a mixture of order and freedom. Where . . . I don't completely agree with Mr Chomsky is when he places the principle of these regularities, in a way, in the interior of the mind or of human nature. If it is a matter of whether these rules are effectively put to work by the human mind, all right; all right, too, if it is a question of whether the historian and the linguist can think it in their turn; it is all right also to say that these rules should allow us to realise what is said or thought by these individuals. But to say that these regularities are connected, as conditions of existence, to the human mind or its nature, is difficult for me to accept; it seems to me that one must, before reaching that point . . . replace it in the field of other human practices, such as economics, technology, politics, sociology, which can serve them as conditions of formation, of models, of place, or apparition, etc. I would like to know whether one cannot discover the system of regularity, of constraint, which makes science possible, somewhere else, even outside the human mind, in social forms, in the relations of production, in the class struggle, etc. (123)

Although Chomsky is interested in the "intrinsic capabilities of mind," Foucault is interested in explaining how infinite possibilities of application arise from a limited number of rules that constitute the social conditions of existence. In this sense a parallel exists between Foucault's model of holism-particularism or system/originality and non-linear theories of determination or causality which are being used in both the physical as well as the social sciences and which show how infinite possibilities and random non-predictable occurrences may be derived from a set of determined rules or laws.[2]

In sociological terms, there are parallels as well between Foucault and Weber in terms of the fundamental form of materialism relating to the conception of social and historical change. While Foucault would agree with both Weber and Marx that capitalism is an historically specific economic form and not due to any ubiquitous human drive, he would side with Weber against forms of deterministic Marxism in relation to the methodological underpinning to the theory of how history changes. With Weber, he would concur that historical events and outcomes, rather than being determined by any single factor such as the economy, instead follow a logic of *unintended consequences*, and on this basis as well cannot be predicted in terms of their future development. This issue concerning different views of history, and the different forms of materialism implied, was central to the dispute among sociologists between Weberian and classical Marxist accounts of historical development (see Ray, 1987: 97–125). Foucault's contribution, then, has been to incorporate a pluralist social ontology into an historicist frame of reference, while preserving the radical impetus of historical materialism as both an oppositional politics and as a rigorous form of critical analysis.

As a stimulus to research Foucault helps us understand the intricate relations between modernism, humanism, liberalism, and Western science as structural forms that occluded difference and remained intolerant to groups caught in underprivileged positions who lacked power. Foucault draws our attention to the underside of modernity and Enlightenment rationality, of our faith in science and in the human will to change and to master. He points to the darker side of the liberal Enlightenment—to Hiroshima, Auschwitz, Chernobyl—to any number of impending crises linked to ecological breakdown, or to crises of health and disease, or to the politics of exclusion and violence, or to the failures of liberalism with respect to people of color, to women, or to those living in the Third World. The failures of liberal humanism are also evident in relation to new developments within mass culture relating to the invention, manufacture, and spread of new forms of technology. While on the one hand this may have resulted in a partial uprising of some previously marginalized groups—now empowered by the new portable forms of technology and new sources of information, sometimes even temporarily resulting in spaces of ungovernability—and created a clash of multiple perspectives from which the world is viewed, on the other hand it leads to increasing surveillance and normalization as those groups who exercise real power effectively seek to extend their control through the insidious mobilization of market strategies and ever-tighter systems of institutional control.

The revolt against liberalism and humanism is for Foucault an opposition to all forms of marginalization and subjugation. It is through such discourses by which citizens are taught and forced to submit to power regimes presently in place. To oppose them is not possible simply at the level of the economy or at the level of the State, for power operates in the present era most effectively at the social and cultural levels as well as through systems of disciplined knowledge. In this sense, in order for political opposition to be effective it must operate against the hegemonies of culture and knowledge by which normalization is achieved. Foucault invites us then to ask questions about a whole series of issues not traditionally a part of the political agenda for debate: questions about the function of the liberal partition between public and private, about the relations between the sexes, about what is normal, about what is possible, about the epistemological status of psychiatry, about the function or nature of mental illness, about minorities, about subjugated knowledges, about the environment, and about delinquency.

Foucault's contribution to the theory of power is to emphasize that modern power, rather than operating as a directive from a sovereign who demands obedience, operates ever more insidiously through disciplinary institutional forms which mask themselves as forms of truth and knowledge pertaining especially to those forms of knowledge relating to mental illness, sexuality, and delinquency. In this sense, Foucault's point is that modern power is *centerless*, located neither in the State nor in any other single source.

Given that power is capillary, the nature of oppositional politics is also altered. As truth is already a particular form of power (sometimes valid and sometimes not), the goal is not to seek to release truth from all systems of power, but to detach it from its forms of hegemony—economic, social, cultural—that it is inescapably wrapped in and which therefore constitute the context of its operation. Although I have argued in Chapter 9 that Foucault adheres ontologically to a form of "thin" communitarianism based upon a consideration of the epistemological and social presuppositions that undergird his analysis, his oppositional politics are not directed to instituting any particular form that communities must take but are directed instead to equalizing power in the interests of the marginalized. The aim is not to replace one hegemony with another, but to replace the idea of a monastically organized community with one characterized according to *difference*. This, more than anything else, is what separates Foucault from traditional forms of communitarian thinking.

The development and spread of technologies of communication linked to the post-Fordist global extension of transnational capitalism is one central material explanation for the disintegration of a centric culture and the growth of multiplicity in relation to truth, values, or styles of life. At one obvious level, of course, such new technologies result merely in a change of *visibility* in terms of which the world is viewed, shaking up power structures and values only to the extent that there is a greater knowledge about and tolerance for differences in style and ethos. There are of course limits to this pluralism of existing values, however, for they can apply only to a margin of flexibility within the discursive in terms of how the real is negotiated, interacted with, and understood. Unless Foucault is to suffer death through incoherence his approach must, in relation to both politics and morality, entail a *minimal universalism* premised upon a complex and sophisticated conception of the good. Although Foucault himself never articulated such a notion, I believe that such a push is warranted. For while *difference* can be respected both for groups and individuals, such a concept itself implies limits in relation to the basis on which such a complex political ideal itself rests. While it has some applicability in relation to lifestyles and values, it is not possible to equally respect different *actual* proposals as to how politics should be conducted, or how the State should be run. Similarly, it is not possible to respect lifestyles which are themselves intolerant and which are not in turn committed to the same ground rules. The principle of *difference* itself must entail a commitment to certain non-negotiable universal values if it can function as a principle at all. In this sense, if it is to be a *minimal* universalism, the "good" must have a "smart button," for while giving pride of place to difference and pluralism it must itself be *dogmatically* committed to those democratic values which are intolerant of styles of life not themselves respectful of the principle. In this sense, democratic values themselves constitute the basis of *difference*, and at a pragmatic level, its necessary foundation.

NOTES

1. This theorization of a non-linear form of materialism has been one of Foucault's central contributions.

2. Chaos theories, for instance, seek to understand free action and novelty within a deterministic, rule-governed context (see Swinney, 1983; Holden, 1985; Gleick, 1987; Sappington, 1990; Ayers, 1997). Other forms of emergentist materialism such as advanced by Bunge (1977a, 1977b), Haken (1977, 1990), Rapp et al. (1986), or Skarda and Freeman (1990) are also analogous to Foucault's theoretical materialism in this sense. *Synergetics*, as advanced by Haken, is a holist-emergentist materialism which seeks to explain how small-scale processes combine to energize qualitatively different forms of behavior on a macroscopic scale (e.g., as in explaining how gasses combine from molecules, or how the human brain functions). As defined by Stadler and Kruse, "[s]ynergetics is . . . defined as an interdisciplinary field of research concerned with the interaction of individual parts of a system that produces macroscopic, spatio-temporal or functional structures and which deals with deterministic as well as stochastic processes" (1994: 212). An emergent property is a property possessed by a system but not by its components. Synergetics, as well as chaos theory, are forms of compositional materialism in which the elements of a system cannot be predicted from a knowledge of the characteristics of its components. Sappington (1990) and Gleick (1987: 251) apply such non-linear theories to the issue of free will and determinism, noting that such systems allow free will to coexist within a deterministic system. It is worth noting also that thought itself may be theorized as an emergent property in that, as represented by Foucault, it supersedes the elemental physico-chemical factors that constitute it. For a similar view in the philosophy of science, see Sperry (1969).

It can also be noted here that, in antiquity, the Stoics sought to reconcile necessity with freedom of choice in a way that parallels the approach taken contemporarily in chaos theory and by Foucault, where it was held that in the "tensional motion" (*toniké kinesis*) of the *pneuma*, every "self-vibration" of matter *imposes a quality of its own*, which is to say, in different terms, that the actual never exhausts or constrains the possible.

Bibliography

Adamson, W. L. (1980). *Hegemony and Revolution: A Study of Antonio Gramsci's Political and Cultural Theory*. Berkeley: University of California Press.

Althusser, L. (1969). *For Marx*. Allen Lane, London: Penguin Press.

Althusser, L. (1970). *Reading Capital*. London: New Left Books.

Armstrong, T. J. (Ed.) (1992). *Michel Foucault: Philosopher*. New York and London: Harvester/Wheatsheaf.

Aronowitz, S. & Giroux, H. (1991). *Postmodern Education: Politics, Culture, and Social Criticism*. Minneapolis: University of Minnesota Press.

Ayers, S. (1997). The application of chaos theory to psychology. *Theory and Psychology, 7*(3), 373–398.

Balibar, E. (1992). Foucault and Marx: The question of nominalism. In T. J. Armstrong (Ed.), *Michel Foucault: Philosopher*. New York and London: Harvester/Wheatsheaf.

Ball, S. J. (Ed.) (1990). *Foucault and Education: Discipline and Knowledge*. London: Routledge.

Barrett, M. (1988). *The Politics of Truth*. Cambridge: Polity Press.

Barry, A., Osbourne, T., & Rose, N. (1996). *Foucault and Political Reason: Liberalism, Neoliberalism and Rationalities of Government*. London: UCL Press.

Barton, S. (1994). Chaos, self-organization, and psychology. *American Psychologist, 47*, 5–14.

Bates, T. R. (1976). Antonio Gramsci and the bolshevization of the PCI. *Journal of Contemporary History, 11*, 15–133.

Benhabib, S. (1989). On contemporary feminist theory. *Dissent, 36* (Summer), 366–370.

Benton, T. (1984). *The Rise and Fall of Structural Marxism*. London: Macmillan.

Bernauer, J. (1991a). *The Final Foucault*. Cambridge, Mass.: The MIT Press.

Bernauer, J. (1991b). Michel Foucault's ecstatic thinking. In J. Bernauer & D. Rasmussen (Eds.), *The Final Foucault* (pp. 45–82). Cambridge, Mass.: The MIT Press.

Best, S. & Kellner, D. (1991). *Postmodern Theory: Critical Interrogations*. London: Macmillan.

Bhaskar, R. (1978). *A Realist Theory of Science*. Sussex: Harvester Press.

Bhaskar, R. (1986). *Scientific Realism and Human Emancipation*. London: Verso.

Bhaskar, R. (1991). *Philosophy and the Idea of Freedom*. London: Basil Blackwell.

Bordo, S. (1988). Anorexia Nervosa: Psychopathology as the crystallization of culture. In I. Diamond & L. Quinby (Eds.), *Feminism and Foucault: Reflections on Resistance*. Boston: Northeastern University Press.

Britzman, D. (1991). *Practice Makes Practice: A Critical Study of Learning to Teach*. Albany: State University of New York Press.

Bukharin, N. (1969). *Historical Materialism: A System of Sociology*. Ann Arbor: University of Michigan Press.

Bunge, M. (1977a). Levels of reduction. *American Journal of Physiology: Regulatory, Integrative and Comparative Physiology, 233*(2) (September 2), 75–82.

Bunge, M. (1977b). Emergence and the mind: Commentary. *Neuroscience, 2*, 501–509.

Bunge, M. (1979). *The Mind-Body Problem*. Oxford: Pergamon.

Bunge, M. (1983). *Epistemology and Methodology II. Treatise on Basic Philosophy*. Dordrecht: Reidel.

Burchell, G. (1996). Liberal government and techniques of the self. In A. Barry, T. Osbourne, & N. Rose, *Foucault and Political Reason: Liberalism, Neoliberalism and Rationalities of Government* (pp. 19–36). London: UCL Press.

Burr, V. (1995). *An Introduction to Social Constructionism*. London: Routledge.

Butler, J. (1990). *Gender Trouble: Feminism and the Subversion of Identity*. New York: Routledge.

Callinicos, A. (1988). *Against Postmodernism*. Cambridge: Polity Press.

Cherryholmes, C. (1988). *Power and Criticism: Post-structural Investigations in Education*. New York: Teachers College Press.

Cocks, J. (1989). *The Oppositional Imagination: Feminism, Critique and Political Theory*. London: Routledge.

Cook, D. (1987). The turn towards subjectivity: Michel Foucault's legacy. *British Journal of Phenomenology, 18*(3), 215–225.

Craib, I. (1997). Social constructionism as a social psychosis. *Sociology, 31*(1), 1–15.

Davidson, A. (1977). *Antonio Gramsci: Towards an Intellectual Biography*. London: Merlin Press.

Davidson, A. (1986). Archaeology, genealogy, ethics. In D. Couzens Hoy (Ed.), *Foucault: A Critical Reader*. Oxford: Basil Blackwell.

Davidson, A. (1997). *Foucault and His Interlocutors*. Chicago and London: University of Chicago Press.

Davidson, D. (1985). On the very idea of a conceptual scheme. In J. Rajchman & C. West (Eds.), *Post-analytic Philosophy*. New York: Columbia University Press.

Davies, B. (1989). *Frogs and Snails and Feminist Tales: Preschool Children and Gender*. Sydney: Allen & Unwin.

Dean, M. (1994). *Critical and Effective Histories: Foucault's Methods and Historical Sociology*. London and New York: Routledge.

Deleuze, G. (1986). *Foucault*. Paris: Editions de Minuit.

Derrida, J. (1973). *Speech and Phenomena*. Evanston, Ill.: Northwestern University Press.

Derrida, J. (1976). *Of Grammatology*. Baltimore: Johns Hopkins University Press.

Derrida, J. (1981). *Positions*. Chicago: University of Chicago Press.

Dewan, M. (1976). Consciousness as an emergent causal agent in the context of control systems theory. In G. G. Globus, S. Maxwell, & I. Savodnik (Eds.), *Consciousness and the Brain: A Scientific and Philosophical Inquiry*. New York: Plenum.

Diamond, I. & Quinby, L. (Eds.) (1988). *Feminism and Foucault: Reflections on Resistance*. Boston: Northeastern University Press.

Donelly, M. (1982). Foucault's genealogy of the human sciences. *Economy and Society 11*(4), 363–379.

Dreyfus, H. L. (1987). Foreword to the California edition. In M. Foucault, *Mental Illness and Psychology* (pp. vii–xiii). Cambridge, Mass.: The MIT Press.

Dreyfus, H. L. (1992). On the ordering of things: Being and power in Heidegger and Foucault. In T. J. Armstrong (Ed.), *Michel Foucault: Philosopher* (pp. 80–98). New York and London: Harvester/Wheatsheaf.

Dreyfus, H. L. & Rabinow, P. (1982). *Michel Foucault: Beyond Structuralism and Hermeneutics* (with an afterword by Michel Foucault). Chicago: University of Chicago Press.

Dreyfus, H. L. & Rabinow, P. (1983). *Michel Foucault: Beyond Structuralism and Hermeneutics* (2nd ed., with an afterword and interview with Michel Foucault). Chicago: University of Chicago Press.

Dreyfus, H. L. & Rabinow, P. (1986). What is maturity? Habermas and Foucault on "What Is Enlightenment?" In D. Couzens Hoy (Ed.), *Foucault: A Critical Reader* (pp. 109–222). Oxford: Basil Blackwell.

Durkheim, E. (1993). *The Rules of Sociological Method*. New York: The Free Press.

Ellesworth, E. (1989). Why doesn't this feel empowering: Working through the repressive myths of critical pedagogy. *Harvard Educational Review, 59*(3), 297–324.

Engels, F. (1978). Letter to Joseph Bloch [orig. 1890]. In R. C. Tucker (Ed.), *The Marx-Engels Reader* (2nd ed.). New York and London: W. W. Norton.

Femia, J. V. (1987). *Gramsci's Political Thought: Hegemony, Consciousness, and the Revolutionary Process*. Oxford: Clarendon Press.

Finocchiaro, M. (1988). *Gramsci and the History of Dialectical Thought*. Cambridge: Cambridge University Press.

Fisk, M. (1993). Poststructuralism, difference and marxism. *Praxis International, 12*, 223–240.

Flynn, T. (1989). Foucault and historical nominalism. In H. A. Durfee & D. F. T. Rodier (Eds.), *Phenomenology and Beyond: The Self and Its Language* (pp. 134–147). Dordrecht: Kluwer Academic Publishers.

Flynn, T. (1991a). Foucault and the spaces of history. *Monist, 45*, 165–186.

Flynn, T. (1991b). Foucault as Parrhesiast: His last course at the Collège de France (1984). In J. Bernauer, *The Final Foucault* (pp. 102–118). Cambridge, Mass.: The MIT Press (also printed in *Philosophy and Social Criticism, 12*, 1987, 213–276).

Flynn, T. (1994). Foucault's mapping of history. In G. Gutting (Ed.), *The Cambridge Companion to Foucault*. Cambridge: Cambridge University Press.

Fontana, B. (1993). *Hegemony and Power: On the Relation Between Gramsci and Machiavelli*. Minneapolis and London: University of Minnesota Press.

Foucault, M. (1965). *Madness and Civilization* (trans. R. Howard). New York: Pantheon.

Foucault, M. (1967). Nietzsche, Freud, Marx. *Cahiers de Royaumont 6: Nietzsche*. Paris: Éditions de Minuit. English translation by John Anderson. *Critical Texts*, 3(2) (Winter), 1986 [paper initially delivered 1964].

Foucault, M. (1970). *The Order of Things*. New York: Random House.

Foucault, M. (1971a). A conversation with Michel Foucault (interview by John Simon). *Partisan Review*, 38, 192–201.

Foucault, M. (1971b). Monstrosities in criticism (trans. R. J. Matthews). *Diacritics*, 1(1), 57–60.

Foucault, M. (1972). *The Archaeology of Knowledge* (trans. A. Sheridan). London: Tavistock.

Foucault, M. (1973). *The Birth of the Clinic: An Archaeology of Medical Perception* (trans. A. Sheridan). New York: Pantheon.

Foucault, M. (1975a). Foreword (trans. F. Jellinek). In M. Foucault (Ed.), *I, Pierre Rivière, Having Slaughtered My Mother, My Sister and My Brother: A Case of Parricide in the 19th Century*. New York: Pantheon.

Foucault, M. (1975b). Tales of murder (trans. F. Jellinek). In M. Foucault (Ed.), *I, Pierre Rivière, Having Slaughtered My Mother, My Sister and My Brother: A Case of Parricide in the 19th Century*. New York: Pantheon.

Foucault, M. (1976). The politics of crime (trans. M. Horowitz). *Partisan Review*, 43(3), 453–459.

Foucault, M. (1977a). *Discipline and Punish* (trans. A. Sheridan). New York: Pantheon.

Foucault, M. (1977b). *Nietzsche, Genealogy, History in Language, Counter-meaning, Practice: Selected Essays and Interviews* (Eds. D. F. Bouchard & S. Simon) (pp. 139–164). Ithaca, N.Y.: Cornell University Press.

Foucault, M. (1977c). The father's "no." In D. Bouchard (Ed.), *Language, Counter-Memory, Practice: Selected Essays and Interviews* (trans. D. Bouchard & S. Simon) (pp. 68–86). Ithaca, N.Y.: Cornell University Press.

Foucault, M. (1977d). A preface to transgression. In D. Bouchard (Ed.), *Language, Counter-Memory, Practice: Selected Essays and Interviews* (trans. D. Bouchard & S. Simon) (pp. 29–52). Ithaca, N.Y.: Cornell University Press.

Foucault, M. (1977e). Language to infinity. In D. Bouchard (Ed.), *Language, Counter-Memory, Practice: Selected Essays and Interviews* (trans. D. Bouchard & S. Simon) (pp. 53–67). Ithaca, N.Y.: Cornell University Press.

Foucault, M. (1977f). Fantasia of the library. In D. Bouchard (Ed.), *Language, Counter-Memory, Practice: Selected Essays and Interviews* (trans. D. Bouchard & S. Simon) (pp. 87–109). Ithaca, N.Y.: Cornell University Press.

Foucault, M. (1977g). What is an author? In D. Bouchard (Ed.), *Language, Counter-Memory, Practice: Selected Essays and Interviews* (trans. D. Bouchard & S. Simon) (pp. 113–138). Ithaca, N.Y.: Cornell University Press.

Foucault, M. (1977h). Theatricum philosophicum. In D. Bouchard (Ed.), *Language,*

Counter-Memory, Practice: Selected Essays and Interviews (trans. D. Bouchard & S. Simon) (pp. 165–196). Ithaca, N.Y.: Cornell University Press.

Foucault, M. (1977i). History of systems of thought. In D. Bouchard (Ed.), *Language, Counter-Memory, Practice: Selected Essays and Interviews* (trans. D. Bouchard & S. Simon) (pp. 199–204). Ithaca, N.Y.: Cornell University Press.

Foucault, M. (1977j). Intellectuals and power. In D. Bouchard (Ed.), *Language, Counter-Memory, Practice: Selected Essays and Interviews* (trans. D. Bouchard & S. Simon) (pp. 205–217). Ithaca, N.Y.: Cornell University Press.

Foucault, M. (1977k). Revolutionary action: Until now. In D. Bouchard (Ed.), *Language, Counter-Memory, Practice: Selected Essays and Interviews* (trans. D. Bouchard & S. Simon) (pp. 218–233). Ithaca, N.Y.: Cornell University Press.

Foucault, M. (1977l). The political function of the intellectual (trans. C. Gordon). *Radical Philosophy, 17* (Summer), 12–14.

Foucault, M. (1977m). Power and sex: An interview with Michel Foucault (trans. D. J. Parent). *Telos, 32* (Summer), 152–161.

Foucault, M. (1977n). Preface. In G. Deleuze & F. Guattari, *Anti-Oedipus: Capitalism and Schizophrenia*, Vol. 1 (trans. R. Hurley, M. Seem, & H. Lane). New York: Viking Press.

Foucault, M. (1978a). *The History of Sexuality*. Vol. 1: *An Introduction* (trans. R. Hurley). New York: Pantheon Books.

Foucault, M. (1978b). Politics and the study of discourse (trans. C. Gordon). *Ideology and Consciousness, 3* (Spring), 7–26.

Foucault, M. (1978c). Interview with Michel Foucault. In R. Bellour (Ed.), *Les Livres Des Autres*. Paris: Union Generale d'Editions.

Foucault, M. (1978d). Second interview with Michel Foucault. In R. Bellour (Ed.), *Les Livres Des Autres*. Paris: Union Generale d'Editions.

Foucault, M. (1979a). Governmentality (trans. R. Braidotti). *Ideology and Consciousness, 6* (Autumn), 5–21.

Foucault, M. (1979b). My body, this paper, this fire (trans. G. Bennington). *Oxford Literary Review, 4*(1) (Autumn), 5–28.

Foucault, M. (1979c). Power and norm: Notes (trans. W. Suchting). In M. Morris & P. Patton (Eds.), *Michel Foucault: Power, Truth, Strategy*. Sydney: Feral Publications.

Foucault, M. (1979d). The life of infamous men (trans. P. Foss & M. Morris). In M. Morris & P. Patton (Eds.), *Michel Foucault: Power, Truth, Strategy*. Sydney: Feral Publications.

Foucault, M. (1979e). The simplest of pleasures (trans. M. Riegle & G. Barbedette). *Fag Rag, 29*, 3.

Foucault, M. (1980a). On popular justice: A discussion with Maoists (trans. J. Mepham). In C. Gordon (Ed.), *Power/Knowledge: Selected Interviews and Other Writings 1972–1977*. Brighton: Harvester.

Foucault, M. (1980b). Truth and power. In C. Gordon (Ed.), *Power/Knowledge: Selected Interviews and Other Writings 1972–1977* (pp. 109–133). Brighton: Harvester Press.

Foucault, M. (1980c). Prison talk (trans. C. Gordon). In C. Gordon (Ed.), *Power/Knowledge: Selected Interviews and Other Writings, 1972–1977* (pp. 37–54). Brighton: Harvester Press.

Foucault, M. (1980d). Body/power (trans. C. Gordon). In C. Gordon (Ed.), *Power/*

Knowledge: Selected Interviews and Other Writings, 1972–1977 (pp. 55–62). Brighton: Harvester.

Foucault, M. (1980e). Questions on geography (trans. C. Gordon). In C. Gordon (Ed.), *Power/Knowledge: Selected Interviews and Other Writings, 1972–1977* (pp. 63–77). Brighton: Harvester Press.

Foucault, M. (1980f). Two lectures (trans. K. Soper). In C. Gordon (Ed.), *Power/Knowledge: Selected Interviews and Other Writings, 1972–1977* (pp. 78–108). Brighton: Harvester Press.

Foucault, M. (1980g). The politics of health in the eighteenth century (trans. C. Gordon). In C. Gordon (Ed.), *Power/Knowledge: Selected Interviews and Other Writings, 1972–1977* (pp. 166–182). Brighton: Harvester Press.

Foucault, M. (1980h). Powers and strategies (trans. C. Gordon). In C. Gordon (Ed.), *Power/Knowledge: Selected Interviews and Other Writings, 1972–1977* (pp. 134–145). Brighton: Harvester Press.

Foucault, M. (1980i). The eye of power (trans. C. Gordon). In C. Gordon (Ed.), *Power/Knowledge: Selected Interviews and Other Writings, 1972–1977* (pp. 146–165). Brighton: Harvester Press.

Foucault, M. (1980j). The history of sexuality (trans. L. Marshall). In C. Gordon (Ed.), *Power/Knowledge: Selected Interviews and Other Writings, 1972–1977* (pp. 183–193). Brighton: Harvester Press.

Foucault, M. (1980k). The confession of the flesh. In C. Gordon (Ed.), *Power/Knowledge: Selected Interviews and Other Writings, 1972–1977* (pp. 194–228). Brighton: Harvester Press.

Foucault, M. (1980l). Georges Canguilhem: Philosopher of error (trans. G. Burchell). *Ideology & Consciousness, 7* (Autumn), 51–62.

Foucault, M. (1981a). The order of discourse (trans. Ian McLeod). In R. Young (Ed.), *Untying the Text*. London: Routledge & Kegan Paul.

Foucault, M. (1981b). Questions of method: An interview with Michel Foucault (trans. C. Gordon). *Ideology & Consciousness, 8* (Spring), 3–14.

Foucault, M. (1981c). Foucault at the Collège de France I: A course summary (trans. J. Bernauer). *Philosophy and Social Criticism, 8*(2), 235–242.

Foucault, M. (1981d). Foucault at the Collège de France II: A course summary (trans. J. Bernauer). *Philosophy and Social Criticism, 8*(3), 349–359.

Foucault, M. (1981e). Is it useless to revolt? (trans. J. Bernauer). *Philosophy and Social Criticism, 8*(1), 1–9.

Foucault, M. (1982a). The subject and power. Afterword in H. L. Dreyfus & P. Rabinow, *Michel Foucault: Beyond Structuralism and Hermeneutics* (2nd ed.). Chicago: Chicago University Press.

Foucault, M. (1982b). Is it really important to think? (trans. with afterword by T. Keenan). *Philosophy and Social Criticism, 9*(1) (Spring), 29–40.

Foucault, M. (1982c). Space, knowledge, and power: An interview with P. Rabinow (trans. C. Hubert). *Skyline* (March), 16–20.

Foucault, M. (1983a). Structuralism and poststructuralism: An interview with Michel Foucault (with G. Raulet). *Telos, 55*, 195–211.

Foucault, M. (1983b). An interview (conducted by Stephen Riggins on 22 June 1982). *Ethos, 1*(2) (Autumn), 4–9.

Foucault, M. (1983c). The power and politics of Michel Foucault. An interview in the weekly magazine of the *Daily Californian: Inside*, April 22, 7, 20–22.

Foucault, M. (1983d). On the genealogy of ethics: An overview of work in progress. In H. Dreyfus & P. Rabinow, *Michel Foucault: Beyond Structuralism and Hermeneutics* (2nd ed.). Chicago: University of Chicago Press (interview conducted by authors).

Foucault, M. (1984a). What is enlightenment? (trans. C Porter). In P. Rabinow (Ed.), *The Foucault Reader* (pp. 31–50). New York: Pantheon.

Foucault, M. (1984b). Le Sourci de la vérité. Interview with François Ewald. *Magazine Littéraire, 207* (May), 18–23.

Foucault, M. (1984c). Nietzsche, genealogy, history (trans. D. Bouchard & S. Simon). In P. Rabinow (Ed.), *The Foucault Reader* (pp. 76–100). New York: Pantheon.

Foucault, M. (1984d). On the genealogy of ethics: An overview of work in progress. In P. Rabinow (Ed.), *The Foucault Reader* (pp. 340–372). New York: Pantheon.

Foucault, M. (1984e). Preface to *The History of Sexuality*, Vol. 2. In P. Rabinow (Ed.), *The Foucault Reader* (pp. 333–339). New York: Pantheon.

Foucault, M. (1984f). Politics and ethics: An interview (trans. C. Porter). In P. Rabinow (Ed.), *The Foucault Reader* (pp. 373–380). New York: Pantheon.

Foucault, M. (1984g). Polemics, politics and problemizations (trans. L. Davis). In P. Rabinow (Ed.), *The Foucault Reader* (pp. 381–389). New York: Pantheon.

Foucault, M. (1984h). Space, knowledge and power (trans. C. Hubert). In P. Rabinow (Ed.), *The Foucault Reader* (pp. 239–256). New York: Pantheon.

Foucault, M. (1984i). Sex, power and the politics of identity. Interview (conducted by B. Gallagher & A. Wilson in June 1982). *The Advocate, 400* (August 7), 26–30, 58.

Foucault, M. (1985a). *The Use of Pleasure: History of Sexuality*, Vol. 2 (trans. R. Hurley). New York: Pantheon.

Foucault, M. (1985b). Final interview (trans. T. Levin & I. Lorenz). *Raritan, 5* (Summer), 1–13 (interview conducted by G. Barbedette, published in *Les Louvelles*, June 28, 1984).

Foucault, M. (1985c). La vie: L'expérience et la science. *Revue de Métaphysique et de Morale, 1*, 6–14.

Foucault, M. (1986a). *The Care of the Self: History of Sexuality*, Vol. 3 (trans. R. Hurley). New York: Pantheon.

Foucault, M. (1986b). Nietzsche, Freud, Marx (trans. J. Anderson & G. Hentzi). *Critical Texts, 3*(2) (Winter), 1–5.

Foucault, M. (1986c). Kant on enlightenment and revolution (trans. C. Gordon). *Economy and Society, 15*(1) (February), 88–96.

Foucault, M. (1986d). *Death and the Labyrinth: The World of Raymond Roussel* (trans. C. Ruas, with introduction by J. Ashberry). New York: Doubleday & Company.

Foucault, M. (1987a). Questions of method. In K. Baynes, J. Bohman, & T. McCarthy (Eds.), *After Philosophy: End or Transformation?* Cambridge, Mass.: The MIT Press.

Foucault, M. (1987b). *Mental Illness and Psychology* (trans. A. Sheridan). Berkeley: University of California Press.

Foucault, M. (1988a). Critical theory/intellectual history (an interview with Michel Foucault by Gérard Raulet). In L. D. Kritzman (Ed.), *Politics, Philosophy, Cul-*

ture: Interviews and Other Writings, 1977–1984 (trans. A. Sheridan et al.) (pp. 17–46). New York: Routledge (originally published as "Structuralism and post-structuralism," *Telos, 55* (Spring 1983), 195–211.

Foucault, M. (1988b). The functions of literature (trans. A. Sheridan et al.). In L. D. Kritzman (Ed.), *Politics, Philosophy, Culture: Interviews and Other Writings, 1977–1984* (pp. 307–313). New York: Routledge.

Foucault, M. (1988c). Confinement, psychiatry, prison (trans. A. Sheridan et al.). In L. D. Kritzman (Ed.), *Politics, Philosophy, Culture: Interviews and Other Writings, 1977–1984* (pp. 178–210). New York: Routledge.

Foucault, M. (1988d). On power (trans. A. Sheridan et al.). In L. D. Kritzman (Ed.), *Politics, Philosophy, Culture: Interviews and Other Writings, 1977–1984* (pp. 96–109). New York: Routledge.

Foucault, M. (1988e). The dangerous individual (trans. A. Sheridan et al.). In L. D. Kritzman (Ed.), *Politics, Philosophy, Culture: Interviews and Other Writings, 1977–1984* (pp. 125–151). New York: Routledge.

Foucault, M. (1988f). Sexual morality and the law (trans. A. Sheridan et al.). In L. D. Kritzman (Ed.), *Politics, Philosophy, Culture: Interviews and Other Writings, 1977–1984* (pp. 271–285). New York: Routledge.

Foucault, M. (1988g). Iran: The spirit of a world without spirit (trans. A. Sheridan et al.). In L. D. Kritzman (Ed.), *Politics, Philosophy, Culture: Interviews and Other Writings, 1977–1984* (pp. 211–226). New York: Routledge.

Foucault, M. (1988h). The masked philosopher (trans. A. Sheridan et al.). In L. D. Kritzman (Ed.), *Politics, Philosophy, Culture: Interviews and Other Writings, 1977–1984* (pp. 323–330). New York: Routledge.

Foucault, M. (1988i). Practicing criticism (trans. A. Sheridan et al.). In L. D. Kritzman (Ed.), *Politics, Philosophy, Culture: Interviews and Other Writings, 1977–1984* (pp. 152–158). New York: Routledge.

Foucault, M. (1988j). The minimalist self (trans. A. Sheridan et al.). In L. D. Kritzman (Ed.), *Politics, Philosophy, Culture: Interviews and Other Writings, 1977–1984* (pp. 3–16). New York: Routledge.

Foucault, M. (1988k). Social security (trans. A. Sheridan et al.). In L. D. Kritzman (Ed.), *Politics, Philosophy, Culture: Interviews and Other Writings, 1977–1984* (pp. 159–177). New York: Routledge.

Foucault, M. (1988l). Contemporary music and the public (trans. A. Sheridan et al.). In L. D. Kritzman (Ed.), *Politics, Philosophy, Culture: Interviews and Other Writings, 1977–1984* (pp. 314–322). New York: Routledge.

Foucault, M. (1988m). The battle for chastity (trans. A. Sheridan et al.). In L. D. Kritzman (Ed.), *Politics, Philosophy, Culture: Interviews and Other Writings, 1977–1984* (pp. 227–241). New York: Routledge.

Foucault, M. (1988n). An aesthetics of existence (trans. A. Sheridan et al.). In L. D. Kritzman (Ed.), *Politics, Philosophy, Culture: Interviews and Other Writings, 1977–1984* (pp. 47–56). New York: Routledge.

Foucault, M. (1988o). The return of morality (trans. A. Sheridan et al.). In L. D. Kritzman (Ed.), *Politics, Philosophy, Culture: Interviews and Other Writings, 1977–1984* (pp. 242–254). New York: Routledge.

Foucault, M. (1988p). The concern for truth (trans. A. Sheridan et al.). In L. D. Kritzman (Ed.), *Politics, Philosophy, Culture: Interviews and Other Writings, 1977–1984* (pp. 255–270). New York: Routledge.

Foucault, M. (1988q). The art of telling the truth (trans. A. Sheridan et al.). In L. D. Kritzman (Ed.), *Politics, Philosophy, Culture: Interviews and Other Writings, 1977–1984* (pp. 86–95). New York: Routledge.

Foucault, M. (1989a). *Foucault Live: Interviews, 1966–84* (Ed. S. Lotringer). New York: Semiotext(e).

Foucault, M. (1989b). Friendship as a way of life (trans. J. Johnston). In S. Lotringer (Ed.), *Foucault Live*. New York: Semiotext(e).

Foucault, M. (1989c). The order of things. In S. Lotringer (Ed.), *Foucault Live: Interviews, 1966–84* (pp. 1–10). New York: Semiotext(e).

Foucault, M. (1989d). The discourse of history. In S. Lotringer (Ed.), *Foucault Live: Interviews, 1966–84* (pp. 11–34). New York: Semiotext(e).

Foucault, M. (1989e). Foucault response to Sartre. In S. Lotringer (Ed.), *Foucault Live: Interviews, 1966–84* (pp. 35–44). New York: Semiotext(e).

Foucault, M. (1989f). The archaeology of knowledge. In S. Lotringer (Ed.), *Foucault Live: Interviews, 1966–84* (pp. 45–56). New York: Semiotext(e).

Foucault, M. (1989g). The birth of a world. In S. Lotringer (Ed.), *Foucault Live: Interviews, 1966–84* (pp. 57–62). New York: Semiotext(e).

Foucault, M. (1989h). Rituals of exclusion. In S. Lotringer (Ed.), *Foucault Live: Interviews, 1966–84* (pp. 63–72). New York: Semiotext(e).

Foucault, M. (1989i). An historian of culture. In S. Lotringer (Ed.), *Foucault Live: Interviews, 1966–84* (pp. 73–88). New York: Semiotext(e).

Foucault, M. (1989j). I, Pierre Rivère. In S. Lotringer (Ed.), *Foucault Live: Interviews, 1966–84* (pp. 131–136). New York: Semiotext(e).

Foucault, M. (1989k). The end of the monarchy of sex. In S. Lotringer (Ed.), *Foucault Live: Interviews, 1966–84* (pp. 137–156). New York: Semiotext(e).

Foucault, M. (1989l). The anxiety of judging. In S. Lotringer (Ed.), *Foucault Live: Interviews, 1966–84* (pp. 157–178). New York: Semiotext(e).

Foucault, M. (1989m). Clarifications on the question of power. In S. Lotringer (Ed.), *Foucault Live: Interviews, 1966–84* (pp. 179–192). New York: Semiotext(e).

Foucault, M. (1989n). Sexual choice, sexual act. In S. Lotringer (Ed.), *Foucault Live: Interviews, 1966–84* (pp. 211–232). New York: Semiotext(e).

Foucault, M. (1989o). An ethics of pleasure. In S. Lotringer (Ed.), *Foucault Live: Interviews, 1966–84* (pp. 257–274). New York: Semiotext(e).

Foucault, M. (1989p). What calls for punishment. In S. Lotringer (Ed.), *Foucault Live: Interviews, 1966–84* (pp. 275–292). New York: Semiotext(e).

Foucault, M. (1989q). The concern for truth. In S. Lotringer (Ed.), *Foucault Live: Interviews, 1966–84* (pp. 293–308). New York: Semiotext(e).

Foucault, M. (1989r). An aesthetics of existence. In S. Lotringer (Ed.), *Foucault Live: Interviews, 1966–84* (pp. 309–316). New York: Semiotext(e).

Foucault, M. (1989s). The return to morality. In S. Lotringer (Ed.), *Foucault Live: Interviews, 1966–84* (pp. 317–332). New York: Semiotext(e).

Foucault, M. (1990). Maurice Blanchot: The thought from outside (trans. J. Mehlman & B. Massumi). In *Foucault-Blanchot*. New York: Zone Books.

Foucault, M. (1991a). The ethic of care for the self as a practice of freedom: an interview (trans. J. D. Gauthier). In J. Bernauer & D. Rasmussen, *The Final Foucault*. Cambridge, Mass.: The MIT Press.

Foucault, M. (1991b). *Remarks on Marx: Conversations with Duccio Trombadori* (trans. R. J. Goldstein & J. Cascaito). New York: Semiotext(e).

Foucault, M. (1994a). *Dits et écrits: 1954–1988* (Eds. D. Defert & F. Ewald with J. Lagrange), 4 vols. Paris: Éditions Gallimard.

Foucault, M. (1994b). Linguistique et sciences sociales. In D. Defert & F. Ewald (Eds.) with J. Lagrange, *Dits et écrits: 1954–1988*, 4 vols. (Vol. 1, No. 70, pp. 821–842). Paris: Éditions Gallimard.

Foucault, M. (1994c). La philosophie analytique de la politique. In D. Defert & F. Ewald (Eds.) with J. Lagrange, *Dits et écrits, 1954–1988*, 4 vols. (Vol. 3, No. 232, pp. 534–551). Paris: Éditions Gallimard.

Foucault, M. (1994d). Méthodologie pour la connaissance du monde: comment se débarrasser du marxisme. In D. Defert & F. Ewald (Eds.) with J. Lagrange, *Dits et écrits, 1954–1988*, 4 vols. (Vol. 3, No. 235, pp. 595–617). Paris: Éditions Gallimard.

Foucault, M. (1997a). Subjectivity and truth. In M. Foucault, *Ethics, Subjectivity and Truth: The Essential Works* (Ed. P. Rabinow, trans. R. Hurley) (pp. 87–94). Allen Lane, London: Penguin Press.

Foucault, M. (1997b). The hermeneutic of the subject. In M. Foucault, *Ethics, Subjectivity and Truth: The Essential Works* (Ed. P. Rabinow, trans. R. Hurley) (pp. 95–108). Allen Lane, London: Penguin Press.

Foucault, M. (1997c). Self writing. In M. Foucault, *Ethics, Subjectivity and Truth: The Essential Works* (Ed. P. Rabinow, trans. R. Hurley) (pp. 207–224). Allen Lane, London: Penguin Press.

Foucault, M. (1997d). On the genealogy of ethics: An overview of work in progress. In M. Foucault, *Ethics, Subjectivity and Truth: The Essential Works* (Ed. P. Rabinow, trans. R. Hurley) (pp. 253–280). Allen Lane, London: Penguin Press.

Foucault, M. (1997e). Technologies of the self. In M. Foucault, *Ethics, Subjectivity and Truth: The Essential Works* (Ed. P. Rabinow, trans. R. Hurley) (pp. 223–251). Allen Lane, London: Penguin Press.

Foucault, M. (1997f). Candidacy presentation: Collège de France, 1969. In M. Foucault, *Ethics, Subjectivity and Truth: The Essential Works* (Ed. P. Rabinow, trans. R. Hurley) (pp. 5–10). Allen Lane, London: Penguin Press.

Foucault, M. (1997g). The will to knowledge. In M. Foucault, *Ethics, Subjectivity and Truth: The Essential Works* (Ed. P. Rabinow, trans. R. Hurley) (pp. 11–16). Allen Lane, London: Penguin Press.

Foucault, M. (1997h). Penal theories and institutions. In M. Foucault, *Ethics, Subjectivity and Truth: The Essential Works* (Ed. P. Rabinow, trans. R. Hurley) (pp. 17–22). Allen Lane, London: Penguin Press.

Foucault, M. (1997i). The positive society. In M. Foucault, *Ethics, Subjectivity and Truth: The Essential Works* (Ed. P. Rabinow, trans. R. Hurley) (pp. 23–38). Allen Lane, London: Penguin Press.

Foucault, M. (1997j). Psychiatric power. In M. Foucault, *Ethics, Subjectivity and Truth: The Essential Works* (Ed. P. Rabinow, trans. R. Hurley) (pp. 39–50). Allen Lane, London: Penguin Press.

Foucault, M. (1997k). Society must be defended. In M. Foucault, *Ethics, Subjectivity and Truth: The Essential Works* (Ed. P. Rabinow, trans. R. Hurley) (pp. 59–66). Allen Lane, London: Penguin Press.

Foucault, M. (1997l). The birth of biopolitics. In M. Foucault, *Ethics, Subjectivity and Truth: The Essential Works* (Ed. P. Rabinow, trans. R. Hurley) (pp. 73–80). Allen Lane, London: Penguin Press.

Foucault, M. (1997m). On the government of the living. In M. Foucault, *Ethics, Subjectivity and Truth: The Essential Works* (Ed. P. Rabinow, trans. R. Hurley) (pp. 81–86). Allen Lane, London: Penguin Press.

Foucault, M. (1997n). Friendship as a way of life. In M. Foucault, *Ethics, Subjectivity and Truth: The Essential Works* (Ed. P. Rabinow, trans. R. Hurley) (pp. 135–140). Allen Lane, London: Penguin Press.

Foucault, M. (1997o). Sexual choice, sexual act. In M. Foucault, *Ethics, Subjectivity and Truth: The Essential Works* (Ed. P. Rabinow, trans. R. Hurley) (pp. 141–157). Allen Lane, London: Penguin Press.

Foucault, M. (1997p). Sex, power and the politics of identity. In M. Foucault, *Ethics, Subjectivity and Truth: The Essential Works* (Ed. P. Rabinow, trans. R. Hurley) (pp. 163–174). Allen Lane, London: Penguin Press.

Foucault, M. (1997q). The battle for chastity. In M. Foucault, *Ethics, Subjectivity and Truth: The Essential Works* (Ed. P. Rabinow, trans. R. Hurley) (pp. 185–198). Allen Lane, London: Penguin Press.

Foucault, M. (1997r). Preface to *The History of Sexuality, Vol. 2.* In M. Foucault, *Ethics, Subjectivity and Truth: The Essential Works* (Ed. P. Rabinow, trans. R. Hurley) (pp. 199–206). Allen Lane, London: Penguin Press.

Foucault, M. (1997s). The masked philosopher. In M. Foucault, *Ethics, Subjectivity and Truth: The Essential Works* (Ed. P. Rabinow, trans. R. Hurley) (pp. 321–328). Allen Lane, London: Penguin Press.

Foucault, M. & Chomsky, N. (1997). Human nature: Justice versus power. In A. I. Davidson (Ed.), *Foucault and His Interlocutors.* Chicago and London: University of Chicago Press.

Frank, M. (1992). On Foucault's concept of discourse. In T. J. Armstrong (trans.), *Michel Foucault: Philosopher* (pp. 99–117). New York: Harvester/Wheatsheaf.

Fraser, N. (1989). *Unruly Practices: Power, Discourse and Gender in Contemporary Social Theory.* Cambridge: Polity Press.

Geras, N. (1990). *Discourses of Extremity: Radical Ethics and Post-Marxist Extravagances.* London and New York: Verso.

Gergen, K. (1985). The social constructionist movement in modern psychology. *American Psychologist, 40,* 266–275.

Giddens, A. (1982). *Profiles and Critiques in Social Theory.* London and Basingstoke: The Macmillan Press.

Giddens, A. (1984). *The Constitution of Society.* Cambridge: Polity Press.

Giroux, H. (1991). Modernism, postmodernism and feminism: Rethinking the boundaries of educational discourse. In H. Giroux (Ed.), *Postmodernism, Feminism and Cultural Politics: Redrawing Educational Boundaries.* Albany: State University of New York Press.

Gleick, J. (1987). *Chaos: Making a New Science.* London: Abacus.

Goldstein, J. (Ed.) (1994). *Foucault and the Writing of History.* Oxford: Oxford University Press.

Gordon, C. (1980). Afterword. In M. Foucault, *Truth and Power in Power/Knowledge: Selected Interviews and Other Writings 1972–1977,* C. Gordon (Ed.). Brighton: Harvester Press.

Gore, J. (1993). *The Struggle for Pedagogies.* New York: Routledge.
Gracia, J. J. E. (Ed.) (1988). *Individualism in Scholasticism: The Later Middle Ages and the Counter Reformation 1150–1650.* Albany: State University of New York Press.
Gramsci, A. (1971). *Selections from Prison Notebooks* (Ed. and trans. Q. Hoare & G. Nowell Smith). London: Lawrence & Wishart.
Grosz, E. (1989). *Sexual Subversions.* Sydney: Allen & Unwin.
Gutting, G. (1989). *Michel Foucault's Archaeology of Scientific Reason.* Cambridge: Cambridge University Press.
Gutting, G. (Ed.) (1994). *The Cambridge Companion to Foucault.* Cambridge: Cambridge University Press.
Habermas, J. (1971). *Knowledge and Human Interests* (trans. J. Shapiro). Boston: Beacon Press.
Habermas, J. (1984). *Theory of Communicative Action*, Vol. 1: *Reason and the Rationalization of Society* (trans. T. McCarthy). Boston: Beacon Press.
Habermas, J. (1986). Taking aim at the heart of the present. In D. Couzens Hoy (Ed.), *Foucault: A Critical Reader* (pp. 103–108). Oxford: Basil Blackwell.
Habermas, J. (1987). *The Philosophical Discourses of Modernity* (trans. F. Lawrence). Cambridge, Mass.: The MIT Press.
Hacking, I. (1979). Foucault's immature science. *Nous, 13,* 39–51.
Hacking, I. (1985). Styles of scientific reasoning. In J. Rajchman & C. West (Eds.), *Post Analytic Philosophy* (pp. 145–165). New York: Columbia University Press.
Hacking, I. (1983). *Representing and Intervening: Introductory Topics in the Philosophy of Natural Science.* Cambridge: Cambridge University Press.
Hacking, I. (1986a). Making up people. In T. C. Heller, M. Sosna & D. E. Wellbery, *Reconstructing Individualism: Autonomy, Individuality and the Self in Western Thought.* Stanford, Calif.: Stanford University Press.
Hacking, I. (1986b). Self improvement. In D. Couzens Hoy (Ed.), *Foucault: A Critical Reader.* Oxford: Basil Blackwell.
Hacking, I. (1990). *The Taming of Chance.* Cambridge: Cambridge University Press.
Hadot, P. (1987). *Exercices Spirituels et Philosophie Antique* (2nd ed.). Paris: Etudes Augustiniennes.
Hadot, P. (1992). Reflections on the notion of "the culturation of the self." In T. Armstrong (Ed.), *Michel Foucault: Philosopher* (pp. 225–232). New York/London: Harvester/Wheatsheaf.
Hadot, P. (1997). Forms of life and forms of discourse in ancient philosophy (trans. A. I. Davidson & P. Wissing). In A. I. Davidson (Ed.), *Foucault and His Interlocutors* (pp. 203–224). Chicago: University of Chicago Press.
Haken, H. (1977). Synergetics—An introduction. *Springer Series of Synergetics, 1.* Berlin: Springer.
Haken, H. (1990). Synergetics as a tool for the conceptualization and mathematization of cognition and behaviour—How far can we go? In H. Haken & M. Stadler (Eds.), *Synergetics of Cognition* (pp. 2–31). Berlin: Springer.
Haraway, D. (1990). A manifesto for cyborgs: Science, technology, and socialist feminism in the 1980s. In L. J. Nicholson (Ed.), *Feminism/Postmodernism.* New York: Routledge.
Hartsock, N. (1990). Foucault on power: A theory for women. In L. J. Nicholson (Ed.), *Feminism/Postmodernism.* New York: Routledge.

Heidegger, M. (1967). *Being and Time*. Oxford: Basil Blackwell.

Henriques, J., Hollway, W., Urwin, C., Venn, C. & Walkerdine, V. (1984). *Changing the Subject: Psychology, Social Regulation, and Subjectivity*. London: Methuen.

Holden, A. (1985). Chaos is no longer a dirty word. *New Scientist, 12–15* (April 25).

Holub, R. (1992). *Antonio Gramsci: Beyond Marxism and Postmodernism*. London and New York: Routledge.

Horrocks, C. & Jevtic, Z. (1997). *Foucault for Beginners*. Cambridge: Icon Books Ltd.

Hoskin, K. (1979). The examination, disciplinary power and rational schooling. *History of Education, 8*(2), 135–146.

Hunter, I. (1994). *Rethinking the School: Subjectivity, Bureaucracy, Criticism*. St. Leonards, New South Wales: Allen & Unwin.

Hunter, I. (1996). Assembling the school. In A. Barry, T. Osborne, & N. Rose (Eds.), *Foucault and Political Reason: Liberalism, Neo-liberalism and Rationalities of Government*. London: UCL Press.

Ingleby, D. (1987). Psychoanalysis and ideology. In J. M. Broughton (Ed.), *Critical Theories of Psychological Development*. New York: Plenum.

Ingram, D. (1994). Foucault and Habermas on the subject of reason. In G. Gutting (Ed.), *The Cambridge Companion to Foucault* (pp. 215–261). Cambridge: Cambridge University Press.

Jameson, F. (1984). Foreword. In J-F. Lyotard, *The Postmodern Condition*. Minneapolis: University of Minnesota Press.

Janicaud, D. (1992). Rationality, force and power: Foucault and Habermas's criticisms. In T. J. Armstrong (Ed.), *Michel Foucault: Philosopher* (pp. 283–301). New York and London: Harvester/Wheatsheaf.

Jones, K. & Williamson. K. (1979). The birth of the schoolroom. *Ideology and Consciousness, 5*(1), 5–6.

Kant, I. (1992). An answer to the question: What is enlightenment? In P. Waugh (Ed.), *Postmodernism: A Reader*. London: Edward Arnold (orig. 1784).

Kenway, J. (1990). Education and the Right's discursive politics: Private vs. state schooling. In S. J. Ball (Ed.), *Foucault and Education: Disciplines and Knowledges* (pp. 167–206). London: Routledge.

Kritzman, L. (1988). *Michel Foucault: Politics, Philosophy, Culture*. New York and London: Routledge.

Kuhn, T. S. (1981). What are scientific revolutions? Center for Cognitive Science, Occasional Paper 18, Massachusetts Institute of Technology.

Lacan, J. (1977). *Ecrits*. London: Tavistock.

Laclau, E. (1977). *Politics and Ideology in Marxist Theory: Capitalism, Fascism, Populism*. London: New Left Books.

Laclau, E. (1983). The impossibility of society. *Canadian Journal of Political and Social Theory, 7*(1&2).

Laclau, E. & Mouffe, C. (1985). *Hegemony and Socialist Strategy: Towards a Radical Democratic Politics* (trans. W. Moore & P. Cammack). London: Verso.

Lash, S. (1984). Genealogy and the body: Foucault/Deleuze/Nietzsche. *Theory, Culture and Society, 2*, 1–17.

Lather, P. (1991). *Getting Smart: Feminist Research and Pedagogy within the Postmodern*. New York: Routledge.

Layder, D. (1994). *Understanding Social Theory*. London: Sage.

Lichtheim, G. (1961). *Marxism: An Historical and Critical Study.* New York: Prae-
    ger.
Lukács, G. (1971). *History and Class Consciousness: Studies in Marxist Dialectics*
    (trans. Rodney Livingstone). Cambridge, Mass.: The MIT Press.
Lyotard, J. F. (1984). *The Postmodern Condition: A Report on Knowledge.* Minne-
    apolis: University of Minnesota Press.
Macey, D. (1993). *The Lives of Michel Foucault.* London: Hutchinson.
Machado, R. (1992). Archaeology and epistemology. In T. J. Armstrong (trans.),
    Michel Foucault: Philosopher (pp. 3–19). New York: Harvester/Wheatsheaf.
Machery, P. (1986). Aux sources de l'histoire de la folie: une rectification et ses
    limites. *Critique, 42* (August–September), 753–774.
Macpherson C. B. (1962). *The Political Theory of Possessive Individualism.* Oxford:
    Clarendon Press.
Mahon, M. (1992). *Foucault's Nietzschean Genealogy: Truth, Power and the Subject.*
    Albany: State University of New York Press.
Manicas, P. (1987). *A History and Philosophy of the Social Sciences.* Oxford: Basil
    Blackwell.
Margolis, J. (1993). *The Flux of History and the Flux of Science.* Berkeley: University
    of California Press.
Marshall, J. (1989). Foucault and education. *Australian Journal of Education, 2,*
    97–111.
Marshall, J. (1990). Foucault and educational research. In S. J. Ball (Ed.), *Foucault
    and Education: Discipline and Knowledge.* London: Routledge.
Marshall, J. (1995). Skills, information and quality for the autonomous chooser. In
    M. Olssen & K. Morris Matthews (Eds.), *Education, Democracy and Reform.*
    Auckland: New Zealand Association for Research in Education/Research Unit
    for Maori Education.
Marshall, J. (1996a). Personal autonomy and liberal education: A Foucauldian cri-
    tique. In M. Peters, W. Hope, J. Marshall, & S. Webster, *Critical Theory,
    Post-structuralism and the Social Context.* Palmerston North: Dunmore Press.
Marshall, J. (1996b). *Michel Foucault: Personal Autonomy and Education.* Dordrecht:
    Kluwer Academic Publishers.
Martin, L., Gutman, H., & Hutton, P. (Eds.) (1988). *Technologies of the Self.* Lon-
    don: Tavistock.
Marx, K. (1904). *A Contribution to the Critique of Political Economy* (2nd ed.) (trans.
    N. I. Stone). New York and London: International Library Publishing Com-
    pany.
Marx, K. (1917). *Capital,* Vol. 2 (Ed. F. Engels). Moscow: Progress Publishers.
May, T. (1995). The limits of the mental and the limits of philosophy: From Burge
    to Foucault and beyond. *The Journal of Speculative Philosophy, 9*(1), 36–47.
McKenzie, D. (1979). Eugenics and the rise of mathematical statistics in Britain. In
    J. Irvine, I. Miles, & J. Evans, *Demystifying Social Statistics.* London: Pluto
    Press.
McLaren, P. & Hammer, R. (1989). Critical pedagogy and the postmodern chal-
    lenge: Toward a critical postmodernist pedagogy of liberation. *Educational
    Foundations, 3*(3), 29–62.
Mead, S. G. (1934). *Mind, Self and Society.* Chicago: University of Chicago Press.
Mercer, C. (1980). Revolutions, reforms or reformulations? In A. Hunt (Ed.), *Marx-
    ism and Democracy* (pp. 102–137). London: Lawrence & Wishart.

Miller, J. (1990). *Creating Spaces and Finding Voices: Collaborating for Empowerment*. Albany: State University of New York Press.

Miller, J-A. (1992). Michel Foucault and psychoanalysis. In T. J. Armstrong (Ed.), *Michel Foucault: Philosopher* (pp. 58–64). New York and London: Harvester/Wheatsheaf.

Minson, J. (1985). *Genealogies of Morals*. New York: St. Martin's Press.

Morea, E. (1990). *Gramsci's Historicism: A Realist Interpretation*. London: Routledge.

Mouffe, C. (1979). Hegemony and ideology in Gramsci. In C. Mouffe (Ed.), *Gramsci and Marxist Theory*. London: Routledge & Kegan Paul.

Mouffe, C. (1993). *The Return of the Political*. London: Verso.

Nietzsche, F. (1966). *Beyond Good and Evil*. New York: Vintage Books.

Nietzsche, F. (1968). *The Will to Power*. New York: Vintage Books.

Nietzsche, F. (1974). *The Gay Science* (trans. W. Kaufmann). New York: Vintage Books.

Nietzsche, F. (1983). *Untimely Meditations* (trans. R. J. Holingdale). Cambridge: Cambridge University Press.

Norris, C. (1993). *The Truth about Postmodernism*. Oxford: Basil Blackwell.

O'Farrell, C. (1989). *Foucault: Historian or Philosopher?* London: Macmillan.

Olssen, M. (1993). Science and individualism in educational psychology: Problems for practice and points of departure. *Educational Psychology, 13*(2), 155–172.

Olssen, M. (1995). Wittgenstein and Foucault: The limits and possibilities of constructivism. *Access: Critical Perspectives on Education Policy, 13*(2), Special Issue: Constructivism in Science Education (pp. 71–78).

Olssen, M. (1996). Michel Foucault's historical materialism. In M. Peters, W. Hope, J. Marshall, & S. Webster (Eds.), *Critical Theory, Poststructuralism and the Social Context*. Palmerston North: Dunmore Press.

Pagano, J. (1990). *Exiles and Communities: Teaching in the Patriarchal Wilderness*. Albany: State University of New York Press.

Patton, P. (1987). Michel Foucault. In D. Austin-Broos (Ed.), *Creating Culture*. Sydney: Allen & Unwin.

Peters, M. (1996). Habermas, poststructuralism and the question of postmodernity. In M. Peters, W. Hope, J. Marshall, & S. Webster (Eds.), *Critical Theory, Poststructuralism and the Social Context*. Palmerston North: Dunmore Press.

Peters, M. & Marshall, J. (1996). *Individualism and Community: Education and Social Policy in the Postmodern Condition*. London: Falmer Press.

Plato (1985). *Alcibiades* (trans. M. Croiset). Paris: Belle Lettres.

Poster, M. (1984). *Foucault, Marxism, History: Mode of Production vs Mode of Information*. Cambridge: Polity Press.

Poulantzas, N. (1978). *State, Power, Socialism*. London: New Left Books.

Putnam, H. (1983). *Realism and Reason: Philosophical Papers: Volume 3*. Cambridge: Cambridge University Press.

Rabinow, P. (Ed.) (1984). *The Foucault Reader*. New York: Pantheon.

Rabinow, P. (1997). Introduction: The history of systems of thought. In M. Foucault, *Ethics, Subjectivity and Truth: The Essential Works* (Ed. P. Rabinow, trans. R. Hurley) (pp. xi–xlii). Allen Lane, London: Penguin Press.

Racevskis, K. (1991). Michel Foucault, Rameau's nephew and the question of identity. In J. Bernauer & D. Rasmussen (Eds.), *The Final Foucault.* Cambridge, Mass.: The MIT Press.

Rajchman, J. (1985). *Michel Foucault: The Freedom of Philosophy.* New York: Columbia University Press.

Rapp, P. E., Zimmerman, I. D., Albano, A. M., de Gusman, G. C, Grenbauri, M. N. & Bashmore, T. R. (1986). Experimental studies of chaotic neural behaviour: Cellular activity and electroencephalographic signals. In H. G. Othmer (Ed.), *Nonlinear Oscillations in Biology and Chemistry.* Berlin: Springer.

Ray, L. (1987). The Protestant ethic debate. In R. J. Anderson, J. A. Hughes, & W. W. Sharrock, *Classic Disputes in Sociology* (pp. 97–125). London: Unwin Hyman.

Riggens, S. (1983). Interview with Michel Foucault. *Ethos, 1*(2) (Autumn), 4–9.

Rorty, R. (1991). *Objectivity, Relativism, and Truth.* Cambridge: Cambridge University Press.

Rose, N. (1996). Governing "advanced" liberal democracies. In A. Barry, T. Osborne, & N. Rose, *Foucault and Political Reason: Liberalism, Neoliberalism and Rationalities of Government* (pp. 37–64). London: UCL Press.

Rouse, J. (1994). Power/knowledge. In G. Gutting (Ed.), *The Cambridge Companion to Foucault* (pp. 92–114). Cambridge: Cambridge University Press.

Said, E. (1983). *The World, the Text, and the Critic.* Cambridge, Mass.: Harvard University Press.

Sappington, A. A. (1990). Recent psychological approaches to the free will versus determinism issue. *Psychological Bulletin, 108,* 19–29.

Sawicki, J. (1991). *Disciplining Foucault: Feminism, Power, and the Body.* New York: Routledge.

Sawicki, J. (1995). Foucault, feminism and questions of identity. In G. Gutting (Ed.), *The Cambridge Companion to Foucault* (pp. 286–313). Cambridge: Cambridge University Press.

Sellars, W. (1963). *Science, Perception and Reality.* London: Routledge & Kegan Paul.

Sheridan, A. (1980). *Michel Foucault: The Will to Truth.* London & New York: Routledge.

Simons, J. (1995). *Foucault and the Political.* London: Routledge.

Skarda, C. A. & Freeman, W. J. (1990). Chaos and the new science of the brain. *Concepts in Neuroscience, 1,* 275–285.

Smart, B. (1983). *Foucault, Marxism Critique.* London: Routledge.

Smart, B. (1985). *Michel Foucault.* London: Routledge.

Smart, B. (1986). The politics of truth and the problem of hegemony. In D. Couzens Hoy (Ed.), *Foucault: A Critical Reader* (pp. 157–173). Oxford: Basil Blackwell.

Sperry, R. W. (1969). A modified concept of consciousness. *Psychological Review, 76*(6), 532–536.

Sperry, R. W. (1988). Psychology's mentalist paradigm and the religion/science tension. *American Psychologist, 43,* 607–613.

Stadler, M. & Kruse, P. (1994). Gestalt theory and synergetics: From psycho-physical isomorphism to holistic emergentism. *Philosophical Psychology, 7,* 211–226.

Stuart Hughes, H. (1961). *Consciousness and Society.* New York: Knopf.

Swinney, H. L. (1983). Observations of order and chaos in nonlinear systems. *Physica, 7,* 3–15.

Taylor, C. (1986). Foucault on freedom and truth. In D. Couzens Hoy (Ed.), *Foucault: A Critical Reader* (pp. 69–102). Cambridge: Basil Blackwell.

Thompson, K. (1986). *Beliefs and Ideologies*. Chichester: Ellis Harwood.

Walkerdine, V. (1989). *Counting Girls Out*. London: Virago.

Walzer, M. (1986). The politics of Michel Foucault. In D. Couzens Hoy (Ed.), *Foucault: A Critical Reader*. Cambridge: Basil Blackwell.

Weber, M. (1930). *The Protestant Ethic and the Spirit of Capitalism*. London: Allen & Unwin.

White, H. (1978). *Tropics of Discourse: Essays in Cultural Criticism*. Baltimore: Johns Hopkins University Press.

White, S. (1991). *Political Theory and Postmodernism*. Cambridge: Cambridge University Press.

Williams, R. (1980). *Problems in Materialism and Culture*. London: Verso.

Wolin, S. (1988). On the theory and practice of power. In J. Arac (Ed.), *After Foucault*. New Brunswick, N.J.: Rutgers University Press.

Index

About the Author

MARK OLSSEN is Senior Lecturer, Department of Education, University of Otago, New Zealand. His published works include articles in *Educational Psychology* and *Access: Critical Perspectives on Education Policy*.

ISBN 0-89789-587-8

9 780897 895873

HARDCOVER BAR CODE